Aesthetics After Finitude

Anamnesis

Anamnesis means remembrance or reminiscence, the collection and re-collection of what has been lost, forgotten, or effaced. It is therefore a matter of the very old, of what has made us who we are. But *anamnesis* is also a work that transforms its subject, always producing something new. To recollect the old, to produce the new: that is the task of *Anamnesis*.

a re.press series

the need for phenomenal stimulation? What happens when perception can see itself? Simultaneous with this shift in neuro-affective technologies is an equally unprecedented cognitive demand: the advent of our recognition of climate change or ecological catastrophe. Conceptually grasping such a large-scale and distributed change in geophysical dynamics makes unprecedented demands on human perception because such changes rarely provide local or visible instantiations.[3] The phenomenon whereby a major event is not experientially available to us is not unique to climate change. This structure is replicated today in the torsions of financial capitalism, a source of major economic crisis and a domain so rapid and complex that it now operates in excess of perceptual traction—even for those whose job it is to understand it.[4]

Although climate science, neuroscience and contemporary theories of the market seem to be radically disconnected domains, they all participate in a broad shift in the possibilities and problematics of perceptive technologies, introducing novel cognitive, environmental and biopolitical circumstances that an aesthetics bound to the human subject has trouble accounting for. The problem that comes into focus here is one of scale. There is a fundamental mismatch between our spontaneous apprehension of reality and the scientific data that contradicts this experience. We can either continue to veer towards ignorance or we can create new ways to grapple with these complexities.[5] Art has a lot to offer this situation.

As well as being formulated in response to the urgency of the human situation at the beginning of the twenty-first century, these pressures arise alongside the recent and profound shift in contemporary philosophy attributed to thinkers such as Quentin Meillassoux, Ray Brassier, François Laruelle and Reza Negarestani, among others.[6] The work of these thinkers is pertinent to the

---

3. For example, how do we comprehend what Timothy Morton calls a 'hyperobject': a thing 'that is massively distributed in space and time relative to humans'? Morton's flattened vision of aesthetic experience develops hyperobjects as constructions or aggregates that have no specific locality, are inter-objective and are widely distributed. Timothy Morton, *Hyperobjects* Minneapolis, Minnesota Press, 2013, p. 1.

4. See Elie Ayache, *The Blank Swan: The End of Probability*, Chichester, John Wiley & Sons, 2010. The aesthetic and ontological implications of high frequency trading and algorithmic capitalism are addressed by Laura Lotti in this volume, see *Enter the Black Box: Aesthetic Speculations in the General Economy of Being*.

5. The recent emergence of the discipline of agnotology, which studies the deliberate manufacture of ignorance, is a good example of a disciplinary response to this increase in both complexity and vulnerability manufactured by the new challenges presented by neuroscience, climate science and the emergence of finance capitalism. Agnotology is briefly discussed in Laura Lotti's paper in this volume, see note 4.

6. Importantly, the way for such thought has been one paved by feminist thinkers (notably those connected to the materialist and techno-feminist movements of the late twentieth-century) such as Donna Haraway, Rosi Braidotti, Elizabeth Grosz, and Sadie Plant. For a discussion of both the pioneering claims and limitations of these thinkers in relation to realist and materialist conceptions of art, see Christoph Cox, Jenny Jaskey and Suhail Malik's introduction to *Realism, Materialism, Art*, Christoph Cox, Jenny Jaskey, Suhail Malik (eds.), Berlin, Sternberg Press, 2015, pp. 23-25. More recently, Catherine Malabou has been a forerunner in suturing naturalist theories of brain plasticity to feminist politics in a way that straddles late twentieth century continental philosophy's investment in deconstruction and twenty-first century neuroscience, see (for example) Catherine Malabou, *Changing Difference*, trans. Carolyn Shread, Cambridge, Polity Press, 2011. Meanwhile, a younger generation of feminist thinkers

problems raised above in their divestment of the primacy of critical and subject-bound dimensions in philosophical thought, instead giving full weight to rigorous speculative and pragmatic modalities of exploration and experimentation. The phrase 'aesthetics after finitude' is a reference to—and refiguring of—the title of one of the key catalytic philosophical works of the early 21st century: Quentin Meillassoux's extended essay *Aprés la finitude* or, *After Finitude*.[7] This essay emerged from a wider philosophical project in which Meillassoux develops a concept of the absolute in order to construct the basis for a realist and materialist philosophy. Meillassoux argues that philosophy has been impaired by the idea that there is an inescapable correlation between thought and experience, perhaps the most powerful presupposition in Western philosophy since Kant. Meillassoux's term, 'correlationism', describes a traditional tenet of modern thought that claims we can only access the world through the distorting lens of experience. The 'correlationist' maintains that reason and thought are bounded by the experiential, and thus any noetic hold on the noumenal is inevitably a contradiction. Meillassoux seeks to construct a habitable space within that contradiction by following its own logic: at once denying a naive purchase on the real whilst also formalizing an escape route 'out of' the phenomenal bind.

After Finitude begins with an appeal to rehabilitate primary and secondary qualities. A secondary quality, following Meillassoux's account, is a sensation that we derive from an object, i.e. we burn when we touch fire. A primary quality is an attribute of an object: for example, its colour. For post-Kantian philosophy, this distinction breaks down almost immediately when we realize that colour, an attribute of the object that is supposed to be independent of our perception or its effect on us, is in fact entirely dependent on the capacities inherent to the unique structures that configure and circumscribe human sense perception. Meillassoux, however, wants to restore the possibility of the primary quality, which severs the idiosyncratic affordances of human perception from that which we know exists. This issue of primary and secondary qualities can be figured as representative of the entire philosophical consensus of 'correlationism'. For Meillassoux, 'what decisively discredited the distinction between primary and secondary qualities is the very idea of such a distinction: i.e. the assumption that the "subjectivation" of sensible properties (the emphasis on their essential link to the presence of a subject) could be restricted to the object's sensible determinations, rather than extended to *all* its conceivable properties'.[8]

---

are responding in their own ways to the challenges outlined above. Alexandra Pirici and Raluca Voinea's *Manifesto for the Gynecene* proposes an 'expanded' and 'inhuman' humanism, compatible with both 'machinic desires and existing forms of life', while Laboria Cuboniks hijacks the formal abstractions of category theory to outline a plan for the construction of a 'transmodern' universalist politics, founded on the anti-naturalist insights of queer theory and transfeminism in *Xenofeminism: A Politics for Alienation*. Both appear (in German translation) in *Dea Ex Machina*, Helen Hester and Armen Avenessian (eds.), Berlin, Merve, 2015, and online (in English): Alexandra Pirici and Raluca Voinea, *Manifesto for the Gynecene*, http://infinitexpansion.net/gynecene.pdf, January 2015; Laboria Cuboniks, *Xenofeminism: A Politics for Alienation*, http://www.laboriacuboniks.net/, June 2015.

7. Quentin Meillassoux, *After Finitude: An Essay on the Necessity of Contingency*, trans. Ray Brassier, London, Continuum, 2008.

8. Ibid., p. 2.

One of the ways in which Meillassoux will return to primary qualities is to reassert a renewed form of the Cartesian thesis that 'all those aspects of the object that can be formulated in mathematical terms can be meaningfully conceived as properties of the object in itself.'[9] He then goes to great lengths to show how a statement such as this is impossible to accept in the current philosophical milieu; a milieu dedicated to the primacy of the subject: 'We cannot represent the "in itself" without it becoming "for us", or as Hegel put it, we cannot "creep up on the object from behind" …'.[10] Meillassoux's strategy is exemplary in its attempt to confront Kant on epistemological terms. After all, this was the *Critique of Pure Reason*'s brilliant maneouvre—to transfer the dispute between dogmatic rationalism and empirical scepticism onto epistemological terrain, a context (inspired by the latter) in which Kant could then reconstruct a philosophical position capable of satisfying the demands of a new critical methodology. Consequently, the legacy of finitude is first and foremost an epistemological problem and—no matter how enthusiastically one wants to hurtle into 'speculative' terrain—it does no good to forget that one of the most important objectives of the first *Critique* was to purge philosophy of spurious metaphysical constructions that cannot furnish a proper epistemological foundation for whatever it is they claim. By engaging Kant's legacy on its own terms and attacking it at its strongest point, Meillassoux's 'speculative materialism' discovers an epistemological loophole that opens onto the real. The path it locates between the 'for us' and the 'in itself', or the phenomenal and the real, is necessarily one cleaved by knowledge.

Importantly, for Meillassoux, speculative activity is constituted by a 'non-correlational mode of *knowing*', which does not necessarily infer a metaphysical standpoint.[11] In fact, he deliberately keeps metaphysics and speculation separate, defining the 'factial' (the absolute facticity of the correlation—the fact that there might be an 'in itself' different from the 'for us' and that this 'might' refers to a real 'in itself') as 'the very arena for speculation that excludes all metaphysics' in accordance with the precision that metaphysics either posits a necessary entity or relies on the principle of sufficient reason to access the absolute.[12] Thus, for the speculative materialist, the speculative act is buoyed up by the absolute possibility that any theory entertained about the 'in itself' is *potentially absolutely true*, while the correlationist 'is incapable of disqualifying any hypothesis about the nature of the absolute'.[13] Mounted, thus, from the epistemological foundation that Meillassoux has carefully and painstakingly laid (via the *deduction* of factiality—and ultimately 'hyperchaos'), the speculative act attains an unprecedented level of gravity.

---

9. Ibid., p. 3.

10. Ibid., p. 4.

11. Ibid., p. 119, italics added.

12. Ibid., p. 128. 'Factiality' is the principle of unreason: 'everything in the world *is* without reason, and is thereby *capable of actually becoming otherwise without reason*'. Alternatively put, factiality is the fact that '[e]verything could actually collapse: from trees to stars, from stars to laws, from physical laws to logical laws; and this is not by virtue of some superior law whereby everything is destined to perish, but by virtue of the absence of any superior law capable of preserving anything, no matter what, from perishing.' Ibid., p. 53.

13. Ibid., p. 65.

At the end of *After Finitude*, Meillassoux evokes Kant's declaration that his critique of reason equates to a Copernican revolution in thought. 'Yet this is where we encounter a rather disconcerting paradox …: when philosophers refer to the revolution in thought instituted by Kant as "the Copernican revolution", they refer to a revolution *whose meaning is the exact opposite of the one we have just identified*', this latter being that of the astronomer Nicolaus Copernicus, who—against reigning theological models of the time—discovered the fact of the earth's revolution around the sun.[14] In light of this decentralization of the human subject's place in the universe by science, Meillassoux argues that Kant's 'Copernican revolution' is in many ways a 'Ptolemaic counter-revolution'. For, at the precise moment that modern science was trying to give us knowledge about 'the nature of a world without us' in which 'the truth or falsity of physical law is not established with regard to our own existence', Kant returned humans to the centre of epistemology. Against Kant, Meillassoux holds fast to the original 'Copernico-Galilean event' which 'institutes the idea of a mathematical knowledge of nature'.[15]

Outside of Meillassoux's own employment of the metaphor, the famous Copernican shift—away from the geocentric model of the universe and the privileged place of humanity within it, to a much less forgiving cosmic viewpoint—can be understood as a parallel event to the recent developments in neuroscience, the possibility of ecological catastrophe, and the era of algorithmic capitalism mentioned above. Furthermore, just as the most significant astronomical revolution of early modernity did not unleash some radical potential of human thought but rather restricted it (buffering the human subject from the world by a rousing philosophical investment in phenomenal being), the 'deracinating effect' (to borrow a favourite phrase of Negarestani's) of these new developments threatens to turn us further inwards, back towards the safety and familiarity of hermeneutics, the unquestioned valuation of subjective perception, and a return to the discourse of authenticity.[16] Speculative philosophy counters this by seeking once again to go 'beyond finitude' (in Meillassoux's words)—to refigure the relation between phenomena, the human subject, and the cosmos that delivered those Copernican truths in the first place.

Meillassoux is not the only philosopher to attempt to recalibrate our conception of the relationship between the real and the phenomenal without ultimately falling back into the human. Over the last decade, several schools of 'speculation' have emerged under the various banners of 'non-philosophy,' 'speculative realism,' 'object oriented philosophy,' 'accelerationism' and 'new rationalism'. The 2007 Speculative Realism conference at Goldsmiths, University of London, was a key event in this history, bringing Ray Brassier, Iain Hamilton Grant, Graham Harman, and Quentin Meillassoux together to sound out novel config-

---

14. Ibid., p. 114.

15. Ibid., p. 124.

16. Recent works notable for their rejection of authenticity as a viable locus for political and social action are Nick Srnicek and Alex Williams' *Inventing the Future: Postcapitalism and a World Without Work*, London, Verso, 2015 and Laboria Cuboniks' *Xenofeminism: A Politics for Alienation*, http://www.laboria-cuboniks.net/, June 2015.

urations of the real. The nomenclature of 'speculative realism' has become increasingly obsolescent as each of these philosophers has gone on to develop the role played by realism in their individual projects, yet the initial impetus to go 'beyond the correlation' remains.

Grant's revision of Schellingian *Naturphilosophie* presents a realism that spans both nature and the domain of Ideas (with nature as primary but co-productive with the thought it thinks through). Grant seeks to understand human thought as the latest product in an asymmetrical, generative, naturalist epistemology. One that can never turn back to capture the conditions of its own production, and therefore, is always necessarily incomplete. Grant understands this epistemological rift as a motor for a form of natural-physical speculation that can only move forwards in time, away from the question-mark of its ground. Epistemology is thus retained in Grant's thought, but under very specific temporal conditions. Just as nature 'mountains' or 'rivers' or 'planetizes', 'nature thinks'—what we discover in thinking nature, is that nature is *thinking us*.[17] This activates, as Ben Woodard has put it, a productive 'relation between speculation and the sciences, between postulates of creative thinking and speculative practices'.[18] Grant suggests that this timely re-elaboration of Schelling's transcendental naturalism operates as an alternative to the static transcendental structure proposed by Kant, and that, if the importance of Schelling's work has been neglected, it is due to a mix of inaccurate criticism and the formidable bulk of the writings he produced. This may, as Woodard points out, invite accusations of 'occultism' from the Kantian critic who would prefer to maintain an inherent ontological separation between the human (marked by the capacity for reason) and nature. But such accusations, Woodard continues, can be countered by the equally virulent claim that the 'very division of the thinker and the thought is just as occult and ungrounded as [Schellingian] hyperconnectivity'.[19] What Grant's Schelling provides, then, is a transcendental structure that immanentizes thinker and thought, explaining thought in terms of its natural constitution. This amounts to a denial of exhaustive interiority. As Grant has written: 'The Idea is external to the thought that has it, the thought is external to the thinker that has it, the thinker is external to the nature that produces both the thinker and the thought of the Idea'.[20] All are different strata of a productive nature, co-ordinated via a sheaf of exteriorities, and animated by contingencies on all levels. What this leaves us with is a vision of nature that is ungroundable and irreducible to its aggregated parts.

Graham Harman, famous for developing an 'object oriented philosophy' (OOP) that refuses the centrality of human consciousness, has perhaps strayed

---

17. Iain Hamilton Grant, 'Speculative Realism', *Collapse III*, Falmouth, Urbanomic, 2007, p. 344.

18. Ben Woodard, 'Ultraviolet' in *Prismatic Ecology: Ecotheory Beyond Green*, ed. Jeffrey Jerome Cohen, Minneapolis, University of Minnesota Press, 2013, pp. 252-269.

19. Ibid. p. 255.

20. Iain Hamilton Grant, 'Speculative Realism', Collapse III, Falmouth, Urbanomic, 2007, p. 339. It is important to note that the notion of 'externality' here is meant to describe the condition of something raised to a new level, rather than something made foreign.

furthest from the original premise of overcoming correlationism.[21] Like correlationism, object oriented philosophy begins with an affirmation of an epistemological limit: we can never know the reality of the objects we encounter. In a fashion similar to Meillassoux's speculative materialism, object oriented philosophy then radicalizes the correlationist position, but where speculative materialism pushes finitude into a positive epistemological premise ('hyperchaos'), object oriented philosophy extends finitude beyond the bounds of the human to bestow it naively upon everything.[22] This extension of the negativity of finitude cannot occur without mobilizing a series of spurious metaphysical assertions. Namely, that nonhuman objects encounter other objects as sensual objects (following a consummately human model), and that all objects have a real, transcendent core that withdraws from access. Rather than presenting a means by which this failure of knowledge might be overcome, however, object oriented philosophy relocates the finitude of the human subject to the object (or from the real object to the sensual object that it relates to with sincerity, in Harman's schema) where it becomes an essential property, and thereby switches an epistemological assertion for a metaphysical, ontological one. For Harman, what begins as a negative epistemological claim about the human subject becomes a positive, though untenable, metaphysical claim about the object.

Perhaps the most attractive aspect of Harman's philosophy for those working in art and aesthetics has been his claim that, for OOP, aesthetics is 'first philosophy'.[23] This is sustained by his concept of 'allure', an 'aesthetic' rather than epistemological mode of access. As a means of apprehension of the real, allure operates akin to Heidegger's broken hammer (in accordance with the model outlined in Harman's realist reading of the tool-analysis).[24] In order to apprehend something of an object's real core, one must experience the detachment of its real, unified essence from its phenomenal accidents. When it surprises us by coming to pieces in our hands, something that exceeds the hammer's phenomenal presence makes itself apparent specifically by not being explicable in terms of the object's phenomenal instantiation. Allure is thus a modality of failure: in failing to capture the real, allusion forces it to separate from certain sensual qualities, purportedly generating a momentary negative image of the unified, real object. Thus, allure rises up to replace knowledge as the exemplary instrument of realist discovery. The claim that all objects relate sensually liberates aesthetics from the human-world relation and allows it to exist as a potential modality for all object relations. Furthermore, following Harman, because the real resides at the heart of every object and necessarily withdraws from access, allure furnishes the sole means of communion between real objects; it is the

---

21. See, for example, Graham Harman, *Guerilla Metaphysics: Phenomenology and the Carpentry of Things*, Chicago, Open Court, 2005 and *The Quadruple Object*. Winchester, Zero Books, 2011.

22. As Peter Wolfendale has put it in his recent book on Harman, 'properly understood, Harman's work should be seen not as a *critique* of correlationism, but a *consolidation* of its central tenets.' Peter Wolfendale, *Object-Oriented Philosophy*, Falmouth, Urbanomic, 2015, p. 6. Italics added.

23. For an AAF critique of this position, see 'Ontology for Ontology's Sake', http://aestheticsafterfinitude.blogspot.com.au/2013/04/ontology-for-ontologys-sake-object.html, April 2013.

24. Graham Harman, *Tool-Being: Heidegger and the Metaphysics of Objects*, Chicago, Open Court, 2002.

singular occasion in which real objects might 'touch without touching'. Aesthetics, then, not only absorbs epistemology, but in a way that has been very seriously problematized by recent criticism, it absorbs causality as well, leading Harman dangerously close the dogmatic metaphysics he so energetically disavows.[25]

Object oriented philosophy has, for understandable reasons, been taken up with great enthusiasm by the art world, ultimately giving artists and other practitioners a 'philosophical' explanation of something they had been doing all along: interrogating the being of the 'stuff' they work with, and relishing the impossibility of resolving art into any definite discursive trajectory. Whether or not object oriented philosophy will eventually proceed to push art and aesthetics beyond the established orthodoxies of the art world remains an open question, one upon which its value as a problematic thought and therefore an enduring philosophy, ultimately rests.

Ray Brassier's work on nihilism and philosophical realism seeks to reinstate 'the coruscating potency' of reason as an 'invigorating vector of intellectual discovery rather than a calamitous diminishment' of the human being in an indifferent world.[26] Brassier is the philosopher who has distanced himself most vehemently from what is—or was—called 'speculative realism', yet his work stands as one of the most powerful cases for a reassertion of a philosophy that goes beyond the creation of meaningfulness in or for human existence; Brassier indeed develops a philosophy of the *meaninglessness* of the human. His best-known work, *Nihil Unbound: Enlightenment and Extinction*, concludes with the claim that 'it is precisely the extinction of meaning that clears the way for the intelligibility of extinction'.[27] This allows Brassier to re-vision philosophy as an 'organon of extinction,' developing the very task of thought in a speculative register by enabling it to think that which it is not, or, more specifically, to place thought 'after finitude'.[28] This move also allows us to think that which goes beyond empiricism; 'extinction,' Brassier reminds us, 'is real yet not empirical'.[29]

Similar themes can be located in the work of Reza Negarestani, whose current philosophical project seeks to sever the umbilical cord between thought and empirical method. Acknowledging the complexly bounded nature of conceptual creativity, Negarestani exhorts us to 'recognize speculative thought as a particular navigational scheme corresponding to schemata of a Universe that explicitly express its contingency, bottomless continuity, invisible layers and alternative passages or conceive the meaninglessness of the free sign, the unbound modality of the eternal and the in-divisibility of 0 qua nothing of nature for thought'.[30] The navigational scheme activates a space in which thought can be unshackled from empiricism, opening passages to futures otherwise foreclosed by a situation that sees thought as receptive rather than enactive. For art, this entails an

25. Peter Wolfendale, *Object-Oriented Philosophy*, Falmouth, Urbanomic, 2015, esp. pp. 97-105.

26. Ray Brassier, *Nihil Unbound: Enlightenment and Extinction*, New York: Palgrave McMillan, 2007, p. xi.

27. Ibid., p. 238.

28. Ibid.

29. Ibid.

30. 'Reza Negarestani, 'Notes on the Figure of the Cyclone' in Ed Keller, Nicola Masciandaro, Eugene Thacker (eds), *Leper Creativity; Cyclonopedia Symposium*, Punctum Books, New York, 2012, p. 290.

understanding of the creative act as part of an ongoing, open-ended and eman-cipatory labour of abstraction, for which art's self-transformation—in complex unity with other modes of thought and practice—is key. Taking its model from contemporary mathematics, this 'labour of abstraction' describes a conceptual movement between local and global contexts, and the dynamic, reciprocal mod-ification of thought and matter set in motion by it.[31] Because thought and matter must be held to the intrinsic demands and constraints of one another, subjective intentionality and objective stubbornness—taken independently—no longer constitute a sufficient explanation for the paths a vector of exploration will take. Instead, thought must be deployed to destabilize matter, and matter must be understood to destabilize thought in a synthetic process of 'differential-integra-tion'.[32] This process is 'emancipative' because it incrementally liberates thought from both external causes (such as material determination) and any teleological exigency that threatens to restrict it in advance. Thus, art participates in a prag-matic dialectics of turbulence that cannot be isolated from broader political, sci-entific and cultural concerns bound up, for Negarestani, with the emancipation of the human qua 'inhuman'.[33]

One of the most interesting aspects of these particular lines of 'speculative' thought is their commitment to non-academic modes of writing. An investment in the conceptual possibilities of science fiction, horror and pulp fiction is com-mon to all the thinkers cited above, and can—at least in case of Brassier, Grant and Negarestani—be traced back to the work of the Cybernetic Culture Re-search Unit and its wild blend of philosophy, fiction, science, occultism and son-ic experimentalism. The Cybernetic Culture Research Unit, or Ccru, was ac-tive at the University of Warwick during the mid nineteen-nineties and reflected the uncompromisingly experimental approach of its founders, Sadie Plant and Nick Land. Plant is best known for her cyberfeminist writings, usually taking the form of feminist reconfigurations of technological histories and presented in a consummately nonlinear fashion, wise to the novel formal exigencies of the nineties internet and hypertext.[34] Although her work has been accused of tech-no-utopianism or even a total disavowal of the material, Plant always espoused a rigorous materialism, one that took the virtuality of cyberspace seriously and attempted to understand the complex nature of the loops that fed embodied fe-male existence into the anarchic and disembodied space of the web.[35] Evoking an imminent shift in agential structures corroborated by the technological de-

31. For a sketch of the mathematical models Negarestani seeks to operationalize as epistemologi-cal modes of exploration, see Fernando Zalamea, *Synthetic Philosophy of Contemporary Mathematics*, trans. Zachary Luke Fraser, Falmouth, Urbanomic, 2012, and Guerino Mazzola, *The Topos of Music: Geometric Logic of Concepts, Theory and Performance*, Basel, Birkhäuser, 2002.

32. Reza Negarestani, *Torture Concrete*, New York, Sequence Press, 2014, p. 4.

33. On Negarestani and Brassier's current philosophical projects in relation to art practice, see Si-mon O'Sullivan, *Accelerationism, Prometheanism and Mythotechnesis*, in this volume.

34. Sadie Plant, *Zeros + Ones*, New York, Doubleday, 1997.

35. See Plant's much overlooked essays, Sadie Plant, 'The Future Looms: Weaving Woman and Cy-bernetics', Body Society, vol. 1, no. 3-4, November 1995, pp. 45-64 and Sadie Plant, 'On the Matrix: Cyberfeminist Simulations' in David Bell and Barbara M. Kennedy (eds.), The Cybercultures Reader, London, Routeledge, 2000, pp. 325-336.

velopments of the time, Plant's works looked forward to an emancipatory future that would empower women, queers and anybody (or thing, for that matter) traditionally sidelined by the Western notion of what counted as 'human'. Nick Land, Plant's co-conspirator during the years of the Ccru (and indeed, throughout much of the nineteen-nineties), has made a name for himself as academia's unassimilable part. His unorthodox approach to philosophy, always conceiving of it as a multiplicitous, experimental and practical pursuit, culminating in some of the strangest lectures, conference papers and intellectual and political experiments of the last two decades, has ensured his near-total effacement from histories of institutional thought, and an almost mythological place in pop histories of the time.[36] The incandescent energy of his deliberately cryptic texts often leads to superficial, although impassioned, responses to his work. This is, perhaps, at the cost of a deeper examination of the consequences of his philosophy, one that contains the germ of many of the strains of speculative thought pursued by the thinkers surveyed in this introduction, as well as those—at one or two generations' remove—contained in this book.[37]

In Land's philosophy, Kant's model of experience appears as the product of a pathological compulsion to control thought's relation to its anarchic outside, with synthetic a priori judgement as the prototype for what would come to be known in the idiolect of Land's experimental fiction as the 'Human Security System'.[38] Auto-prophesying the eventual payoff of his heterodox way of 'doing' academia, Land opens 'Spirit and Teeth', an essay bearing the polemical subtitle 'A Preliminary Post-Mortem', by referring to an outmoded Hegelian *Geist* as nothing more than 'parody or nostalgia', a development that has been 'trafficked to the edge of worthlessness' by Hegel's successors, 'before finally succumbing to an irreparable marginalization by the scientific advances of experimental and behavioural psychology, neurology, neuroanatomy, cognitive science, cybernetics, artificial intelligence, until it becomes a sentimentalism, a vague peripheralized metaphor, a joke.'[39] At its core, Kantianism enervates the noumenal by stabilizing it in advance through the consistency of its relation to the human subject. Radical exteriority proves troublesome for phenomenology because it can only be examined in this repressed form: its utter indifference is always already reconfigured as human-correlated difference. True openness to alterity appears only in the lineaments of death, a folding of the exterior

---

36. Simon Reynolds, 'Renegade Academia: The Cybernetic Culture Research Unit' (unpublished feature for *Lingua Franca*, 1999), Energy Flash, http://energyflashbysimonreynolds.blogspot. sg/2009/11/renegade-academia-cybernetic-culture.html, 3rd November, 2003.

37. See Marc Couroux, 'Xenochronic Dispatches from the Domain of the Phonoegregore'; Adam Hulbert 'Folding the Soundscape: A Speculative ad hoc Account of Synthes/is Plateaux in relation to Actual Control'; Simon O'Sullivan 'Accelerationism, Prometheanism and Mythotechnesis', Chris Shambaugh 'The Emergence of Hyperstition', and Amy Ireland 'Noise: An Ontology of the Avant-garde' in this volume.

38. Nick Land, 'Meltdown,' in *Fanged Noumena: Collected Writings 1987-2007*, Robin Mackay and Ray Brassier (eds.), Falmouth: Urbanomic, 2011, 443. Elsewhere, Land refers to Kant's critical philosophy as 'the most elaborate fit of panic in the history of the Earth.' Nick Land, *The Thirst for Annihilation: Georges Bataille and Virulent Nihilism*, London, Routledge, 1992, p. 2.

39. Nick Land, 'Spirit and Teeth: A Preliminary Post-Mortem', *Fanged Noumena: Collected Writings 1987-2007*, Robin Mackay and Ray Brassier (eds.), Falmouth: Urbanomic, 2011, p. 175.

back into the interior, the inscription of an irrecuperable excess into the system which must expel it in order to persist.[40] Like Meillassoux, Land sees Kantian critique as modernity's founding anxiety (a pre-apprehension of capitalist synthesis), but where Meillassoux deploys a reinvigorated philosophical rationalism against philosophical irrationality, Land actuates his critique of critique beyond the frontiers of both philosophy and the transcendental human subject, returning during the night to smuggle heterogeneous matter over their borders.[41] 'To repeat Kantianism' he writes 'is to perpetuate the exacerbative displacement of critique, but to *exceed* it is to cross the line which divides representation from the real, and thus to depart both from philosophy and from the world that has expelled it into its isolation. Critique is a matter of boundaries... It is inherent to critique that a terrain of unthinkability is delineated, or that limits are set to the exercise of theoretical endeavour'.[42] Whatever it is that lies beyond the jurisdiction of the Human Security System, something other than philosophy will be required to make contact with it.

This willingness to move beyond the domain of legitimate philosophical expression arises from a shared desire (inherent to the thought of the real) to speak from or with the outside, as well as being indicative of a more general drive to collapse theory into practice. This connection has been developed more recently by Eugene Thacker in his *Horror of Philosophy* trilogy, in Negarestani's crypto-fictive text *Cyclonopedia*, Jussi Parrika's *The Anthrobscene*, and Benjamin Bratton's *Dispute Plan to Prevent Future Luxury Constitution*.[43]

The essays in this volume approach the question of an aesthetics after finitude with a variety of different concerns. The 'post-empirical' world imagined in the philosophies detailed above is also about new power structures. Laura Lotti's essay considers neoliberalism as a regime that secures and distributes power via aesthetic means. By investigating the aesthetic operations of neoliberal hegemony, Lotti elucidates several hypotheses for what it means to make 'sense' of power today. Other essays approach what we take to be the companion phenomenon to this age of fiscal crisis: climate change and the advent of the Anthropocene. Three essays deal directly with speculative approaches to the environment. Prudence Gibson delves into the puncturing possibilities of a fictional and hyper-objective fly. She enacts environmental adaptation and sustainability by writing alongside French artist Herbert Duprat's caddisfly artworks, and as

---

40. See Nick Land, 'Teleoplexy' in *#Accelerate: The Accelerationist Reader*, Robin Mackay and Armen Avenessian (eds.), Falmouth, Urbanomic, 2014, pp. 509-520.

41. Nick Land, *The Thirst for Annihilation: Georges Bataille and Virulent Nihilism*, (London, Routledge, 1992) p. 27. In his later work Land would hand critique over to an a-subjective, materialist technics that is 'increasingly thinking about itself', invoking the dissolution of theory into the pure practicality of self-generating matter as a means of subverting the distinctions between cognitive representation and fictional speculation, as well as human and machinic agencies.

42. Nick Land, *The Thirst for Annihilation: Georges Bataille and Virulent Nihilism*, (London, Routledge, 1992) pp. 5-6.

43. Eugene Thacker, *Horror of Philosophy* vols.1-3 (*In the Dust of this Planet, Starry Speculative Corpse, Tentacles Longer than Night*), Winchester, Zero Books, 2011-2015; Reza Negarestani, *Cyclonopedia*, Melbourne, re.press, 2008; Jussi Parikka, *The Anthrobscene*, Minneapolis, University of Minnesota Press, 2015, and Benjamin H. Bratton, *Dispute Plan to Prevent Future Luxury Constitution*, Berlin, Sternberg, 2015.

an encounter between theory and fiction. Douglas Kahn's chapter is a heliolog-ical examination of the geologic, and the ascendancy of the geological during the Anthropocene, whilst urging us to keep carbon in the ground. His reinter-pretation of the Icarus myth, 'Reverse Icarus', tells the provocative story of the burning earth. In 'Picture that Cyclone' Stephen Muecke considers the bugar-rigarra vision of a cyclone. For Muecke, the bugarrigarra ('the Dreaming') ren-ders the cyclone both a 'strange-attractor' and a 'hyperobject', providing a mod-el by which to rupture the 'zone of exclusion' around Nature characteristic of modern thought.

As Muecke has written elsewhere, a speculative aesthetics opens up a defi-nition and field of practice for art that protects the autonomy of the artwork: 'The point of a speculative aesthetic is that space is opened up for artworks to engage with even more force than before. Engage with what or with whom? With the viewer, certainly. With the art institutions, certainly... with politics, even with the sciences... But without *reducing* art in each case to something else: to a human emotion, to making a living or a reputation, to a political necessi-ty or a scientific truth'.[44] Thomas Sutherland's essay tackles this problem direct-ly, addressing the philosophical tradition that views art as secondary to the a priori, in terms of the seemingly contradictory philosophical 'use' of art to il-lustrate that very a priori. Sutherland develops a rigorous account of Laruelle's non-standard aesthetics, showing how it offers a way out of these traditional aes-thetic stalemates.

Alongside these examinations of the economic and ecological implications for aesthetics, four essays consider 'aesthetics after finitude' in relation to narra-tive, poetics and signification more broadly. Baylee Brits investigates a theory of 'generic literature' in terms of theories of infinity and totality. Her essay looks at the way that the generic sign—a concept developed in Meillassoux and Badiou's work—can be found in narrative fiction. A generic literature is the form of a lit-erary aesthetics that is 'after finitude.' Christian Gelder considers the relation-ship between mathematics and poetry through Stéphane Mallarmé's 'Ses purs ongles', arguing that sound remains poetry's minimal condition, even when it is dealing with 'nothing', in contrast to Cantorian mathematics. Tessa Laird un-scrambles the nested vagina of the chaotic mother goddess Tiamat in Reza Ne-garestani's *Cyclonopedia*, focusing on the preface by Kristen Alvanson. She charts the trope of the colour pink as a feminine gnosis throughout this text and as lip-stick, matching sweaters, nail polish and flowers in related film, sci-fi and video art. Amy Ireland's contribution dramatizes the limits of human modes of rep-resentation, drawing creative production out of its restricted domain within the arts and applying it to the cosmos itself. Alien cities, parables about rats, Ital-ian futurism, the steam engine and the cybernetics of Nick Land and Michel Serres come together in the construction of a receiver for signals transmitting from outside.

Hyperstition and sonic theory infiltrate further chapters, converging in ex-perimental approaches to categories of knowledge and experience. Chris Sham-

---

44. Prudence Gibson, *The Carpentry of Speculative Things*, UNSW Sydney 2012, n.p.

baugh, faced with the problem of elaborating the concept of hyperstition, presents us instead with an enigmatic document, skating through strange temporal loopholes to demonstrate hyperstition in the only way truly appropriate to the concept itself—via the apocryphal intensification of coincidences. Marc Couroux and Adam Hulbert's texts conspire with each other, extending this trajectory in the direction of sound studies, deploying the concept of hyperstition to explore modes of resistance, co-optation, and reconfiguration of the phono-affective control structures inherent in late capitalism. In 'The Nuclear Sonic: Listening to Millennial Matter' Lendl Barcelos seeks a way to 'sonically interrogate' zones of exclusion created by nuclear catastrophes. Barcelos initially looks at work by Jacob Kirkegaard and Peter Cusack to elucidate a form of 'nuclear sonic investigation', before turning to analyse sound works of exceptionally long duration by Jem Finer and John Cage. Barcelos' preliminary questions and speculations on 'millenial matter' open up the possibility of nuclear listening or listening radioactively. Finally, Simon O'Sullivan's essay surveys the strengths and weaknesses of Accelerationism and Prometheanism in relation to art practice and subjectivation, focusing on different forms of 'fictioning'—from the afrofuturist mythologies of Sun Ra and the assemblages of Mike Kelley to the hyperstitional practices of the Ccru—and finds them wanting. In response to what he perceives as a dearth of libidinal content and an adequate theory of the subject, O'Sullivan proposes the practice of mythotechnesis, a form of collective experimental and synthetic modelling that operates on a diagonal between rational and affective modes of apprehension in order to generate unforseen and unknowable possibilities in the midst of the given and the known.

The varied and fractious 'new realisms' and 'new materialisms' explored at the beginning of this introduction have inevitably stultified into camps divided by allegiances to one or another thinker. The volume that we present here has no such allegiance, and does not seek to present or develop a single line or type of thought. Indeed, we attempt to move past the groups and disputes of this decade of speculation to present cutting edge work that exceeds the parameters of what is now an entrenched 'scene'. Equally, these essays are not beholden to the original 'anti-Kantian' requirement that characterised germinal speculative thought. Rather, the essays in this volume present different positions on speculation and participate in different readings of Kant and the tradition of critique, appropriate to a rapidly transforming constellation of ideas and practices liberated from the strictures of factional fidelity.

I

Xenochronic Dispatches from the Domain of the Phonoegregore

Marc Couroux

In December 1995, I found an unsigned note tacked to the student board in the music building of McGill University. It stated (in broken English) that shortly after I had participated in a series of neurological experiments testing *perfect pitch* ability, a conversation had been overheard which suggested there was more to these sessions than met the ear. The message, destroyed in a house fire ten years later, alleged that a neural program or 'algorithm' could be implanted in subjects with substantial mnemonic capacities who are also 'good hummers', though the modalities of this invasive operation remain to this day utterly mysterious. A stimulus of some kind was to trigger an internal generation of melodies, each of which would get stuck until expunged, externalized by humming, jumpstarting contagious circulation. Though the experimenters were apparently of mixed feelings concerning the effectiveness of this implantation (as the note indicated, if in a tortured tongue), the intention was that these generations would proliferate as anticipations of corporately-valenced melodies-to-come.

What follows is an attempt, admittedly provisional, to digest the implications of this still-cryptic transmission. It traverses multiple creative iterations tasked with pinging some of the still-murky domains adumbrated by the haunting frequency of this aberrant missive, concretized by subsequent investigation into corporate technologies of viral sonic infestation before online modalities definitively entered their metastatic phase. This method is adopted in order to situate the 1995 event as a lynchpin in the elaboration of a network of sonically abductive procedures instantiated by the imperatives of emergent neuromodulatory research. To dismiss this communication (however roundabout) as the practical joke of a conspiratorial crank would occult the opportunities it affords to induce effective revalencings of psychosonic capture operations into forces hurtling towards a future beyond capitalist instrumentalization.

What concerns us here pertains to the domain of the *phonoegregore*, a spectral sonic cabal. Though the diagram (fig. 1) which accompanies this debriefing appears split into upper and lower realms—the upper assembling elements constitutive of cybercapitalist circulation, the lower, techniques for intensifying, neutralizing, subtending such elements—it is in reality a totality the parts of which can be equally appropriated by any phonomagus, and employed to leverage the disposition of a given spacetime. In other words and at all times, the descriptive modes used below to frame contemporary *cyberaffordant* machinations can be simultaneously thought as prescriptive invocations, taking as credo that any position asserting that neurobiological abduction by Capital is inevitable and hermetically foreclosed to any possible escape is insufficiently nuanced. The notion that art and its constitutive assemblages might become preemptive again, functionally virulent, instead of playing perpetual catch-up to the new (military-industrial-entertainment-etc.) avant-gardes of our era, is absolutely key.

Edison is said to have expressed his fear of a shadowy phonic consortium gaining access to the disembodied, objectified words of an individual, ripe for circulatory contamination. His anxieties were well founded. The *schizophonical-ly*[1] mobilized effects of recording and transmission technologies were indeed appropriated by the few to gain power over the many—see Hitler's use of radio (and Roosevelt's fireside chats), as well as the fake broadcasts (ferried by a CIA-run radio station, overseen by future Watergate co-conspirator E. Howard Hunt) that precipitated the fall of Guatemalan president Jacobo Árbenz in 1954 (the *Árbenz Effect* moniker applies to any *mètic*[2] hijack of technological predispositions to achieve maximal results). One might do well to also recall the brutally effective *hyperphonochasmic* operations targeting Democratic candidate Howard Dean in 2004,[3] acoustically, electronically isolating the excitable politi-

---

1. Schizophonia = *split sound*, referring (especially) to the electronic decoupling of sound from its source both spatially and temporally. Coined by Canadian composer and acoustic ecologist R. Murray Schafer. However, as sonic theorist David Cecchetto points out, sound, *in general*, 'only comes to be at all through the differential act of hearing, which is the very act that would place it where it isn't.' In this sense, all sound is properly schizophonic. See David Cecchetto, *Humanesis: Sound and Technological Posthumanism*, Minneapolis, University of Minnesota Press, 2014, p. 2.

2. From mètis, *cunning intelligence* in Ancient Greece. According to Detienne and Vernant, mètis "implies a complex but very coherent body of mental attitudes and intellectual behaviour which combine flair, wisdom, forethought, subtlety of mind, deception, resourcefulness, vigilance, opportunism, various skills, and experience acquired over the years." Mètis functions in situations that are "transient, shifting, disconcerting and ambiguous...which do not lend themselves to precise measurement, exact calculation or rigorous logic." Because of its essentially deceptive, resourcefully stratagematic character, mètis was "thrust into the shadows, erased from the realm of true knowledge," though it is enjoying a renaissance in contemporary times. See Marcel Detienne & Jean-Pierre Vernant, *Les ruses de l'intelligence: La mètis des grecs*, Paris, Éditions Flammarion, 1974. See also these recent publications: François Jullien, *A Treatise on Efficacy: Between Western and Chinese Thinking*, Honolulu, University of Hawai'i Press, 2004. Robert C. H. Chia & Robin Holt, *Strategy Without Design: The Silent Efficacy of Indirect Action*, New York, Cambridge University Press, 2009. Nandita Biswas Mellamphy, 'Ghost in the Shell-Game: On the Mètic Mode of Existence, Inception and Innocence', *The Funambulist Papers*, 45, 2013. (http://thefunambulist.net/2013/12/04/funambulist-papers-46-ghost-in-the-shell-game-on-the-metic-mode-of-existence-inception-and-innocence-by-nandita-biswas-mellamphy)

3. Lisa Parks, 'The 2004 Presidential Election and the Dean Scream' (February 4, 2005), available at

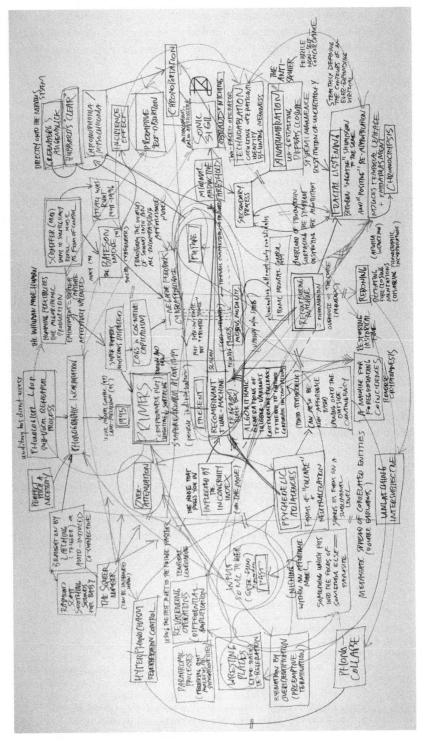

Fig. 1—The Domain of the Phonoegregore
http://xenopraxis.net/domainofthephonoegregore.tif

cian from the crowd whose enthusiasm spurred him on in the first place, a case study of phonoegregoric media manipulation reaping the advances made by Glenn Gould and his multiple microphone *phonochasmic* experiments from the mid 1970s.[4]

However, the phonoegregore of note here is presumed to operate quite differently, exerting control through the mobilization of biosonic propensities of select individuals—musicians with *perfect pitch*—converting the latter into hosts for a continuous production of abductive melodic tropes through embodiment and externalization. In 1995, I underwent a series of experiments charged with uncovering the neural correlates of perfect pitch.[5] Neural activity occurring during pitch recognition exercises was visually tracked via a Positron Emission Tomography scan. As far as I knew then, these probes were exclusively conducted for this purpose. Though the additional abilities pertaining to memorization and humming were part of the introductory questionnaire, they had not been flagged as experimental variables. The note's most compelling allegation concerned the implantation of a tune-generating algorithm, a detail which resonated retrospectively during a very strange period beginning one month after the last experiment, in which curious melodies began to surface in my mind while transiting through various public spaces. These fragments of tunes emerged spontaneously, like slogans, taglines or streaks of graffiti appended to the particular structure being traversed. It wasn't quite like the phenomenon of *cryptomnesia*, in which something memorized is experienced as new on recollection, as these tunes were autonomous, paradoxical entities at once familiar yet indubitably alien.[6]

Regardless of their provenance, these melodies functioned as *earworms*, sonic aberrations that obsessively reiterate without conscious intent, often ingrained by febrile attempts to recollect a hastily adumbrated musical passage, now inaccessible. (The Shazam app and its robust fragment identification would later render such mental efforts redundant.) The common technique of earworm neutralization consisting in replacing the fragmented hook into its original context by listening to the entire piece from whence it came (thus recovering the integral whole, an overall structural picture in which every element is in its place,

---

http://flowtv.org/2005/02/the-2004-presidential-election-and-the-dean-scream. The "crowd" version of the "Scream" is available at http://www.youtube.com/watch?v=-3Meg3CEyUM, while the broadcast version can be found at http://www.youtube.com/watch?v=D5FzCeVoZFc.

4. These recordings involved the alignment of an array of microphone pairs extending from the interior of the piano (close mic) to the back of the hall, allowing for cinematic zooming away from and into the musical *object* of attention, enabling constant shuttling between an intimate closeness devoid of context to an overpowering of the putative signal by its resonant effects. See Gould's mixing session for Scriabin's *Désir* and *Caresse dansée* (Op. 57) at https://www.youtube.com/watch?v=mhdJZyDhjHs.

5. An individual who can effortlessly identify a pitch (by its letter name or Hertz value) or can (inversely) reproduce one accurately on request is said to possess *perfect* or *absolute* pitch, in contrast with an individual with *relative* pitch for whom the relations between pitches take precedence.

6. It was closer to L=A=N=G=U=A=G=E affiliated poet Hannah Weiner's clairvoyant writing: 'I SEE words on my forehead IN THE AIR on other people on the typewriter on the page.' (Epigraph to the *Clairvoyant Journal 1974: March-June Retreat*, New York, Angel Hair Books, 1978.) See http://eclipsearchive.org/projects/CLAIRVOYANT/Clairvoyant.pdf

pace Adorno[7]) was singularly ineffectual. The worm lacked affiliation with any previously extant entity. In effect, these slogans were not synecdoches for greater totalities, but simply splinters that referred to nothing but themselves, lying in wait for future associations. The infectious nature of these self-generated *superearworms* induced an irrepressible urge to surface them by humming them out, thereby donating them to unsuspecting, temporarily adjacent bystanders (perhaps in the vain hope that the latter's attenuated aptitude for *phonographic incorporation* might neutralize the bug).

In retrospect, I began to understand how the recipient might function as a cog, a temporary way station for a symbiant intelligence within a larger system. A virtual superearworm fund, latently percolating in each subject, periodically engenders singularly robust iterations affected with a sufficiently high glischroidal[8] index. The need for a 'good hummer' began to make sense, externalization being integral to transfer. According to the tenets of cognitive capitalism, in full swing by that time, the individual is enslaved via the capture of what Marx termed *general intellect*; her affects, ideas, communicational skills vampirized, creative intensities sucked out and put to work. The evolving earworm diagram described here appeared to function analogously to emergent *cyberaffordant* modes, proper to the *just-in-time* phase of capitalism, which requires a cybernetic system of instant feedback in order to minimize stockpiling and continue accumulation. The constant extraction of information from every domain of an individual's life (that occurs most often in the background of daily activities) operates to preempt future initiative by constantly predicting her next consumptive move, thereby embedding her ever deeper. Noise, far from being a nuisance to the system, is in fact essential to periodically restart it. 'There is no failure, only feedback'—a fundamental maxim of neuro-linguistic programming.

This actualization of the future in the present effectively (but stealthily) closes off any options the system cannot *afford*, pretending to openness (and convincing the subject of this) while operating within a set of clearly delimited boundaries. Norbert Wiener's first-order cybernetics[9] aimed to predict the movement and behaviour of enemy aircraft during WWII, by continuously gathering information about the opponent and feeding it back into the system, gradually improving the latter's predictive ability. After the war, the Macy Conferences provided the impetus for an improved, second-order cybernetics to be applied to the social realm, in order to keep the death drive from exploding into actualiza-

---

7. Theodor Adorno, 'On the Fetish Character in Music and the Regression of Listening', in *The Culture Industry: The Selected Essays on Mass Culture*, London, Routledge, 1991, pp. 29-60. Adorno lamented the manner in which the listener is absolved of the responsibilities of *structural listening* through new-found abilities allowing ingress to a unified work *outside* of its linear (irreversible, ephemeral) unfolding, resulting in its fragmentation into islands of "sensual pleasure torn away from the functions which give them meaning"; the greater concern being the depletion of the individual's ability to patiently construct a long-term narrative by negotiating discrepancies, contradictions, polarities.

8. Glischroid, from the Greek γλισχρος (viscous), is a term appropriated by psychiatrist Françoise Minkowska-Brokman to describe the "epileptoid personality structure" and reappropriated by Félix Guattari to characterize "affect (that) sticks to subjectivity." See Anna Munster, *An Aesthesia of Networks: Conjunctive Experience in Art and Technology*, Cambridge, MIT Press, 2013, pp 110-113.

9. Cybernetic, from *kubernesis* (Gr.) = steering, governing.

tion again. 'How would we rig the maze or problem-box so that the anthropomorphic rat shall obtain a repeated and reinforced impression of his own free
will?' dixit Gregory Bateson.[10] Indeed, the *Bateson Nudge* is still employed today by the mavens of *choice architecture*, to preemptively and strictly limit possibility under-the-radar. (The *hyperphonochasm*[11] is a particularly astute version of
it.) The *möbius modality* is the means by which an individual, a culture, a society
become *system immanent*. It governs imperceptible condition mutations through
a creeping incrementation, each notch insufficiently distinct from the previous
to significantly rupture a perception of status quo. It is the regime under which
the emergence of a new stratum of abduction cannot be apprehended by dint
of an individual's submission to an endless succession of presents, steadily pro-
gressing through control and communication feedback processes. Radical sys-
temic shifts—phase changes—are only meant to be detected retrospectively (if
at all), by which time reversal potential has been fully quashed into impotent
acquiescence.[12]

The public spreading of inscrutable melodic tags might be better understood in terms of later developments in *priming*, indispensable to the cyberaffordant model, involving a slow, background introduction of information that becomes creepingly pervasive, such that the figure—or product—that eventually
emerges against this inscrutable canvas appears inevitable, logical.

Where memory is concerned, musicians, given the mnemonic imperatives
of the profession, constitute the greatest percentage of individuals disposed to
storing *phonographic incorporations*, internalized auditory material of extended duration (most typically of a musical nature) that can be recalled at will. Details regarding frequency, rhythm, dynamics, timbre, and associated effects are all internally *audible* and accurately reproduced on cue. Auditory resolution increases
dramatically among musicians endowed with perfect pitch abilities. A particular instantiation of the incorporation will often be triggered by an environmental factor—linguistic, musical, affective—that engenders internal *playback* (a
phenomena known more commonly as *phonomnesis*). Baddeley suggests that recorded material might be incorporated via a *subvocal rehearsal process* that continuously refreshes the memory trace through the use of one's inner voice.[13] This

---

10. Gregory Bateson, 'Social Planning and the Concept of Deutero-Learning', in *Steps to an Ecology of Mind*, Chicago, University of Chicago Press, 1999, p. 170.

11. The *hyperphonochasm* surgically severs a subject from its acoustical milieu, delivering it into schizophonic chaos through a judicious control of reverberation. Beyond its acoustical valence, reverberation indexes relative (*critical*) distance from an originary impulse via the attendant distortions the latter has shouldered along the way; the inevitable accretion of rumours (*noise = rumore (It.)*), latencies and
other détournements makes plain the need for robust reverb management, and a more vigorous pro-
motion of vectors deemed useful to persist (and to be reinjected into actuality) once the original emission has died off.

12. The möbius strip is a paradoxical entity with only one boundary, simultaneously one-sided and
two-sided: the tracing of a continuous line on its surface—without ever breaking contact—involves the
contouring of what appear to be two loops, which one might term *introductory* and *normalization* cycles.
The first cycle is completed when the point on the opposite side of the inceptive point is paradoxically
reached (without deliberately changing sides); the second, when the original point on the initial side is
regained. In fact, there is only one global loop that encompasses both cycles.

13. Alan Baddeley and Barbara Wilson, 'Phonological Coding and Short-Term Memory in Patients

process appears indispensable in extending the length of the incorporation beyond that afforded by the capacities of the *phonological store*, which can only maintain three to four seconds of material in active memory before decay sets in.

It still remained unclear why particular fragments became obsessively lodged. I returned to the idea of noise as that which tethers one more securely to a cybernetic system. The day before leaving for an extended vacation, I watched a 1970s TV movie entitled *Strange Homecoming*,[14] which included a scene enveloped by an oddly memorable musical theme. Away from my *hypomnesic* environment, I spent an entire week fruitlessly attempting through various mental procedures to surface the irritant. Back home, I maniacally scrubbed over the same music[15] until it began looping in my mind autonomously. Though the incongruity of this particular theme fostered the fixation, it could not have become ingrained without my vigorous efforts. (Mètic intelligence would be impotent without an understanding of how one is as implicated in the mechanisms of entrapment as the putative target.)

The *incongruity index* expresses the degree of deviation from normative melodic, harmonic, and rhythmic conditions that requires excess cognition on the part of the listener, absorbed in the effort of identifying the anomalous nature of the mysterious event. This surplus effort to *pull back* perceived incongruity into an existing category induces an *earworm*—a more or less deeply lodged fragment, most often of music, that appears to have no purpose other than its obsessive reenactment in the mind of the afflicted individual—which is why sonic branders (inspired by the work of Dr. James Kellaris, among others) are interested in mathematizing a particular hook's deviation in order to more effectively abduct. In addition, formulas exist that calculate the average amount of repetitions needed to *naturalize* a deviation, contingent on its incongruity index. This naturalization process is tantamount to the half-life of the deviation—its gradual decay into the normative where it can do no more direct harm, though all the while it effectively conditions future potential by withdrawing into an expanding virtual. Types of deviation include: an awkward melodic leap of incipient unattractiveness, an unexpected harmonic modulation, rhythmic asymmetries and foreshortenings, metric aberrations, etc. These deviations are often sucked into controllable territory by the conscious mind without undue effort and without lasting parasitic effect, which is why the magickal art of deviation requires constant practice and perpetual amendment in alignment with prevailing sensible distributions of cultural matter.

I had no recourse but to design a *recontouring machine*, given that *ironic mental control* (as theorized by Wegner[16]) only redoubles earworm embedding. Such a device is populated by an inalienably local (therefore provisional) set of devi-

---

without Speech', *Journal of Memory and Language*, 24, 1985, pp. 490-502.

14. http://www.imdb.com/title/tt0072216/

15. A video work, *Strange Homecoming: A Structural Comedy*, restaged the febrile backwards and forwards scrubbing described here (this time silent, unlike the sonorous rewinds and fast-forwards of *Adumbrate_57*): https://vimeo.com/100080594

16. Daniel M. Wegner, 'Ironic Processes of Mental Control', *Psychological Review*, Vol. 101, No. 1, 1994, pp. 34-52.

ational functions feverishly tasked with the de-emphasis qua defusing of a resil-
ient earworm, especially of algorithmic, superearworm variety. This machine
discretizes the melodic, harmonic, rhythmic components of an earworm in order to calculate iterated deviations, peculiarly calibrated to donate a subliminal impression of change whilst preserving coherent contour-identity—a fractal
positioning, in other words, erratically vacillating between familiarity and *par-
amnesia* (déjà entendu). The recontouring machine operates in real-time via *deaf
recording* procedures that segregate components within a given textural totality
from one another, capturing them in strict indifference to adjacent context in
order to curtail the temptation to produce deliberately memorable gestalts. Recontouring machines have been known to backfire, chiefly from insufficiently
rigorous deviation design: an anomaly that too drastically exceeds parametric
boundaries risks becoming a new object of obsession for the listener, unaware
that an earworm is about to ingress. 84 recontourings of the *Strange Homecoming*
theme were generated and chained to each other without pause, yielding a surface impression of perpetual restarting—*as if* looping back to the beginning—
even as each variation secretes a remaindered, *infra_legible* difference from the
next. A delicate operation.[17]

   With this in mind, I remembered that not all of the *self-generated* melodies
had successfully lodged themselves. Only those with a sufficient *incongruity index* managed to gestate until expulsion. The next stage was crucial: the *reboning*,
bodily reappropriation of the recombinant tune-machine's automated generations through humming. An affectively valenced, flexibilized, boned hum considerably lubricates transfer to unsuspecting temporarily adjacent individuals.
Glenn Gould attributed his increasing incapacity to accurately perform a giv-
en musical passage to the overwhelming influence of foreclosing mentations,
preemptions of the future, the anticipation of difficulties ahead in a given time-
line physically blowing back in the present. Gould's solution to this debilitating
condition consisted of obliterating any acoustical evidence of ongoing physical
efforts, masking it by the massed effects of multiple vacuum cleaners, televisions,
and radios operating at full blast.[18] Once a properly embodied relationship with
the passage in question was restored, so was its sonorous resultant (i.e. the noise-
makers were shut off). Some accounts report successful displacement of phonographic incorporations through humming, though the testimonies of many
primers suggest that this form of repeated externalization has little long-term effect on the integrity of the inner recording.

   In my case, the accretion of a number of debilitating, self-perpetuating fail-
ure-inducing algorithms quickened the demise of my career as contemporary
music interpreter, no longer able to negotiate the affordance model of the linear concert ritual still predicated on *structural listening*,[19] a collapsing crystalliza-

---

17. This accumulated bundle of infra-variations was later entitled *Structural Listening*, accessible at
http://infranationale.net/X_structurallistening.aif

18. Jonathan Cott, *Conversations with Glenn Gould*, Boston, Little, Brown & Company, 1984, pp. 36-41.

19. In this modality, listening is organized according to a constant push and pull between parts of a
given structure and the latter's gradual, temporally irreversible consolidation. Such a framework, mobilized by constant dialectical interchange within linear evolution, reflected a more general conception

tion of past-present-future much favoured by Adorno. My brain was anticipating a model that had not yet arrived. A few years after the onset of this algorithmic condition, which could not seemingly be put to any productive use, I attempted an exorcism of these embedded modalities via the fractal playing-out of infra_legibly distinct contrapuntal entanglements, one indistinguishable from the next. *le contrepoint académique (sic)*—performed at the hallowed *Festival de Musique Actuelle de Victoriaville* in 2000[20]—was a rather desperate venture constituted by a permanent refusal to settle on any possible object of obsession, seeking to outwit mental melodic production through a logic of constant rupture and bodymind short-circuiting.

The *Squier number* (named after Major General George Owen Squier, founder of the Muzak Corporation) describes the composite degree of discrepancy between a recording and the (phonographic) incorporation of it by a subject. Internal playbacks of incorporations are often induced via *auditory latching*, within the general purview of *entrainment*, a mode by which a subject attunes to environmental signals, often manifesting through the autonomic synching of bodily movements with adjacent rhythms. (Entrainment is also indispensable in the maintenance of collective egregoric synchronization.) Latching will occur most often without one being aware of it—given a generalized passivity towards music's *schizophonic ubiquity*—frequently coming to consciousness retrospectively, after the original signal has dissipated; the simple realization of the just-heard sound's disappearance may internally reinstate it, automatically inducing the playback of an extant phonographic incorporation. A significant enough deviation between the subject's incorporation and its analogue diffused through the air may foster, on becoming aware of the discrepancy (on *reentry*), a feeling Keats might have described as *embarrassment*, a surreptitious coming-upon-oneself, a momentarily unsettling non-self-concordance. Raymond Scott's 1964 *Soothing Sounds For Baby* series, consisting for the most part of extended repetitive rhythmic structures, was marketed as music to put your child to sleep. In fact, portions of his work may well have been used to investigate latching potential in very small infants temporarily caught in the gap between conscious and unconscious mind. Though cybercapitalist power has harnessed the autonomic valences of entrainment, binding them to individual consumption, any publically disseminated stimulus risks fomenting unlikely bonds between subjects mutually interpellated by it, who may choose to negotiate and overpower it together, through discrepant reappropriations, rebonings.

However, concomitant with the gradual substitution of the *jingle-slogan* by the *brand-password*—in the wake of sensory overload and the increasing unrelia-

---

of life as an ongoing narrative, in which one's self-situation depends on the ability to form continuities, establish polarities. Such auto-fashioning requires for its continuing potency a foundational stability hard to come by within post-Fordist precarity, which dissolves permanent horizons into expedient, expendable presents, anxious instants insufficiently energetic to foment productive bonding.

20. Fragments of this performance can be viewed at https://vimeo.com/142216720. The performance garnered hyperbolic reviews symptomatic of a generalized inability to ground its paradigm-evading strategies. For an assessment 10 years on, see Marc Couroux, 'Introductory note to *le contrepoint académique (sic)*', Le Merle, Vol. 0, No. 0, Autumn 2011, pp. 49-52 (https://www.academia.edu/4302558/le_contrepoint_académique_sic_preamble).

bility of time—audio branders had developed the technique of *preemptive self-distortion,* initially to defeat issues glaringly exposed by the 1989 release of John Oswald's *Plunderphonics* album in which the genetic structures of iconic pop were subjected to disfiguring manoeuvres of urgent concern to the corporate phonoegregore, fearing disastrous and potentially irreversible image-damage. (This explanation runs contrary to the general consensus that the records were destroyed purely for reasons of copyright violation.) Researchers speculated that if they endowed their *sigils* with capacities to absorb distortion from all sides with no loss of integrity—chiefly through the timbral engineering of a unique *soundprint*—any future attempt at détournement by phonoinsurgents could be preemptively forestalled.[21] As Teilhard de Chardin put it: 'All real integration is based on prior differentiation. [...] Only union within diversity is creative. It increases complexity, and brings about higher levels of organization'.[22]

I then understood why the phonoegregore was not content to simply implant a robustly immutable earworm, but instead a program for generating embodied variations. It was preemptive self-distortion in full florescence, correlated to the subtleties of the incongruity index. Instead of running the risk of a melodic trope decaying into ineffectiveness, better to constantly induce variations displaying sufficient incongruity to force automatic pullback and redoubled implantation. When a melodic figure in the same lineage eventually emerged in the context of an advertisement, it would appear as new (*incipience effect*), and yet distinctly primed for by a multiplicity of same-but-different entities. This avoidance of a too crude ground-to-figure correlation might explain the success of the phonoegregore at covering its tracks.

A faultline in the cyberaffordant paradigm rears its head: the possibility of *ruination by overidentification,* in which too-rapid dispersal blows back, prematurely terminating the future effectiveness of a particular viral entity. This was acutely evident in 2001 with the punctual ascent and quick oversaturation of Kylie Minogue's *Can't Get You Out of My Head,* the title itself reflective of a cavalier arrogance too sure of its abductive potency. Never underestimate the indeterminate potential of bad connections.

Ejection from the cybernetic folds of the perpetually preemptive phonoegregore can be equally dispatched via the strategic deployment of *psychedelic adjacencies,* formations inevitably spawned within a colloidal[23] dispersion in which

---

21. PSD recasts a common technique among institutions of control, involving the integration of plausibly comprehensive internal critique and dissent into a corporate image, multiple alibis conspiring to disguise a severely curtailed range of possibilities, such that resistance is promptly declawed. The perception of sufficiently legitimate options encourages the continued occlusion of the operating system (normalized, therefore inaccessible to direct engagement) within which each choice has already been predetermined.

22. 'Toute intégration réelle se fonde sur une différenciation préalable. [...] Seule l'union dans la diversité est créatrice. Elle accroît la complexité, conduit à des niveaux plus élevés d'organisation.' Cited in Tiqqun, 'L'hypothèse cybernétique', in *Tout a failli, vive le communisme!*, Paris, La Fabrique éditions, 2009, p. 278. English translation: https://cybernet.jottit.com/chapter_5

23. Colloid: 'A homogeneous non-crystalline substance consisting of large molecules or ultramicroscopic particles of one substance dispersed through a second substance. Colloids include gels, sols, and emulsions; the particles do not settle, and cannot be separated out by ordinary filtering or centrifuging like those in a suspension.' (OED)

perpetually recombinant auditory surfaces enter into temporary electrical relationships with one another by virtue of haphazard temporal and spatial proximities. (*Psyche* + *delos* = made manifest to the mind). The *baker's dough* analogy is fitting: two extreme points on a slab become adjacent after a mathematically-determinable number of folds.[24] Terms need only hang together in the same general spacetime for factual coalescence to occur.[25] Phonoegregoric propaganda understandably deplores the waning of attention and concentration characteristic of colloidal capitalism (a lachrymose pining for an empty category considering William James's reminder of how focus and distraction are perpetually complicating each other), fearful of an uncontrolled festering of the viral powers of psychedelic adjacency. Indeed, a state of permanent distraction—the primary perceptual modality of the twenty-first century—unlocks unprecedented capacities to induce synchronicities, making effective previously unsuspected correlations. A metastatic spread of such entities may indeed constitute an indigestible challenge to the stealthy incorporation of phonoegregoric earworms, given the unstable fracturing and resynthesizing typical of mutant rhythmanalyses.[26]

Predictably, Burroughs's insistence on the functionalizing of art to unshackle its capacities to effectuate changes in reality was deliberately downplayed. Genesis P-Orridge recounts a story of the author casting a spell on an eatery whose proprietors had maligned him by walking back and forth in front of it playing a barely audible tape on which 'trouble noises' were *cut into* characteristic field recordings captured in that location. Shortly after the action had begun, the joint closed without explanation.[27] With the volatility and *accessibility* of schizophonic practices thus exposed—their capacities to fold time and space— it was deemed preferable to defuse Burroughs within the equivocating realm of postmodern stylistic experimentation, rather than let him further expedite the mass propagation of techno-actualization principles.

In a Sedimental Mood (alien furniture music[28]) is a work of concentrated adjacency-making constituted by convulsive reorderings of a set of concatenated variables, syzygetically (and paradoxically) tasked with eluding the abductive

24. 'N comme Neurologie' in *L'abécédaire de Gilles Deleuze*, Directed by Pierre-André Boutang, 1989, Paris, Éditions Montparnasse, 2004, DVD. See also Charles Stivale's summary and translation of the abécédaire at http://www.langlab.wayne.edu/CStivale/D-G/ABC3.html.

25. Immediately after 9/11, a minority of Americans were inclined to ascribe co-conspiratorial responsibility to Saddam Hussein; contrast with the 70 per cent endorsement garnered in the weeks leading up to the invasion of Iraq following copious media efforts at engineering adjacencies (Atta, Al Qaeda, Prague, Hussein, 9/11, etc.), without explicitly declaring inviolable causal linkage.

26. The notes to DJ xenaudial's *Adjacent Exposure* mention 'double earworm inductions' and 'hearing one thing through another, semi-permanently'. The album kicks off with a stunning superimposition of Al Green's *I'm Still in Love With You* and the theme from the 1971 tearjerker *Love Story*, amusingly titled *I'm Love Still Story In Love Love Story With Love You Story*. Free download at https://xenaudial.bandcamp.com/album/adjacent-exposure

27. Genesis Breyer P-Orridge, 'Magick Squares and Future Beats, The Magical Processes of William S. Burroughs and Brion Gysin', in Richard Metzger (ed.), *Book of Lies*, New York, Disinformation, 2003, p. 106.

28. IaSM was released under the moniker *Algorithmic Moods Inc.*: https://algorithmicmoodsinc.bandcamp.com. For a discussion of the work's occult valences (including a rundown of its generative conceits in the form of classifieds), see eldritch Priest, *Boring Formless Nonsense: Experimental Music and the Aesthetics of Failure*, London, Bloomsbury, 2013, pp. 222-5.

properties of memorability while compelling and maintaining attention in the moment. This returns us back to the process of *fractal listening* impelled by the recontouring machine. In a fractal listening experience, an affective intuition of non-repetition is perpetually undercut by a cognitive ratification of identity. It shuttles the listener between local specifics (deviations with various capacities to be registered *as* deviations) and an accumulating shadowy shape-shifting totality, constantly updated by information from this transient matter, forever deferring its termination into a graspable gestalt. The incapacity to categorically identify ongoing recursion within the convulsions of unresolution almost inevitably engenders temporal anomalies, folds, a general buckling of teleological integrity, and an expedition of uncontrollable interpenetrations of past, present, and future; all the while, a virtual field of potential stealthily expands, unceasingly leveraging the perception of change. Any isolated iteration is thus summarily demoted to transient status, lacking the resilience to firmly establish itself. This modality takes into account the inevitable process by which repetition pressures incongruity to reverse into new forms of congruity (through a gradual ablation of idiosyncrasy); it therefore must remain constantly on the move. *Anadumbration* is the process that effects the perpetual postponement of any unifying perceptual paradigm through the febrile shuffling of parameters. Adumbration is a term developed by philosopher-phenomenologist Edmund Husserl denoting the continuous accumulation of various perspectives (*shadings = abschattungen (Ger.)*) of an object into a multi-dimensional mental consolidation. Appropriating Husserl's theory by détourning it (for highly practical purposes), English artist Norman Wilkinson originated[29] at the tail end of World War I one of the most notorious applications of anadumbration via *dazzle camouflage*, a technique involving the painting of stripes of contradictory size and directionality on a vessel, such that the opponent's ability to coherently grasp its coordinates (size, speed, heading, etc.) is accordingly impeded.

Any attempt to defeat a listener's propensity to terminate perception when confident that an experience has been identified, categorized, captured is invariably enhanced by the use of anadumbrative tactics. Indeed, the *ungestalting* deviations of anadumbration forestall any preemptive extraction from a system by preventing conscious seizure of its modalities; ungraspable from an extrinsic vantage point, their mysterious implications cannot be comfortably integrated qua dismissed. System immanence is guaranteed by a rapid containment of discrepant surfaces powered by the efficient operations of the Freudian *secondary process*, by which a subject backtracks into a rational second-order justification from an incoherent first impression, summarily deleted. Anadumbration is a *chronocrypsic*[30] operation, tasked with time camouflage, asymmetrically imbricating incongruent temporalities while prosecuting integumentary impressions of a wholly illusory kind.

29. Roy R. Behrens, 'The art of dazzle camouflage', *Defense & Security Analysis*, 3.3, 1987, pp. 233-243. Behrens suggests that the technique of dazzle camouflage was already in existence by the time Wilkinson arrived on the scene to "invent" it (1917).

30. Crypsis: Defensive maneuver characteristic of certain species consisting in altering appearance to match the (background) environment.

Adumbrate_57 (infra_legible training music for the late capitalist subject[31]*)* investigates such templexing wormholes through *rewind, fast-forward, stutter* and *drop-
out* procedures. Dazzle camouflage's use of differential blending—breaking up
surface continuities by collapsing portions of the figure into the (back)ground—
also works effectively in the time domain via the abutment of inconsistent, incomplete iterations of a given material that increasingly destabilize the constitution of an accumulated ground in memory. Intimate knowledge of the shifty,
time-dependent operations of the *möbius modality* can betray the boundaries of
the (cyber)affordant model and its perpetual upgrading (qua normalizing) of
fictional entities to the status of inviolable fact (the contingent provisional promoted to generalized permanence), prying open channels within which synthetic constructs may be insinuated (*illapsus* = flowing, gliding in), inf(l)ecting
feedback loops accordingly. Such infradermal infiltrations behave parasitically,
forcing the distorting operations of time into consciousness. Moreover, the möbius modality affords the recovery of occulted valences from historical practices—by retrospectively surf(ac)ing un-adumbrated (un-normalized) pasts—in order to gain expedited access to the future.[32] To boot, this particular experiment
is wholly dependent on the mètic ruses of *technoablation*, charged with blunting
incipience through the möbiusoidal occulting (backgrounding and consequent
disappearing) of a technology's operational identity, such that certain valences
associated with contiguous materials are suppressed from conscious attention.
Technoablative stratagems simulate and mutate the infrastructural shibboleths
of a given device—exploiting the listener's propensity to accept the latter as
relatively immutable—thereby opening the floodgates to prodigiously productive bait-and-switch potentials. In *Adumbrate_57*, each time forward playback re-
sumes (after any of the four interruptive incursions), it does so with another version of itself, functioning *as if* the same, which occasions subliminal alterations
of the listener's capacity to form a coherent gestalt.[33]

Given the messy contingencies and vampire effects inevitably engendered
by the passage of time, it's no surprise that the chronically *chronophobic* phonoegregore would want to arrest its deleterious progress. Melody and rhythm
require time to unfold, whereas a vertical, timbral structure can detonate in-
stantly, according to the principles of *sonic niching*, by which highly effective in-
tra-species communication operates in the animal world (see Bernie Krause's
work).[34] Bare traces requiring no more than a few milliseconds to be actualized can intercalate themselves rhythmically between other signals without any
undue effort—affectively tuned *passwords* promptly accessing worlds of associa-

31. Listen at http://infranationale.net/X_adumbrate_57.aif

32. Nick Land describes the task of the 'hyperstitional cyberneticist' as 'closing the circuit of history
by detecting the convergent waves [that] register the influence of the future on its past.' Delphi Cars-
tens, 'Hyperstition', 2010 (http://merliquify.com/blog/articles/hyperstition).

33. Further details re. *Adumbrate_57* can be found in Marc Couroux, 'Towards Indisposition', in
Marc-James Léger (ed.), *The Idea of the Avant Garde—And What It Means Today*, Manchester, Manchester
University Press, 2014, pp. 255-262.

34. Bernard L. Krause, 'The Habitat Niche Hypothesis: A Hidden Symphony of Animal Sounds',
Literary Review, 36/1, Fall 1992, pp. 40-45; Bernard L. Krause, 'Bioacoustics, Habitat Ambience in Ecological Balance', *Whole Earth Review*, 57, Winter 1987.

tion through chronoportation. In the absence of suitable crannies for tactical in-cursion, a judiciously constituted timbral cocktail riding unoccupied frequency bands can superimpose itself on a complex acoustic scene with no loss of com-municational integrity. The quest for an ever-reduced abductive threshold is therefore a matter of intense speculation and experimentation. While cruder methods simply splinterize extant references into immediately legible, timbral-ly specific incarnations, autonomically activating prior phonographic incorpo-rations (capitalism functions most effectively when the subject does its work), recent branding tendencies privilege the development of radically contained, psychoacoustically tweaked fragments without history, that more effectively re-sist the subject's attempts to expunge them. The construction of these overcom-pressed units is highly inflected by research on human phylogenetic develop-ment and the somatic effects (breathing / heart rate) of specific acoustic wave patterns that activate deeply embedded survival mechanisms tied to hearing, though in this case it is the survival of the cybercapitalist system that motivates the abductive project.[35]

A chronophobic individual, a *clear* in the parlance of père-scientologue L. Ron Hubbard, thinks in instantaneous bursts, without the digressive, delibera-tive ramblings of an inner voice, without time. Clement Greenberg's *Augenblick*: the totality of the artwork is accessible in the blink of an eye, before cognition takes things up. Francis Bacon conjured paintings meant to explode *directly onto the nervous system*. Strategically deployed formalisms with the capacity to preempt conscious apprehension can effectively delimit the range of available experi-ence. Control requires time for its feedback operations, but needs to conceal this fact—by parcelizing it into manageable presents—lest the enslaved subject ap-propriate its modulatory effects to foster embodied continuities and self-eject from the communicative bind with capitalism.

Pierre Schaeffer, a French telecommunications engineer and anti-nuclear activist, believed the world could be altered by coding its sounds into the musi-cal realm, developing the technique of *reduced listening* after WWII to empty out the semantic register of sound, the linguistically corrosive, while maintaining intact its affective, psychosomatic valences. In sympathy with the Darmstadt *tabula rasa* compositional faction—but in a far more powerful fashion, for having the insight to employ the technology of his time as medium for psychic trans-formation—Schaeffer sought to zero out in order to fill, this time squarely with-in the stabilizing machine of music. Perhaps Jacques Attali was right after all in alleging that cyclical transformations in the sacrificial order of music antic-ipate the social world to come.[36] Schaeffer's particular preemption was to pla-

---

35. Diego Rinallo, a marketing professor, equates brands with egregores, and encourages the use of magic methods to gain non-rational insights into a brand's meaning. Paco Xander Nathan has written extensively on corporate egregores. See in particular Paco Xander Nathan, 'Chasing Egregors', *The Scarlet Letter*, Vol. VI No. 1, March 2001 (http://www.scarletwoman.org/scarletletter/v6n1/v6n1_egre-gors.html); Nathan, Paco Xander, 'Corporate Metabolism', 2000 (http://www.tripzine.com/listing. php?id=corporate_metabolism)

36. Jacques Attali, *Noise: The Political Economy of Music*, Minneapolis, University of Minnesota Press, 1985.

giarize Attali's theory *avant-la-lettre*, flipping it from descriptive to prescriptive, formalizing a new, totalizing musicalized affordance model—from the bottom up—that would help induce the future through the transformation and regulation of natural sounds, channelling the impersonal, inhuman death drive (*positive* feedback) into homeostatic equilibrium (*negative* feedback). Schaeffer didn't know that the cybercapitalist phonoegregore, already anticipating the decline of Fordism, was seeking such a set of schizophonic modulatory modalities to further its capture operations.

Though much of what surrounds the events of 1995 remains open to conjecture, the subliminal hum of machinic earworm generation continues to do its work inside me, undoubtedly long past the obsolescence of this mode of aural dissemination. All the while, the premises outlined herein (and then some), flowing from (and entangled with) this condition, have already begun mapping—*hyperstitionally*[37]—the coordinates of a *phonoegregore-to-come*. As mentioned at the outset, the tight, noise-absorbent negative feedback of capitalist modulation is but a limited, affordable compromise. Indeed, portals can already be glimpsed, *earwormholes*, in which psycho-somatic-machinic constructs can be carefully engineered to differentially compact and distend temporal flow between gaseous, viscous, and solid states in order to pressure memory retention, dislocate bodily time from clock time, preempt the normalization cycle by introducing figures into a not-yet-primed ground, leveraging music's occult proclivities in the name of an as yet dimly adumbrated futurity.[38]

---

37. A portmanteau term coined by Nick Land and the CCRU (Cybernetic Culture Research Unit) in the mid-1990s, combining hype (or hyper) and superstition, *hyperstition* operates via (at least) four vectors: 1. Element of effective culture that makes itself real; 2. Fictional quantity functional as a time-traveling device; 3. Coincidence intensifier; 4. Call to the Old Ones. See http://hyperstition.abstractdynamics.org/archives/006777.html.

38. The theoretical vectors deployed here have also been worked through in a *Preemptive Glossary for a Techno-Sonic Control Society*, accessible in its current form at http://xenopraxis.net/MC_technosonicglossary.pdf

2

Art Theory/Fiction as Hyper Fly

Prudence Gibson

Fiction within theory texts (and vice versa) can be an effective way of recording encounters that take place at the nexus of imagination and argument. Theory fiction emerges when the activity of reasonable articulations of information becomes blocked. Fear of the finite takes hold and, at that point of pulsating energy, a membrane needs to be punctured. The membrane is the boundary between art fiction and theory, the puncturing equipment is the fictional deviation, announced (or not) by a commentating narrator. The discussion in this chapter is both an analysis of that deviating, fictional phenomenon, as it relates to several artists and their artworks, and also an enactment of it.

French artist Hubert Duprat is a naturalist whose interests extend to creating man-made microscopic reconstructions of crystals and caddisfly larvae.[1] Duprat carefully collects the caddisflies and transports them to his lab, where he separates them from their aquatic larvae cases. These cases were originally made by the caddisfly using sticks, bark and moss gathered from their immediate environments. He then placed them in an aquarium, alongside small nuggets of gold and semi-precious stones. Soon, these versatile creatures constructed new sheaths out of the introduced materials. The resultant caddisfly hybrids were an emergent species that have evolved from their original biological course.

The ability of the caddisfly to self-generate, using unconventional materials and by creating elaborate abiotic casings, reminds me of Timothy Morton's concept of the 'hyperobject', as a thing that exists outside chronological time, that is not fully visible for certain periods (like the moon) and that won't decay like undistributed local biotic matter. A hyperobject, in this instance, functions as a unified but uncontained object with inter-objective relations to other things and also as a pluralised object with adaptive possibilities and multiple, expansive applications.

---

1. Jeffrey Kastner, 'Artist Project Trichopterae: Hubert Duprat,' *Cabinet Magazine*, 25, 2007, accessed July 17, 2014, http://www.cabinetmagazine.org/issues/25/duprat.php.

The caddisfly's capacity for cross-material change, for experimental modi-
fication and for acclimatisation to a new ecosystem relates to some of these general qualities of hyperobjects, as devised by Morton. The fly creates a mutant
home (ever so monstrous in its glitziness), having lost its former, shabby incar-
nation. As hyperobject, it is not limited by its locality, because we are bound by
our distinctly human apprehension of what locality might mean and hyperobjects exist beyond that apprehension.

In terms of specific hyperobject qualities, the caddisfly is 'viscous' because it
sticks to other materials: it is pervasive. The caddisfly is not just in front of me;
it is attached to me; it is around me; it is me. It is 'nonlocal' because the insect
can thrive in a natural and unnatural environment at the same time; it can be
both anatomically conventional but also synthetically aggregated, at once. Stephen Muecke discusses the hyperobject's 'phased' nature in a review of Morton's
book. He says that Morton's hyperobjects act simultaneously, but with time/
space existing within them, rather than as an external event, and that this is
their viscosity, because they display a lack of discreteness.[2] So, they are not indi-
vidually separated but are, instead, mutually attached.

Finally, the caddisfly conforms to Morton's definition of a hyperobject, due
to its 'interobjective' and vicarious connections with other objects. Also, it exists
in shared space, not so much in space-time, but as space-time.[3] This means that
Duprat's interruption of time and causation (with his scientific experimentation,
his disciplinary regime and his laboratory discretions) is not acting upon the
caddisfly to precipitate change. Instead, the caddisfly has already been changing, simultaneously, in its relation to all other things.

So, I am attracted to the little caddisfly, because it is a hyperobject and
adapts well to a new situation, without being compromised (despite the potential
peril of too much bling.) I would like to apply the *readiness to reorganise contextual
structures* of the caddisfly and the hyperobject to fictive art writing, in an attempt
to extend the metaphor of versatility. However, narrative fiction is a tricky beast,
as its process requires working a-chronologically, and using omissions and metaphors to generate narrative threads. Nothing can be explicitly stated or told
in fiction: it must be shown through characterisation, dialogue and imagery. In
contrast, scholarly writing, requires an expositional mode of outlining, confirm-
ing and supporting—a chronological movement of argument from proposition
to conclusion. These genres seem to work against each other. The challenge is
to infuse the one with the other and to create a dialectic regarding their inter-
objective relation.

ART THEORY/FICTION AS A HYPEROBJECT CROSS-DISCIPLINE

Fiction-infused art writing might be considered an adaptive cross-discipli-
nary critical practice similar to the caddisfly. It follows the trend, in contemporary art, of incorporating fiction, particularly science fiction, into art practice,

---

2. Stephen Muecke, 'Global Warming and other Hyperobjects,' *LA Review of Books* February 20, 2014,
accessed May 15, 2014, http://lareviewofbooks.org/review/hyperobjects.

3. Timothy Morton, *Hyperobjects*, Minneapolis, Minnesota Press, 2013, p. 81.

including the practice of art writing. I propose that this can best be discussed/analysed through Object Oriented Ontology theories and especially through Timothy Morton's notion of hyperobjects, with which I began.

In his review of Morton's *Hyperobjects*, Stephen Muecke writes:

> The pressing reality of hyperobjects now has the effect of destroying this critical distance, of making it impossible to separate causality from art (as if art were mere decoration on top of the 'real workings'), and of forcing us to abandon the modern habit of redemptively imaging a better future, for now we have to hesitate in front of what hyperobjects are placing right in front of us: that we are not in charge of the future anymore, because it might well be *without us*.

Muecke illustrates how hyperobjects afford a wider space (outside human existence) to be more than inert and sonorous sentinels, watching time. Instead, their activity, enactment, actuality and action are liberated. This is potentially exciting for analyses of things as aesthetic works. The disciplines of environmental ecology and aesthetics might appear to be different, but the 'real workings' that Muecke mentions are a reminder that the habit of hopeful faith has been foreclosed.

I subsequently pose that fictive art writing is, itself, a hyperobject (which seems logical, since language itself is probably hyperobjective), due to its uncanny knack of superimposing or simultaneously engaging two things at once. Morton writes of the difference between climate change and global warming as the difference between thing and phenomenon; however, he yields to an update of the distinctions by saying they are a package rather than choices.[4] In application to fictive art writing, the hyperobjectivity of this concept lies in the packaging of the two, alongside a third, whereby the 'story' is a phenomenon, the 'narration' is a thing and the art is the discourse.

We feel the narrative as a mood, as a voice, as some kind of tale that affects us, materially and corporeally. The narration is an aggregate of literary elements: techniques and crafts used to build the text (via dialogue, description and omission). There is a gap between the phenomenon and the thing (and, therefore, between the story and the narration), as with all OOO objects, but Morton writes, 'There is a gap, but I can't find it. The best term for this is nothingness, by which I mean meontic nothing'.[5] He argues that meontic nothing is not absolutely nothing at all, but a flickering distortion, a quality of nothing.[6] If fictive art writing can be termed a hyperobject, then this quality of nothing (but not absolutely nothing) becomes important and relates to the cosmic, the esoteric, the speculative, the horrifying nothing, the black matter of intergalactic space and how it is manifested in science fiction . . . and increasingly, in contemporary art.

---

4. Morton, *Hyperobjects, p.8.*

5. Timothy Morton, 'Same As It Ever Was,' *Libre* 35, 2014, p. 21, accessed April 17, 2014, https://www.academia.edu/3200652/Biosynthesis_Same_as_It_Ever_Was.

6. Ibid.

THEORY/FICTION'S LOVE AFFAIR WITH SCI-FI

A corresponding mushrooming of pseudo-science and fictional concepts has also occurred in theory fiction, examples being Reza Negarestani's *Cyclonopedia* and the Confraternity of Neoflagellants' *th.N Lng folk2go*.[7] In the latter, we find the following statement,

> What follows is a schizo-comic fictioning that lays bare the connections between our hyper-modernity and a medieval-ism that is its appropriate accompaniment and frame of ref-erence (this being precisely, neomedievalism, or, in short, the laying out of a 'Medieval-Tech®'as the only adequate frame of reference for these Troubled Times). Old World meets New World in an untimely assemblage (or, 'Mall') in which, in fact, all temporalities—futures, pasts, future-pasts, past-futures—are deployed, mashed up and then realigned so as to open, at last, a space for something different (this most cramped court allows us, at last, to breathe!)[8]

Schizo-comic fictioning, in this second text, is a fictionalisation of rigorous discussion regarding the neo-medievalist systems of disorder and disobedience as a result of eroded sovereignty and the massive distribution of digital media imagery and information. No longer are we so slavishly dependent on facts, as distinct from social structures and conventions. If our lives have become de-centralised and de-temporalised, no longer can we follow chronological story-telling formats.

In the preface to the collectively written book, Simon O'Sullivan describes their seven writerly logics as fictioning, acceleration, geopolitics, the spectacle, scenes, gifts and things. To this thesis, an active articulation of fictive and novelistic elements in a theoretical treatise that is also subsumed with experiential art passages (fictioning) is most relevant. In an excursion close to the aims of this chapter, O'Sullivan charts the group's movement through ideas of neo-medievalism and art and subject and ontology, looping around to medieval times to explain speculative thought. It is interesting, in light of OOO and Speculative Realism, that 'fictioning' plays a substantial role. It reflects the re-introduction of fictive elements and narratorial qualities in traditionally non-fictional forms of writing.

INTERGALACTICA

Another artist whose work is an encounter with theory and fiction is Melbourne-based Sam Leach. His artwork incorporates strange science fictions as subject matter. A recent exhibition comprised a series of paintings and objects hung on a hand-crafted or carpentered wooden rack, which sat out from the wall and curved past the corner.[9] Several paintings had small shelves jutting from their bases, upon which geological specimens sat. Leach has used archery imagery before (as references to illusionism and the extinction of animals; that is, targets), and the concentric circles were evident in this body of work, too.

However, the reason my heart skipped a beat when I saw the exhibition was

---

7. The Confraternity of Neoflagellants, *th.N Lng folk2go*, New York, Punctum Books, 2013, pp. i-v.
8. Ibid.
9. Sam Leach exhibits with Sullivan Strumpf Fine Art, Sydney. His exhibition *Dymaxion* was held in April 2013.

its other-worldly, supernatural elements. The works incorporated evolutionary biology, the Anthropocene and sci-fi speculation, all at once. The rocks, like H.P. Lovecraft's cosmic rocks, were alive. In his story *The Colour Out of Space*, the town of Arkham slowly rots and decays to dust, due to the strange arrival of a galactic meteor, which slowly and malevolently poisons all life forms.[10] Leach's rocks, too, vibrated with vital, malevolent energy. The paintings and rock specimens were immanent, existing for and in themselves.

A large mapped painting by Leach, structured in triangular shapes (utilising the method of opening out or flattening the globe into an isocohedron), charted a strange ecological crisis. Apes, skulls, and geometric imaging of utopian landscapes formed an overall artistic vision of disaster and a desire 'to see' with a fresh, mapped and unified perspective.

University of Plymouth academic Robert Jackson,[11] in writing about Leach's 2010 *Present-at-Hand* exhibition, which clearly refers to Heidegger, cited the artist's work as fitting into an Object-oriented aesthetic. And for his 2012 exhibition, Leach wrote:

> When we use an axe, we do not theorise about it. It is ready to hand, as Heidegger says, ready to be used for chopping. But while we are actually using it, the axe itself cannot be at the forefront of our minds. It becomes less visible. When we stop using the axe, when it ceases to be functional, it becomes more visible - it is present at hand. If it is only non- functioning tools that can be present at hand, then something is always missing in these present at hand entities.[12]

Leach is referring to Harman's books and papers on Heidegger's ready-to-hand, present-at-hand concepts. Harman points out that this latency is true of all entities, not just tools, and that they withdraw, not just from human attention, but from each other's attention, as well.[13] Even in the realm of the non- or pre-human, unfathomable space, the deep sea, the sub-microscopic places where no human sees, objects interact without being fully revealed to each other. When a wave laps against a rock, both the rock and the wave see only part of each other—a caricature.[14] For an art writing ontology and for a writing practice that seeks to escape description and explanation, an enactment of writing using a meta-fictive voice (divested of expert authority) fits into this latent philosophy of being. My computer is my tool, but I frequently forget to position it into my practice and theory of writing. For, surely, the computer, my scribe, has applications, networks and systems of knowledge well beyond the finitude or limits of my writing.

I met Leach in his Melbourne studio, shortly after his *Dymaxion* show, to talk object theory, science fiction and cosmic enterprises. Leach's house sits on

---

10. H.P. Lovecraft, 'The Colour Out of Space,' in *The Call of Cthulhu and Other Weird Stories*, London, Penguin Modern Classics, 2002, pp.170-199.

11. Robert Jackson, 'The Anxiousness of Objects and Artworks: Michael Fried, Object Oriented Ontology and Aesthetic Absorption,' *Speculations, Vol. II*, 2011.

12. Sam Leach, artist statement, exhibition page, Sullivan Strumpf gallery web site, *Present At Hand* 2010, accessed July 9, 2013, www.sullivanstrumpf.com/exhibitions/90/intro/.

13. Graham Harman, *Heidegger Explained*, Chicago, Open Court Publishing, 2007, 64.

14. Leach, *Present To Hand*.

a wide suburban street, lined with large plane trees. Leach's house had vegetable garden beds, topped with hay, bordered with hardwood, raised above higgledy piggledy bricks. The entrance was down a side path, where small people's clothes flapped on a line.

I dodged a pink sparkly dress and knocked on the glass paned door, which was covered in specks of misapplied white paint. Sam Leach answered the door and we stood awkwardly, like primary school students, incapable of making small talk. 'Shall I come in?' I finally suggested. He opened the door wider, but I suspected ambivalence. Even once I was inside the entry hall, he blocked my way and seemed hesitant to lead me further back, further in. It's not uncommon for artists to feel equivocal about showing an art writer where they work, how they practise. I had experienced such irresolution a hundred times before.

Leach's studio was a sunny room in his home, with white-painted floorboards, walls and ceilings creating a white cube. Half-finished works hung on a far wall. His wife and two daughters were not home, but their shadows lingered in the mess of children's toys poking out of doors, shoes of various sizes scattered about, drawings stuck on fridge and door jambs. Leach paused in the kitchen, almost offered me a coffee, but then led me straight out through the back playroom, which the pots of paint, piles of kids' drawing paper and a light dusting of glitter managed to brighten. Onwards, to an outside shed.

There, in a room smelling of wet blankets, a projector was set up and directed towards a bare wall. Movie night? In the morning? As I looked around the dark room, which had only one bubble glass window, I noticed some of Leach's earlier works on the walls. These were very small paintings, without the usual resin surface. They were illusionistic. The concentric circular forms began to dazzle and warp my vision, like a fairground funhouse. There were eight small paintings, which began to move and tilt, recede and shimmer in sickening syncopation. 'This is where *Dymaxion* started,' said Leach, breaking the nauseating spell. 'It began with this documentary and I think it will help you understand my paintings. It's an illegal copy. From the military, in the US.' I decided not to ask how Leach came to have this illicit film and instead hoped he might make popcorn.

So, the movie started. No popcorn, but there were three punnets of baby tomatoes piled up on a side table next to the chair Sam directed me into. It was a little confusing at first. It was real footage of the interior of a confined space. A simulator? A space craft? The camera angles were shaky, suggesting the film was not a formal documentation but a home-job. It functioned like a Sensecam, those small camera devices that hang around your neck to aid memory and emotive experience, and take images every thirty seconds. In other words, it was a stuttering and unsophisticated sequence of images, rather than a film. Difficult to watch but compelling, it had been edited too, because there were gaps and glitchy interruptions of natural time.

That was the form of the film. The content was something else entirely. I never saw the face of the protagonist wearing the Sensecam but he (or his camera, rather) had recorded an oral narrative at the same time as the photographic sequence. 'What is this?' I asked Leach but he only shook his head and pointed to the wall, indicating I should keep watching. 'US military. Space personnel,' he said, tightly. So I watched, from inside the craft's small space, which had limited views to the outside. There were no clues as to the name of the project or the other two passengers in the craft. However, there was the commentary.

'We are close to the destination,' the Sensecam guy said. 'Johnno reckoned we were going to take much longer on this mission. He's got a thousand bucks that says we will be back by Thursday but I reckon he's overestimated. We'll be back on Wednesday. So that means a tidy little sum for me to spend on my girlfriend' (laughter). The film showed Johnno looking pissed off, or maybe just sulky, while attending to several computer screens and what looked like cables running everywhere. 'Johnno doesn't like to lose a bet, even out here' (more laughter). Indeed, Johnno looked increasingly irritated by the owner of the Sensecam.

The film (loosely termed) flickered and glitched for a few seconds, but Leach tapped my hand and mouthed 'just wait.' Sure enough, the sequence started again, for the third time. It was unclear how much time the film covered, overall. This section had no narration for a few minutes. The images showed Johnno being slowly fascinated by a light that seemed to have appeared out of nowhere. Like a Tinkerbell glow, the light hovered near Johnno's ear—a tiny fairy. It trembled and emanated energy as though it might spontaneously combust.

It didn't. Instead, it expanded to twice its size, soon as big as a plum. Then it aggregated into a million tiny self-replicated glowing lights and moved towards Johnno. In a nanosecond, Johnno was fragmented into atomic dust particles. One minute there, the next gone. A second later, the view shifted as the Sensecam fell to the floor. 'I don't understand, Sam,' I said to Leach. 'What is this? Some kind of mockumentary?' He pulled out his laptop and clicked onto a Nanotechnia software site, slid across a still from the film (exactly when the glows seemed to fragment poor Johnno into a constellation) and zoomed closer and closer. 'Look at that?' said Sam. 'Just look.' We peered at the screen and I found it difficult to make sense of what I saw. At the nano-level, the organisms were clearly biotic.[15] A blossoming of tiny moving creatures, with wriggling legs and mercury-like bodies. Leach explained that there were two fatalities on a recent mission to take light and sound readings on the far side of the moon. The mission's grim end was not evident in the media, or not that I had heard of.

'Did you tell anyone about this, Sam?' I asked. 'Did you report it?' He told me he wouldn't be reporting it; it wasn't his business and it wasn't my place to get involved either. He had only shown it to me to elaborate on the relevance and importance of his recent body of artwork, *Dymaxion*. This was something I needed to know if I *insisted* on writing on his work. I was disturbed by Leach's film. Perhaps I was overreacting, but it seemed incomprehensible that this story was now known to me, and a small group of other individuals, but not known by the world at large. It was also an unusual and bleak source of his creativity.

---

15. This element is highly influenced by Wil McCarthy, *Bloom*, New York, Del Rey, 1999.

There was the sound of a wheelie bin being dragged along Sam's path, out-side the back shed. The wet blanket smell was churning my stomach again, but not enough to miss the look of fear on Sam's face. 'Are you okay Sam?' He jumped up and snatched a folder from the side table and thrust it at me. 'You have to sign this agreement. To say you won't divulge what I've shown you.'

My mouth was open. I wasn't sure how to respond, so I glanced at the fold-er, which had a contract with my name, all ready for the signing. Perhaps it was that Sam had prepared the document before I came, or it was the overbearing stink of wet wool, but I resisted signing. Just as I prepared to tell him I wouldn't be able to do as he'd asked, I noticed a silhouette move outside the opaque shed window. Then another. I saw Sam see the shadows, too. 'Hurry, do it now,' he said, 'Then, head off.' It may have been his family returning home? A friend, come to visit? Or something else. Sam stood and shifted his weight from one foot to the other, wiped his hands on his jeans and looked at his watch. So I scribbled my name, thrust the paper at his chest and strode back through his front door. Glancing down each end of the street, I took off up the footpath, fast as I could.

FICTION ART/THEORY

In art, the inferences of fiction and speculation create an added element, a harbouring of esoteric implications, a further hyperobjective layer of experi-ence. The question is posed: should the lines be blurred between the disciplines? Are we allowed to muck about with established genres like this?

In this vein of fictional interlayering, Donna Haraway wrote an essay as part of 2012 *Documenta(13)*'s 100 Notes. Titled, 'Sf: Speculative Fabulation and String Figures,' it contained a manifesto for Terrapolis (an earth city) as a mul-ti-species, multi-temporal, multi-material equation: fabulism or fictive specula-tions, as a means of becoming more aware of all things. Each line led from the preceding one. Haraway preferred the term 'companion species' to 'post-hu-man' and cited her interpretation of Isabelle Stengers' cosmopolitics as 'playing cat's cradle,' a complex and addictive game of web-like manipulations of wool, usually requiring another person as collaborator. Haraway is yet another inter-national theorist contributing to an experimentation with cosmic alternatives, within transdisciplinary literature, specific to art.

For Haraway, 'Sf' is speculative fabulation, speculative feminism, science fiction, science fact, science fantasy and string figures. She says, 'In looping threads and relays of patterning, this sf practice is a model for worldling.'[16] She also sees it as an opening up of what is yet to come. This conjecture and con-tingent possibility are complementary to an OOO view of the flat ontology of things and of actions that transgress normal chronology. Things can loop back or spiral together—in play or in competition. One art thing does not lead to the next and the next, even though art history may have lulled us into thinking it is so. Incorporating fiction into art writing might be seen as a type of contin-gent worldling, a sophisticated cosmopolitanism, in the sense that fiction shifts

---

16. Donna Haraway, 'Sf: Speculative fabulation and string figures,' *Documenta (13)* 100 notes, Ostfil-dern, Hatje Cantz, 2012, p.4.

time away from the present alone, and incorporates hyper-time, where chronology is halted and sometimes even slowed down or sped up. Fiction sits outside human time, and, in this way, fits into the model of a hyperobject. For me, 'fiction as a hyperobject' reinforces being as beyond the wordlings and outwards to the universelings.

ART FICTION/THEORY = HYPEROBJECT

Sticky, Gooey

An example of a hyperobject is Einstein's space-time.[17] Hyperobjects beckon us with their familiarity: we know it's getting hotter, a condition preceding climate change. Morton says that, as we approach objects, more and more objects emerge.[18] Fiction might fit that category due to its removal from usual chronology, which is disallowed outside fictional realms. Fiction, as storytelling, is massively distributed and endlessly familiar, in the sense that narratorial activities are multiplied across generations and cultures . . . and species. Stories have transdisciplinary modes of operation, structure, characters and complications. Take, for example, the spin of the atom. The spin momentum is a quantum phenomenon that has implications for theory as well as industry/science. It also has implications for preserving, processing and recovering data. The history of the spin makes a good story, but its qualities (as a human-told story) already are elements of a story. It changes and is affected by various environments but is, ultimately, a tale told by humans while existing without them too, in the sense that they will still exist, anyway. So, do the atoms start the story? Or are they the story? Stories stick with us, creating the strange familiarity of temporal undulation.

It is not just humans who, upon waking, begin the narrative of the day. All creatures have consciousness that is connected to what we term the inner monologue, or stream of consciousness, or self-organising qualities. By this I mean that the principles of fiction are deeply embedded in humans and other creatures alike, thereby sticking or adhering to everything.

Phased

We don't feel the hyperobject global warming and we can't see it in any human-oriented three-dimensional way, but we feel the tsunami. Likewise, we don't feel the narrative (the structure in place to make it happen), we feel the story (the quality). The multitudinous nature of fiction, its millions of threads, its abundant iterations, its never-ending variations, lead me to think that it would comply with hyperobjects' multidimensional state.

Interobjective

Interobjectivity is an interesting hyperobjective property to align with art theory/fiction. Transdisciplinary by nature, interobjective relations between various elements also leave a footprint on other kinds of objects, as informa-

---

17. Morton, *Hyperobjects*, 61.

18. Ibid, 55.

tion.[19] This means that a cross-over between art writing, theory and fiction is formed by its various individual parts. However, it is made apparent through the sequence of symptoms, academic interest in writing and talking about fiction in art and, finally, science fiction in art. Fiction is the hyperobject that leaves its imprint on these other disciplines at the point where they meet.

Non-local

Think of nuclear radiation, invisible to the human eye until its symptoms are visible on other objects. Radiation leaks, global warming and nicotine addictions are not here in the palm of my hand, yet they are more than abstract nouns. They are undeniably things, with concrete evidence in their manifestations. 'Non-locality' is a term borrowed from quantum theory. In an OOO context, things are irreducible and indivisible. Two entangled electrons can communicate across a distance. Simultaneously. This simultaneity is of recurring relevance to OOO.

Fiction or the fictioning act is non-local/phased in that certain qualities will always be obscured from our view and it eludes our real grasp. It has temporal undulation in the sense that stories are suspended along with our disbelief and we experience them as disconnected from reality. Stories are phased because they pass through so many sieves of belief and disbelief, emerging as new information at the end.[20] Finally fiction discloses interobjectivity, which is a kind of abyss that floats between objects.

A DARKER AESTHETIC ECOLOGY

Speaking of dark realities, in the process of researching this thesis, particularly the work of Hubert Duprat, I heard an interesting story about the artist's past. This is strictly confidential and deeply illegitimate but it turns out that he spent many weeks collecting his caddisflies. They were located in water environments—streams in the mountains, creeks in the hills. These small creatures were hard to find, being so microscopic. However, Duprat had perfected the skills required to find them and capture them. His scientific methodology was pre-eminent, respected across Europe; his ability to process his experiments according to OHS and contamination rules was without question; it was only his sense of dress that sat outside accepted standards.

Duprat was an average sized man. He has been described as dead-sexy, with an arbitrary ability to look appealing whilst simultaneously choosing quite inappropriate garments. For instance, his favoured apparel for his caddisfly jaunts comprised leather jacket, suit pants, flip flop sandals and a silk singlet. This silky sheath looked a little unusual, being conventionally a feminine piece of clothing; however, Duprat's reason was that the fabric felt soft against his skin, and he frequently experienced nipple rash . . . so he apparently had good cause. Despite the assorted combination of fashion styles, he managed to elicit from women many admiring looks. Those who were usually well-mannered and self-com-

---

19. Ibid.
20. Ibid, 77.

posed, found themselves glancing at his groin. Women, who prided themselves on their modesty and discretion, allowed their eyes to linger over his heavy brow and gentle eyes. His legs were muscled from cycling and his hair was tinged blond by the sun, though pleasantly greyed in patches.

The point is that Duprat was a women's man. He wasn't interested in men or their rugby or their choice of superannuation funds. It was women he sought. This caused trouble at the lab, where he occupied a booth. Firstly, he was unwelcome for compromising the other lab workers' scientific reputations, by introducing art to their cluster. Secondly, women could not resist him. Sara had pulled his body against hers in the adjacent photocopy room. Genevieve had cornered him in the change rooms and pulled her clothes off, before he could take a side-step. Hannah had followed him home one night and strapped on some leather apparatus and killer stilettos, providing the artist with a series of 'memory frames' for many moons afterwards.

On a different sensual level, Duprat enjoyed salami and soda bread, with unsalted butter. He preferred red wine to beer. He liked to sleep fully clothed and his favourite song was Abba's 'Fernando'. The soil was muddy from overnight rain and Duprat revelled in and reviled the feeling of that earthy substance oozing between his toes (his flip flop sandals exposed his feet to the elements). Some woodpeckers were knocking on the trees in pleasing syncopation and an occasional breeze scattered leafy water drops all around him.

When he found the stream bend he sought, where he had found the caddisflies before, he noticed an unusual sound. Like plastic sheets rubbing together, interrupted by an unearthly clacking sound, like no natural specimen Duprat had ever known. Some kid using a computer in the woods, he wondered? Unlikely. But the noises certainly sounded like a computer game—for instance, Minecraft. Duprat decided he must be a little weary, having begun a relationship with a beautiful woman, Elise, who harboured an endless sensual appetite. A petite and sweet-tempered woman, she also liked to cook his favourite coq au vin, using hand-picked field mushrooms from her home town (she had her mother post them, to make this dish exceptional), though he had not yet worked out how she knew coq au vin was his favourite evening meal.

As he unloaded his sterile bottles and sealed containers from his pack, he saw a cluster of caddisflies beside a mossgreen rock. His job, that day, would be quick. No more than a few minutes. He smiled at his good fortune. But as he knelt by the side of the trickling water, which he occasionally splashed on his face for refreshment, an enormous shape reared up from behind the rock, blocking the sunlight. The rock was about one metre high, but this thing rose higher and higher, its shadow casting across poor Duprat's silk singlet.

It was a horrifying spectacle. An enormous caddisfly rose up to three metres high, its antennae clacking together: the source of the fearful clacking noise Duprat had heard. This fly was not like the regular species Duprat collected. It had morphed into the casings, which his experiments had divined. Somehow, his specimens must have become contaminated. This fly had not created a casing from gold, but had formed into a monstrous form, grotesquely expanded into a giant creature.

Although it did no more than appear, in all its horrifying and symptomatic ghastliness, Duprat ran. He did not collect his provisions (bottles and jars), but ran back to his vehicle and skidded back to town, back to Elise, feeling shocked and looking white. Elise asked no questions but uncorked a lovely bottle of red and served him a plate of soft brie and baguette. Strange, he supposed, that she did not notice his distress; however, it soothed him to adjust to his home environment in peace and to wonder if it had been no more than sleep deprivation or low blood sugar levels. A conjured spectre of his imagination.

Later that night, as Duprat moved into Elise's body, his face buried in her soft blonde hair, he thought he heard a very distant, very faint sound coming from Elise's lips. He fell back against his pillows and soon welcomed the beginning of sleep, for his exhaustion had irrationally made him think it was a clacking noise, accompanied by the rubbing of plastic against plastic. Enjoying the silky feel of the pillows, he allowed the allure of sleep to overwhelm him, not understanding this was the worst thing that he could possibly do.

CONCLUSION

Morton expounds that hyperobjects become visible during eco-crises but are also a signal or symptom of that crisis. Infusing ecological issues into art and art writing via sci-fi and fictioning methodologies draws attention to the horrors of ecological, technological and psychological demise. His hyperobject theory makes sense of the way humans tend to document and explore crises through tangential or metaphoric modes. Art, art writing, theory and fiction are phased so that it is difficult to identify them within any given text simultaneously. The elements of this thesis are viscous as they pervade critical art analysis, the experiential art-writer's anecdotes, theory/fiction and an attitude of meta-fictive self-awareness. For these reasons, theory/fiction looks good in the meshed red lace dress of the hyperobject.

If theory/fiction, heavy with sci-fi elements, can scrub up well in a cocktail dress, then how might telepathy stand at the drinks party? Perhaps in green silk shift with a long amber bead necklace and pumpkin Jimmy Choo shoes. This familiar detail might be memory, or madness, or it is a crucial transmission in the network of Speculative Aesthetics.

3

Art, Philosophy, and Non-standard Aesthetics

Thomas Sutherland

> In Laruelle the aesthetic stance is the same as the utopian
> stance. In the most prosaic sense, non-philosophy describes a
> kind of non-place where conventional rules seem not to apply.
> —Alexander R. Galloway, 'Laruelle: Against the Digital'

Reflecting upon the relationship between aesthetics and philosophy, according to which the former typically submits to the aegis of the latter, François Laruelle observes that

> [a]esthetics was always a carbon copy of art in philosophy and subsequently art was always understood as a deficient modality of philosophy. It is the phenomena of self-modeling of philosophy in regards to art, where philosophy finds its model in art, but a model which is philosophically pre-formed or pre-decided.[1]

It is precisely this treatment of art, by philosophy, as an inferior clone, even as the latter draws upon its resources, that I examine in this chapter, focusing on the various ways that metaphysicians have internalized artistic modalities of thought. I begin with an investigation of Plato and his expulsion of all artists and poets from his idealized republic (an outright exclusion of art from philosophical discourse which paradoxically guarantees its essential interiority within the structure of this very form of thought), and then, following a brief discussion of the birth of aesthetics in the eighteenth century, move onto the interiorization of an artistic mentality within the work of Friedrich Nietzsche and Henri Bergson. I will lastly turn to the place of non-standard aesthetics within Laruelle's project as a potential remedy to this fraught relationship between artistic practice and philosophical theory, and try to understand the various ways in which philosophy as a discipline risks sidelining specifically artistic modes of experience in its drive toward a totalizing self-sufficiency.

---

1. François Laruelle, *Photo-Fiction, a Non-Standard Aesthetics*, Trans. Drew S. Burk. Minneapolis, MN: Univocal, 2012, p. 4.

For Laruelle, we do not need to take it for granted that philosophy, and aesthetics particularly (which in its normal operation is a type of categorization and judgment intimately tied to the philosophical schema) should have a monopoly over art:

> [w]e propose another solution that, without excluding aesthetics, no longer grants it this domination of philosophical categories over works of art, but limits it in order to focus on its transformation. It's about substituting for the conflict of art and philosophy the conjugation of their means regulated on the basis of a scientific model.[2]

This so-called scientific model is not so much a means of understanding art (which would in turn mean capturing it as an object of knowledge) as it is an immanent artistic practice, suspending philosophy's categorial boundaries. It does not propose yet another theory of art, but instead emphasizes the possibilities for a non-conceptual, non-reflexive artistic practice that is already given to us, and which would allow us to transform the undecidable coupling art and aesthetics (the philosophy of art) that homogenizes the former in the name of the latter.

PLATO AND THE ARTISTS

Plato (and the simulative image of his mentor Socrates that pervades his writings; a form of dissimulation, one might argue, inasmuch as Plato's words are never his own, always blended with those figurative interlocutors between which his arguments are constructed) was certainly not the first to denounce visual representation. The third commandment inscribed upon Moses' stone tablets is quite clear in this respect: 'Thou shalt not make unto thee any graven image, or any likeness of any thing that is in heaven above, or that is in the earth beneath, or that is in the water under the earth'.[3] Whilst this aspect of Judaic law is certainly important, it has less specifically philosophical significance in comparison to the Platonic interdiction.

In The Republic, Plato denounces artists—painters and poets in particular—as nothing more than frauds, who deal in 'things which are, in fact, two generations away from reality'.[4] The painter, for instance, is merely a 'representer of others' creations', not attempting to craft objects in accordance with the eternal truth of the Ideas, but instead producing simulacra of these Ideas' already corrupted sensorial representations.[5] This is why artists are described as working 'two generations away from the throne of truth'[6], producing a superficial resemblance to the singular being of these Ideas (good enough at least to fool the ignorant masses, who lack education and are thus easily swayed by appeals to their passions) and yet operating through an entirely separate logic of multiplicity and becoming. A painter, or visual artist more generally, is capable of producing a seemingly endless chain of distinct pieces of art 'only because

---

2. Laruelle, *Photo-Fiction, a Non-Standard Aesthetics*, p. 1.

3. Exodus 20.4

4. Plato, *The Republic*. Trans. Robin Waterfield. Oxford: Oxford University Press, 1993, p. 348.

5. Ibid. p. 348.

6. Ibid. p. 348.

his contact with things is slight and restricted to how they look'.[7] The practical reality, suggests Plato, is that no one who is capable of producing a truly original work (i.e. one that is not merely the distorted copy or simulacrum of another preexisting object) would sully themselves by instead opting to make pale imitations: if the painter 'really knew about the things he was copying in his representations, he'd put far more effort into producing real objects than he would into representations'.[8]

Plato's critique of poets, at a time when the orally transmitted poetry of Homer and Hesiod still formed the basis of Greek education, is similarly reproachful, insisting that all the poet really knows is

> how to represent things in a way which makes other superficial people, who base their conclusions on the words they can hear, think that he's written a really good poem about shoemaking or military command of whatever else it is that he's set to metre, rhythm, and music.[9]

Once again, his arguments regarding art are grounded in a distrust of ordinary citizens (and non-citizens, who of course formed the majority within the Greek city-state), and an unwavering belief that it is the philosopher exclusively who is able to discern the ontological gap between the turbulent flux and multiplicity of the empirical realm that constitutes everyday perceptual experience (and which is not only perpetuated, but amplified by the creation of artistic objects, the misguided moralities of the poets, and the shonky word-games of the sophists and rhetoricians), and the transcendent clarity of the Ideas. 'Philosophers are those who are capable of apprehending that which is permanent and unvarying, while those who can't, those who wander erratically in the midst of plurality and variety, are not lovers of knowledge'.[10]

Plato makes a separation or cut between two terms—the ideal and the sensible; that which is merely coming to be and that which is; the One and the Indefinite Dyad—in order to then both valorize the philosopher in their recognition of this division, and laud the ontological primacy of the former term in each instance, which binds these contraries under the sign of the Good. This is why he so eagerly wished to expel all painters and poets from his hypothesized and idealized city-state. Their works are mere simulacra: not even just copies, but copies of the copies; not merely distorted, corrupted imitations of the Ideas, but representations totally divorced from that ideality. They create an image of the world that he, as the philosopher, must denigrate and dispatch in order to uphold the unity-of-contraries that, according to Laruelle, constitutes the basis not only of his philosophy, but of all philosophies. Plato attempts to think the One, in the form of the Good, but can only do so in a unitary (rather than unified) manner, conceiving of the reciprocal duality of the Ideas and their baneful imitations (since the former are posited as the a priori conditions of the latter, the necessity of the latter is implied), whilst also, at the very same time, elevating

---

7. Plato, *The Republic*. p. 348.
8. Ibid, p.349.
9. Ibid, p.352
10. Plato, *The Republic*, p.203.

the Ideas to the position of transcendental unity through which this reciprocal relation is given. Such a unity is at once immanent and transcendent to this relation—internal and external. The philosopher, in the Platonic account, is consequently torn between thinking the purity of being in itself, and thinking the mixture of being with the aesthetic realm he despises, in order to demonstrate his superiority over it.

Art is, for Plato, a deficient modality of philosophical discourse: it is a distraction, whose representations and manipulations garble the truth contained within the Ideas, and detract from the masses' ability to comport themselves in a manner appropriate to the position of philosopher. The paradox of this, however, is that Plato's philosophy needs art. One of the invariant characteristics of philosophy, argues Laruelle, is its auto-position, where the aforementioned mixture of immanence and transcendence, empirical experience and idealized abstraction, given and givenness, is posited as determinative and exhaustive when it comes to thinking the real, thus placing philosophy 'in a state of overseeing in relation to itself'.[11] This is illustrated clearly in Plato's strange (and yet within the disquisitions of philosophy, utterly normal) equivocation, where the real is thought not in the blinding purity of the Ideas themselves, but in an empirico-ideal mélange that gives the philosopher a privileged view of the relationship between the Ideas and the various representations (both copies and simulacra), that are divorced from them and yet able to be judged by them. We have here a truth that claims to transcend the world (even whilst conditioning it), and yet nonetheless exists seemingly to legislate over and pass judgment upon it.

This is, extrapolating from Laruelle's account, the fundamental problem when art is incorporated into philosophy: the subordination (or outright dismissal, as in this case) of artistic practice is a characteristic component of philosophical discourse (keeping in mind of course that both Xenophanes and Heraclitus dismissed the rhapsodic epic poetry of Homer, even prior to Plato's sustained attack), and in particular, a constituent element of philosophy's auto-position, situating itself as superior to all regional disciplines and knowledges; yet at the same time this dismissal is required for said positioning. Artistic practices and products, as we see in Plato's description, are pre-given within the strictures and structurations of his philosophy. Integrating this purportedly mimetic, degraded exteriority into his philosophy in order to then denigrate it, art becomes an exteriority that is always already an interiority, insofar as it is already homogenized under the spatialized representation of the philosophical decision (the schism between the empirical and ideal, immanent and transcendent which only the philosopher in her or his wisdom may suture). This is what Laruelle calls the auto-givenness or auto-donation of philosophy. Whereas auto-position designates 'the dimension of ideal transcendence, of objectifying activity over itself, of auto-formation, auto-production, of Philosophical Decision', auto-givenness by contrast signifies that 'philosophy is, in a way to be determined each

---

11. François Laruelle, *Principles of Non-Philosophy*, Trans. Nicola Rubczak and Anthony Paul Smith, London and New York: Bloomsbury, 2013, p. 68.

time, its own presentation, its own offer and givenness'[12] such that only it is able to fulfil the necessity that it gives itself within the world (noting that for Laruelle, the 'world' must be understood as an object that is inherently philosophizable). In other words, the givenness of the philosophical decision is posited by itself, such that regional knowledges, disciplines, and practices (in this case the arts) are always already contained within this decisional form and structure, making any external access to or analysis of it seem impossible.

THE EMERGENCE OF AESTHETICS

Of course, Plato is perhaps a bad example to choose for this topic insofar as his outright exclusion of both aísthēsis (from which we get the copies of the Ideas encountered in our everyday experience) and the more deliberately artistic forms of tékhnē (from which we get the phantasmic representations of representations that he so despises) is, with quite good reason, never really replicated by any other philosopher. With the exception of Aristotle who, in defiance of his former teacher's dogmatism, wrote an appreciable quantity of material on the judgment of beauty in the arts, especially poetry and rhetoric (defending techniques of imitation in his Poetics as essential to human nature), art is not of much interest to ancient and early modern philosophers. It is predominately viewed as too mundane, too technical (in the aforesaid sense of tékhnē), and contributing little to the far loftier concerns of the philosophical elite. Saint Thomas' description in the Summa Theologiæ of the arts and crafts as 'regulation by reason of the making of things'[13] is instructive in this regard, bearing little resemblance to the championing of artistic autonomy and inspiration we tend to take for granted. This exclusion (as opposed to a dismissal, which is what we get from Plato)—as Umberto Eco describes it, 'a sort of devaluation of artistic as opposed to theoretical knowledge, from the idea of imitation of an imitation to the idea of a gnoseologia inferior'[14]—is perhaps most pronounced during the Age of Enlightenment, when philosophers on either side of the English Channel saw little intellectual value in these practices which seemed to contribute little to a rapidly expanding body of scientific and technical knowledge.

It is only in the eighteenth century, at the summit of Enlightenment thought (and thus also the precipice from which it would subsequently tumble) that aesthetics proper, as a distinct field of study, emerges. The term itself, which in its Greek origin refers primarily to sense perception, comes to refer specifically to the judgment of taste and beauty in the writings of the German philosopher Alexander Gottlieb Baumgarten, one of many at the time working to fill in the gaps left by Christian Wolff, the preeminent German-language philosopher of the age. Hoping to develop a science of aesthetics, Baumgarten was convinced that he could discover universal rules of beauty via individual judgments of taste. His great philosophical innovation, outside of mere nomenclature, was his

---

12. Laruelle, *Principles of Non-Philosophy*, pp. 234-235.

13. Saint Thomas Aquinas, *Summa Theologiæ: A Concise Translation*, Trans. Timothy McDermott, Notre Dame, IN: Christian Classics, 1989, p. 376.

14. Umberto Eco, *Kant and the Platypus: Essays on Language and Cognition*, Trans. Alastair McEwen, San Diego, CA: Harcourt, 1999, p. 32.

conviction that such judgments, and the feelings of pleasure and displeasure that come along with them, were not merely inferior substitutes or imitations of rational thought (a line of argument that persisted through the Enlightenment, assuming that aesthetic judgment was something to be passed through and transcended, rather than encouraged or analysed), but were a viable alternative to the intellect: the beginning, we might say, of a new expression of philosophical discourse, with art as a necessary component of its operations. 'Without art, philosophy lacks sensitivity and without philosophy, art lacks thought'.[15] It is at the origin of aesthetic theory in the mid-eighteenth century that this imbrication is directly explicated, rather than occluded (as it is in Plato).

With this development of aesthetics, a new emphasis upon the importance of subjective judgment—and the pitfalls of the oft-corrosive rationality that characterized Enlightenment rationalism—gradually arises:

> [a]s the validity of this knowledge was gradually questioned, and limited to highly circumscribed universes of discourse, there gradually emerged the possibility of an area of certainty that would definitely come very close to the Universal but through a quasi-numinous revelation of the particular.[16]

With the first signs of a nascent romanticism (or counter-Enlightenment) emerging, we begin to witness the contingencies of individual experience lauded as not only a complementary form of knowledge, but one that is actually superior, over and above the universals of natural science and its philosophical correlates. A new aesthetic modality of perception and thought springs up within philosophy, seen in the work of the British philosopher and politician Edmund Burke, who sought to catalogue 'those faculties of the mind which are affected with, or which form a judgment of the works of imagination and the elegant arts'[17], hoping to locate the root causes of all of such judgments within the human psyche. Likewise, the French philosopher Charles Batteux developed the notion of the fine arts as a realm of inherently beautiful objects, created by great talents, which is conspicuously separate from technical practices, and hence also autonomous of all quotidian concerns.

Perhaps most important though is the work of Kant—another follower of Wolff, and one who also relied greatly upon the writings of Baumgarten as the basis of his metaphysical research—who in his third Critique argues that judgments of taste 'lay claim to necessity and say, not that everyone does so judge—that would make their explanation a task for empirical psychology—but that everyone ought to so judge, which is as much as to say that they have an a priori principle for themselves'.[18] Kant perceived the work of Burke, in particular (from whom he borrows and augments the notion of the 'sublime'), as too focused upon the crude empiricisms of psychology, and sought instead the transcendental basis of such judgment. In the first Critique, Kant is also somewhat critical

---

15. Laruelle, *Photo-Fiction, a Non-Standard Aesthetics*, p. 4.

16. Eco, *Kant and the Platypus: Essays on Language and Cognition*, p. 32-33.

17. Edmund Burke, *A Philosophical Enquiry into the Origin of Our Ideas of the Sublime and Beautiful*, Oxford: Oxford University Press, 1990, p. 13.

18. Immanuel Kant, *Critique of Pure Reason*, Trans. Paul Guyer and Allen W. Wood, Cambridge: Cambridge University Press, 1998, p. 39.

of Baumgarten, declaring that his project is founded upon the 'failed hope ... of bringing the critical estimation of the beautiful under principles of reason, and elevating its rules to a science'[19], and suggesting that, like Burke, he is trapped within the confines of empirical research, unable to determine the a priori rules that must direct our aesthetic judgments.

It is this constant desire on Kant's part to identify and philosophically schematize the conditions of possible experience that provides Laruelle with the arche-example of philosophical decision, for in the Kantian model '[t]he transcendental withdraws from experience ... only in order to better return to it', attempting to identify the basic conditions of empirical thought in order to then judge this thought under the authority of a unified, transcendental subject according to which the empirical and ideal components of experience are synthesized as objects of knowledge.[20] Kant 'understood that perpetual war was the essence of ancient philosophy, what he called metaphysics, and that philosophy was being eaten up from the inside by a drive to auto-destruction'.[21] The irony of the Kantian project, however, is that as much as it wants to limit traditional philosophical hubris (exemplified by both Wolff and Baumgarten's dogmatic conviction that all fundamental truths could be derived through the testing of analytic a priori definitions via the principle of non-contradiction), and its propensity to speak on matters like the existence of God or the immortality of the soul (topics that Kant regards as little more than the fanciful flights of a reason constantly driven to extend beyond its boundaries), it still retains a decisional schism between an empirical datum (studied through the transcendental aesthetic) and an a priori factum (likewise through the transcendental logic), with the former effectively subordinated to the latter.

It is only following Kant, who understands art as a purposively purposeless mode of representation—and thus incorporates art within his already-developed transcendental schema—that aesthetics becomes a distinct and crucial component of philosophy. In regard to Eco's comments, it is interesting that he views this growing interest amongst eighteenth century philosophers regarding aesthetic judgment and taste as a (momentary) surrender of philosophy to the forces of artistic practice. Its ascendency weakened, philosophy retreats to a position in which its attempts to rationalize and systematize thought are tempered by the subjective judgment of a different, more artistic mode of thought. Is this actually the case though? Baumgarten was, of course, an unrepentant rationalist in the Wolffian fashion, emphasizing the need to develop a truly objective, scientific field of aesthetic theory, and Burke was convinced that 'the standard both of reason and taste is the same in all human creatures'.[22] Even Kant, who is so critical of what he perceives as these authors' vulgar empiricism, suggests that

19. Kant, *Critique of Pure Reason* p. 156.

20. François Laruelle. *From Decision to Heresy: Experiments in Non-Standard Thought*, ed. Robin Mackay, Falmouth: Urbanomic, 2012, p. 145.

21. François Laruelle, *Intellectuals and Power: The Insurrection of the Victim*, trans. Anthony Paul Smith, Cambridge and Malden: Polity, 2015, p. 21.

22. Burke, *A Philosophical Enquiry into the Origin of Our Ideas of the Sublime and Beautiful*, p.11.

the power of judgment first makes it possible, indeed necessary, to conceive in nature, over and above its mechanical necessity, a purposiveness without the presupposition of which systematic unity in the thoroughgoing classification of particular forms in accordance with empirical laws would not be possible.[23]

In all of these cases, what we see is not so much the surrender of philosophy to art as simply a change in the nature of philosophical ideality, shifting the terms of critique whilst still preserving art as a regional object and practice subordinated to philosophical categorization and legislation.

'What is standard within aesthetics, is that philosophy alone would be able to justify art attaining the real and that philosophy alone can provide its proper description'.[24] Aesthetics is, from this perspective, the means by which philosophy perpetuates its hegemony: the explicit incorporation, rather than dismissal of art does not mitigate its subordination within the basic philosophical decision, for it still appears as a supplement used to prop up the superiority of the philosopher's transcendent categories (in Kant's case the transcendental subject, forming the condition for all possible experience). Art is shrunk-to-fit, so to speak, within an already-delineated categorial schema. In the case of Kantian aesthetics, the free play of the faculties of the imagination and understanding that defines the judgment of beauty is still preformed by the faculty of intuition (i.e. of sensible space-time) and the transcendental aesthetic by which these a priori forms are studied. Art is thus still thought in philosophical terms, as a philosophy of art. 'Taken as a whole, aesthetics is a market of theories about art supported by the art market itself'.[25]

NIETZSCHE, BERGSON, AND THE PROBLEM OF TECHNICAL AÍSTHĒSIS

Perhaps the apogee of this gradual inclusion of art, and of aesthetics as a legitimate philosophical field of study, occurs within the work of Nietzsche, who attempts to not merely think art as an object of philosophical study, but to transform thought into an artistic, creative mode of practice. For Nietzsche, 'the real is fictional and the fictional real'.[26] This goal traverses his corpus. It begins with his distinction between the Apolline and Dionysiac aims of art, as synthesized within the tragic form, in The Birth of Tragedy, and his claim that the only real purpose of art is 'the conquest of subjectivity, release and redemption from the "I", and the falling-silent of all individual willing and desiring',[27] making clear parallels between such artistic practices and the broader aims of his philosophy (which in its emphasis upon contemplation as a means for transcending the boundaries of the subject still evinces the Schopenhauerian sympathies that he would soon disavow). It continues through to his later emphasis upon the will

---

23. Kant, *Critique of the Power of Judgment*, pp. 21-22.

24. Laruelle, *Photo-Fiction*, p.13.

25. Ibid, p. 4.

26. Laruelle, *Philosophy*, p. 228.

27. Friedrich Nietzsche, *The Birth of Tragedy and Other Writings*. Trans. Ronald Speirs. Cambridge: Cambridge University Press, 1999, p. 29.

to power as a dynamic and productive affirmation of the power of being, contrasted against the ascetic, nihilistic, and scientistic will to truth, which he describes as a 'logicizing, rationalizing, systematizing' mode of thought, which seeks truth as an end in itself, and in doing so reifies it as a stable, external, metaphysical entity.[28]

Nietzsche effectuates a thorough internalization of artistic practice within philosophical thought, incorporating the former into the latter whilst maintaining its subordinate or inferior position by establishing the superiority of an aesthetic philosophy over any specific objects of aesthetic judgment or contemplation. We can perhaps understand this distinction more clearly by looking briefly at Schopenhauer, who generally hews quite closely to Kantian transcendentalism, arguing that:

> [t]he artist allows us to look into the world through his eyes. The fact that he has these eyes, that he has cognition of the essential aspect of things lying outside of all relations, is precisely the gift of genius, and it is innate; but the fact that he also can lend this gift to us and allow us to use his eyes: this is acquired, it is the technical aspect of art.[29]

For Schopenhauer—who views art as the means toward a contemplative state wherein the empirical specificities of the artwork itself dissolve so as to reveal the Ideas that lie at the foundation of thought—the artistic genius is not a philosopher, but contains within herself the ability to attain (at least partially) such a state of contemplation, and in doing so, to impart this unto others through the production of art. What is unique to the philosopher then is the ability to systematize and articulate this process. 'In regard to knowledge of truths,' argues Nietzsche by contrast, 'the artist possesses a weaker morality than the thinker; he does not wish to be deprived of the glittering, profound interpretations of life and guards against simple and sober methods and results'[30]: the philosopher is now actually able to outshine the artist in this regard, preserving a clear-headed solemnity that the latter lacks.

In this way, Nietzsche internalizes the precepts of both aesthetic theory and practice so that he, the philosopher, may declare himself equivalent to artists themselves. Given what we have already seen though, this should not be interpreted as a philosophical colonization of terms once the sole domain of artists; rather, we must keep in mind that aesthetics has always been a means of thinking art in philosophical terms. Philosophy, as Laruelle notes, is not at all homogeneous in its aims and approaches, but it nonetheless 'possesses a homogeneous limit that is its auto-encompassing or auto-specular drive: philosophizability'.[31] Nietzsche, therefore, is not appropriating terms once foreign to philosophy (for

---

28. Friedrich Nietzsche, *The Will to Power*, trans. Walter Kaufmann and R. J. Hollingdale, New York: Vintage Books, 1967, p. 299.

29. Arthur Schopenhauer, *The World as Will and Representation, Vol 1*, trans. Judith Norman, Alastair Welchman, and Christopher Janaway, Cambridge: Cambridge University Press, 2010, p. 219.

30. Friedrich Nietzsche, *Human, All Too Human: A Book for Free Spirits*, trans. R. J. Hollingdale, Cambridge: Cambridge University Press, 1996, p. 80.

31. François Laruelle, *Struggle and Utopia at the End Times of Philosophy*, trans. Drew S. Burk and Anthony Paul Smith, Minneapolis, MN: Univocal, 2012, p. 111.

they originated within this discourse), but merely turning their direction inward, such that they are now virtues of philosophers themselves. The same could be said for Bergson, whose strict dualism between a spatialized, discretized, and externalized intellection and the continuous, temporal, intuitional interiority that precedes it effectively projects categories that since Kant had been deemed the domain of aesthetics (e.g. novelty, originality, etc.) onto thought itself. This means that the intuition, which is constantly oriented in its non-mechanistic causality toward a non-predictable future—its durée being 'that in which each form flows out of previous forms, while adding to them something new'[32]—is an aesthetic mode of thought, inasmuch as we understand aesthetics as aiming toward, in Kant's words, an awakening of the artist's 'own originality, to exercise freedom from coercion in his [sic] art in such a way that the latter thereby itself acquires a new rule, by which the talent shows itself as exemplary'[33]: the production of the genuinely new and original.

This aestheticization is framed as an attempt to bypass the stifling homogeneity of conscious thought:

> Plato was the first to set up the theory that to know the real consists in finding its Idea, that is to say, in forcing it into a pre-existing frame already at our disposal—as if we implicitly possessed universal knowledge. But this belief is natural to the human intellect, always engaged as it is in determining under what former heading it shall catalogue any new object; and it may be said that, in a certain sense, we are all born Platonists.[34]

Nonetheless Bergson, like Plato (and like Nietzsche also, whose aforementioned distinction between the will to power and the will to truth can be understood primarily as a critique of an increasingly positivistic mode of logico-mathematical scientific thought) is not always kind when assessing the new forms of artistic representation and mediated transmission that were appearing during his lifetime. In particular, Bergson is highly skeptical of both photography and cinematography, viewing them (like language as a whole) as technical instantiations of a preexisting psychological and philosophical tendency to divide experience up into discrete, homogeneous chunks: 'we end in the philosophy of Ideas,' he claims, 'when we apply the cinematographical mechanism of the intellect to the analysis of the real'.[35]

Both Nietzsche and Bergson agree that one of the problems with Platonic Idealism is the essential immutability of the Ideas. On this point Bergson writes that Plato's theory

> starts from the form; it sees in the form the very essence of reality. It does not take form as a snapshot of becoming; it posits forms in the eternal; of this motionless eternity, then, duration and becoming are supposed to be only the degradation.[36]

---

32. Henri Bergson, *Creative Evolution*, trans. Arthur Mitchell, Mineola, NY: Dover, 1911, p. 362.
33. Kant, *Critique of Judgment*, pp. 195-196.
34. Bergson, *Creative Evolution*, pp. 48-49.
35. Bergson, *Creative Evolution*, p. 315.
36. Bergson, *Creative Evolution*, p. 318.

As a consequence, they are entirely divorced from the continuity of one's internal duration. And for Bergson, cinema in particular is just the return of this mentality under a new guise, or in a new technical manifestation: it proffers a false image of time, convincing us that movement is just composed of series of still images played in front of our eyes one-after-another, and in doing so distracts us from any possible encounter with that primal, originary time contained within us, and which forms the foundation of all time-consciousness. Bergson, in other words, falls right back into art as tied to explicitly moral judgment: although he has little time for photography and cinema, at least within a specifically philosophical context, he has a much greater fondness for music (especially Beethoven), because its perceived temporality tends to fit more closely with his concept of duration. 'A melody to which we listen with our eyes closed, heeding it alone, comes close to coinciding with this time which is the very fluidity of our inner life'[37], Bergson writes, whilst also noting that even a melody—which appeals to him because it cannot be comprehended as just a series of individual notes; it only makes sense as a melody when in motion—is not fully analogous, for the simple reason that there is still too much discontinuous differentiation between intervals.

So this is the problem then, if we once again extrapolate from the perspective of Laruelle, who describes aesthetics as 'the claimed domination of philosophy over art by which philosophy claims to unpack its meaning, truth, and destination after the event of art's supposed death'[38]: Bergson internalizes characteristics once confined to aesthetics within his broader psychology and metaphysics, but he does so in order to reinforce (rather than undermine) the auto-position and auto-donation of philosophy. Rather than treating art as an autonomous knowledge or practice, it still remains a regional discipline, which philosophy claims to both condition (insofar as Bergson views philosophical thought as synonymous with the duration that acts as the foundation of such thought) and legislate over (insofar as Bergson uses his dualistic ontology in order to judge and classify forms of art and media). It would seem that there is no genuine artistic thought here; rather, what we see is still a philosophical thought situating itself both under and above art, even whilst assimilating certain characteristics from it. Bergson reduces art, so that his judgment in relation to it becomes a question of the extent to which it conforms to his chosen categories, the transcendent a prioris of intuition, duration, continuity, and so on and so forth.

One might observe that this is not dissimilar to one of Alain Badiou's critiques of Gilles Deleuze: reflecting upon Deleuze's clear fascination with the filmic medium (in sharp contrast to Bergson, who he attempts to reshape into a form more amenable to such interests), Badiou argues that 'in the volumes on the cinema, what one learns concerns the Deleuzian theory of movement and

---

37. Henri Bergson, *Duration and Simultaneity*, trans. Leon Jacobson, Indianapolis, IN: Bobbs-Merrill, 1965, p. 44.
38. Laruelle, *Photo-Fiction*, p. 1.

time, and the cinema gradually becomes neutralized and forgotten',[39] effectively criticizing him for only using this medium in order to illustrate preconceived
categories of thought. Laruelle would surely agree with this, but he would also
go further, for he views this mode of categorial exchange—the way in which
the philosophical decision does not and cannot think the One in itself, but
only by projecting various attributes upon it, such as 'Being, God, Thought,
Reason, and other humanistic and anti-humanistic fetishes'[40]—as an invariant component of philosophical discourse. If, as Alexander Galloway puts it,
Deleuze's aesthetics are grounded in 'the productive capacity of matter', revealing a vitalism that effectively subordinates art itself to life, and in doing so
raises the latter to the position of an abstract universal, Laruelle's by contrast
are founded upon 'the immanent and generic logic of the real' which necessarily forecloses all such abstraction through the impossibility of thinking it as an
object of knowledge.[41]

TOWARD A NON-STANDARD AESTHETICS?

What is it then that Laruelle offers instead, outside of what he views as the
domineering and presumptuous sufficiency of philosophical discourse? In a general sense, the aim of his project of non-philosophy (or non-standard philosophy,
as he has come to refer to it in recent years) is to think according to or alongside the One (which is, in non-philosophical terms, the ordinary human individual or ego, stripped of all attributes other than a simple, wholly positive sufficiency)—noting that the immanence that is proposed by philosophers 'always
corresponds to models, and so they are always somewhat transcendent, and
never sufficiently radical in order to determine a thought according to immanence'[42]—and in doing so, to thus think philosophy as a transcendental material
or object, rather than as a truth or unquestioned authority. To think philosophy
in such a fashion is to understand it as 'the aesthetic form and transcendental
logic that posits and gives the World',[43] rather than that which conditions and
legislates over the world.

'If philosophy already claims to fulfil a transcendental task,' Laruelle writes,
'the issue now is to define a generalized transcendental thought, equally "for"
philosophy itself reduced to the state of a priori, deprived of its proper "real"
claim by a more "powerful" thought, capable precisely of a "transcendental reduction" of the philosophical posture itself'.[44] In order to achieve this, he rela-
tivizes the previously discussed Kantian division between the transcendental
aesthetic and the transcendental logic, such that these categories (unlike in the
Kantian mode) precede the subject: the former studies philosophy as material

---

39. Alain Badiou, *Deleuze: The Clamor of Being*, trans. Louise Burchill, Minneapolis, MN: University of Minnesota Press, 2000, p. 16.

40. Laruelle, *Struggle*, pp. 3-4.

41. Alexander R. Galloway, *Laruelle: Against the Digital*, Minneapolis, MN: University of Minnesota Press, 2014, p. 167.

42. Laruelle, *Introduction*, p. 45.

43. Laruelle, *Principles*, p. 282.

44. Ibid, p. 289.

(which gives the world) and the latter studies it as a formal object (with a specific position in relation to this world). Attempting to avoid the disjunction between the sensible and ideal, he argues that rather than the latter conditioning and legislating over the former, they are both in their own rights equal and autonomous, interacting only in the last instance, as identical according to the One. The outcome of this is that there is no longer an external, extra-philosophical world or given—'that of idealizations destined to be philosophically seized again'[45]—over which the philosopher may demonstrate her mastery; conversely, the world is now seen as given through philosophy as an inert material. This is the beginning of a process of creation that Laruelle refers to as philo-fiction, which is the 'conjugation of disciplines outside their disciplinary incarceration as terms in themselves', defining the parameters for 'a new space for thought'.[46] In this sense, the non-standard view of philosophy is congenitally aesthetic, giving the world rather than the dominating it: 'every philosophical project would have its own style that could individuate it.'[47]

Another upshot of this then is that non-standard philosophy, by virtue of its attempt to establish the relative autonomy of regional practices and knowledges, is determined to enable other types of thought, outside the aegis of philosophical sufficiency. It affords the opportunity to challenge the presumption that 'philosophical aesthetics is the lone possible theory of art, especially if it considers itself as fundamental to the works rather than being merely descriptive of the works, styles, and historical and artistic codes.'[48] What Laruelle wishes to create, in short, is a non-standard aesthetics—an artistic thought; a thought according to art, rather than a mere philosophy of aesthetics (i.e. Kant or Hegel) or an aesthetic philosophy (i.e. Nietzsche, Bergson, or Deleuze)—and in doing so, to release art from its domination by philosophy. This is not simply the quest for yet another theory of art, which would in turn instantiate yet another philosophical form of aesthetics (thus perpetuating philosophy's constant warfare against itself); instead, it is the question of whether art can engender its own aesthetics, and in addition to this, whether we can produce an art of philosophy, rather than a philosophy of art. This would be a truly immanent art—that is, art as an immanent act, or more precisely, an act that is immanent to itself, neither representative nor expressive. A non-conceptual form of art, that does not need to extract concepts from elsewhere, nor to have such concepts impressed upon it, for it is an art that is already aestheticized, already given. An art that does not exist for the purpose of engendering a new 'concept of function or of sensation',[49] for we already have enough concepts (and can say with some certainty that the font of philosophical decision will continue to produce them).

The purpose of a non-standard aesthetics in regard to such art would be specifically to render it intelligible, 'producing a science of it instead of a philos-

---

45. Ibid, p. 237.

46. Laruelle, *Anti-Badiou*, p. xxiii.

47. Laruelle, *Dictionary*, p. 76.

48. Laruelle, *Photo-Fiction*, p. 5

49. Deleuze and Guattari, *What is Philosophy?*, trans. Hugh Tomlinson and Graham Burchell, London and New York: Verso, 1994, p. 199.

ophy',[50] science in this context referring not to a positivistic or mechanistic determination of a preexisting truth or essence, but instead a practice of relativization (or 'generalization', as it is oft-referred to in Laruelle's writings), proffering 'a science of essences each time determined in the final instance by real lived experiences, and codetermined by means and supports drawn from the World.'[51] This would not involve the outright exclusion of philosophy, but the recognition of its relative autonomy in relation to the arts, such that we are 'only deprived of excess of philosophy's pretensions of the absolute'[52]: a science (rather than a philosophy) of aesthetics, in other words, would be the means by which an immanent form and practice of art might be extracted from the supposed shackles of philosophical homogeneity. In doing so, what can be achieved is not the radical autonomy of these disciplines (a unilateral duality reserved for the relationship between the One and its clones), which would ensure their utter disseverment and thus incommensurability; rather, it is the reciprocal determination of art and philosophy, and their identity in-the-last-instance. The potential here, as Laruelle sees it, is to effectively make an art out of philosophy, and given that the arts 'have a more obvious relation to the lived included in their procedures'[53], we might come closer to a modality of thought that operates according to the lived finitude of the One, cloned through philosophical materials as the ordinary human subject.

A quite consistent theme running through Laruelle's oeuvre is the notion of a mystical indifference to the world (the latter of course being viewed in its inherent philosophizability as equivalent to philosophy itself), and as a corollary to this, a certain detachment from the empirical or ontic content of philosophy or its regional phenomena. Non-standard philosophy is, he states, 'not a worldly engagement even if it constantly busies itself in the world or if it takes worldly engagement as its materials'[54]—focusing instead upon the decisional schism between such content and the categories to which it is subordinated within the formal structure of philosophy. The practical consequence of this is that he rarely speaks of either philosophy or art in terms of their empirical objects of study, remaining at a potentially quite alienating level of formal or axiomatic abstraction. 'Can aesthetics become a second power of art itself,' Laruelle asks, 'can an art engender or determine its own aesthetics instead of suffering it as being philosophically imposed upon it?'[55] This is the provocation that he offers us, in straightforward terms: it is not that we should cease discussing art through philosophical concepts, but that we should acknowledge that such concepts do not monopolize the possibilities for theories of art. It is possible, he surmises, that we can unleash an aesthetics constructed upon artistic, rather than philosophical concepts.

Yet in making such an assertion, is there not a risk that this non-standard aesthetics merely falls back into yet another form of post-Idealist irrationalism—

50. Laruelle, 'First Choreography: Or the Essence-of-Dance,' Qui Parle, 21.2, 2013, p. 143.

51. Laruelle, 'First Choreography: Or the Essence-of-Dance', p. 147.

52. Laruelle, Photo-Fiction, p. 18.

53. Laruelle, Anti-Badiou, p. 124

54. Laruelle, Intellectuals, p. 25.

55. Laruelle, Photo-Fiction, p. 5.

the reduction of aesthetics to a form of incommunicable, internal truth? 'In that Laruelle is interested in the performance of philosophy, while also rendering it non-representational,' contends John Mullarkey, 'he comes close to Henri Bergson's idea of non-symbolic intuition.'[56] This silent intuitionism—characterized in this particular case by an essentially non-worldly conception of art which, although drawing from the inert (philosophical) materials that give the world, does not actually take place within the world, but is instead an immanent act of creation that is able to transform our thought of the world—is terribly abstract, evincing very little correspondence with artistic practice as we would normally conceive of it. In this respect, it shares features with the Laruellian understanding of science, which also does not bear much resemblance to either the natural and formal sciences or the structuralist conception of a self-sufficient theoretical practice, although it does borrow from the latter a marked disinterest regarding empirical phenomena. Non-philosophy sometimes gives the impression of a borderline-solipsism reliant upon a 'lived experience—that of the immediate self- and vision-application, the very passion or affect of vision'[57] which is not in itself ineffable (insofar as the One can be described, but this description will never actually affect or determine it in any way), but nevertheless cannot be conflated with any form of empirical (and thus philosophical) experience as we would normally understand it.

In the typically biting words of Ray Brassier, the Laruellian project can be situated within a tradition of increasingly radicalized post-Heideggarian phenomenological reduction, endlessly seeking the conditions of conditions of experience, the result being that 'the deeper it digs towards the pre-originary, the greater its remove from "things themselves" and the more impoverished its resources become', burrowing deeper and deeper into its own reflexivity 'in order to unearth the pre-reflexive, exacerbating abstraction until it becomes reduced to plying its own exorbitant vacuity.'[58] This, I would suggest, should not indicate the inherent futility of a non-standard aesthetics (or a non-standard philosophy more broadly), rather, it is indicative of the need to take the insight of such a method as a starting-point, instead of as an end in itself, and to utilize this in order to produce new potential conceptualizations of art which challenge, rather than reinforce the auto-position and auto-givenness of philosophical sufficiency. This is exactly why Laruelle speaks of creating 'an artistic fiction out of aesthetics'[59] for the indifference to the world that he proposes is not an escape from the world (in the manner of the neo-Platonists or gnostics, although he draws resources from both of these traditions), but an attempt to relativize or generalize the materials through which this world is given so that they might be transformed through an artistic practice of thought: art thinking philosophy,

56. John Mullarkey, 'Film Can't Philosophise (and Neither Can Philosophy): Introduction to a Non-Philosophy of Cinema.' *New Takes in Film-Philosophy*. Eds. Havi Carel and Greg Tuck. New York: Palgrave Macmillan, 2011, p. 90.

57. Laruelle, *The Concept of Non-Photography*, p. 13.

58. Ray Brassier, *Nihil Unbound: Enlightenment and Extinction*, Basingstoke: Palgrave Macmillan, 2007, p. 254.

59. Laruelle, *Photo-Fiction*, p. 2.

rather than vice-versa. What this approach emphasizes is the relative autonomy of the arts, insofar as they contain a non-reflexive kernel of immanent practice irreducible to and independent of all philosophical conceptualization and
regionalization.

4

The Nuclear Sonic: Listening to Millennial Matter[1]

Lendl Barcelos

> Sometimes the poisonous vegetation which has grown out of
> such decomposition poisons life itself for millennia.
> —Friedrich Nietzsche, *Twilight of the Idols*

The nuclear accidents at both Chernobyl and Fukushima 'received the same level 7 (severe accident) designation on the International Nuclear Event Scale'.[2] To develop ways of sonically interrogating these equally evaluated events and the global nuclear regime in its varied registers, it seems appropriate to initiate an inquiry with what has been done before. Sound artist Jacob Kirkegaard and sonic journalist Peter Cusack approach sound quite differently, although they both have produced audio projects whose central subject is the irradiated *zone of exclusion* located in Chernobyl, Ukraine. The first part of this paper will explore these two projects in detail. In attentively listening to the differences and similarities of these approaches, murmurs of a methodology of *nuclear sonic* investigation may begin to sound. Since this is only a preliminary investigation into the nuclear sonic, hints at a methodology may remain inchoate, but the unknown and non-knowledge tend to provoke discourse. Nuclear radiation is an invisible phenomenon and, in consequence, we require forms of mediation that transduce it into our sensory modalities in order to perceive it. Of course, simple sonification—such as that found in a radiometer or Geiger counter—only partially captures minute aspects of the global nuclear regime. The globalized, inter-connected networks that fuel ongoing nuclear production—military and domestic—continue to expand and engulf more and more of our planet, transforming the Earth, techno-capitalist production and discursive practices. As Japanese writer Sabu Kohso puts it:

---

1. Thanks to Marc Couroux & Kodwo Eshun for lent ears and catalysing comments; also, to those as yet to come whose ideas anachronically leaked.

2. The National Diet of Japan. *The Fukushima Nuclear Accident Independent Investigation Commission.* Japan, The National Diet of Japan, 2012, p. 75.

What capitalism has been building has been merging with the planetary body to the extent that the interconnectivity of everything has surpassed a condition that can be grasped in terms of dichotomies ... It is necessary to grasp everything as One, either as a planetary apparatus or a planetary machine.[3]

To approach the truly nuclear sonic is to develop an orientation to sound outside the confines of local myopias. The nuclear cannot be fully contained: it is contagious millennial material.

With this in earshot, the second part of this paper will investigate music of extremely extended duration, specifically focusing on two examples: Jem Finer's 1000-year composition *Longplayer* and John Cage's *Organ²/As Slow As Possible*, a work whose current performance is scheduled to last for 639 years. Pieces of such scales point to soundscapes beyond any individual human lifespan, although their construction consists and persists by means of a considered human finitude. The development of spent nuclear fuel repositories such as that of Onkalo in Finland also requires careful planning at scales that dwarf the average human lifespan. These meditations on extended duration force thought to speculate on human extinction and how human commitments might continue to ramify beyond humankind's own annihilation. To resonate with Kohso above, the two extended yet finite artworks of Finer and Cage cannot be considered as situated against the indefinite continuum or 'Nature', but—as will be developed below—must be grasped as One in what might be termed an *anthroposonic*. The latter can be defined as an audible mode of the Anthropocene, a geological time where the human becomes an integral aspect of the tellurian ecosystem. If the anthroposonic develops a humanly affordable (negative) feedback loop of organized sound, the nuclear sonic stretches our ears to an alternate acoustic ecology. The vibratory continuum affords a specific anthropocentric niche that intersects with the bandwidth of human audibility, but this range is only a small portion of the vibrations that affect us. Any formulation of the nuclear sonic must take into account our precariousness qua listeners, for our ears are always open to hear. Yet, even this is not entirely appropriate. Models of listening based on affordance—such as the one deployed in the anthroposonic— will fail to give an account of the nuclear sonic. Nuclear radiation and decay do not wait for you to be ready for them. On the contrary, the nuclear capitalizes on your vulnerable, porous body and works you to death. You begin to decompose and all of your energy is depleted. No matter how open you are to the nuclear sonic, it opens you still further: a positive feedback loop.[4]

MEDI(T)ATIONS

Ultrasound is used to inspect welds, establish the uniformity and quality of poured concrete, and monitor metal fatigue.

---

3. Sabu Kohso, 'Turbulence of Radiation and Revolution' in *through europe*, 3 March 2012, available at: http://th-rough.eu/writers/kosho-eng/turbulence-radiation-and-revolution (accessed 13 June 2015).

4. See Reza Negarestani, *Cyclonopedia: Complicity with Anonymous Materials*, Melbourne, Re.press, 2008, especially the chapter 'A Good Meal: The Schizotrategic Edge' for a detailed statement of the logic of 'being open' as contrasted with the logic of 'being opened'.

> Partially as a result of the Three Mile Island nuclear reactor
> accident in 1979, an increased number of ultrasonic inspec-
> tion procedures are now performed on the structural compo-
> nents in nuclear reactors.
> —Richard E. Berg and David G. Stork[5]

A soft, multi-layered drone resonates in your ear. Partially occluded, fog-
gy machine pulses occupy intensities at the threshold. The sound is not threatening. Actually, it is quite soothing. There is little movement here, save sound
waves cycling against each other. Over time a shift occurs and a throbbing tone
pronounces itself, mimicking the machine pulses still faintly heard. We read
that this hypnotic sound is an audio portrait of an old church now abandoned.
The congregation must assemble elsewhere, for its place of worship rests in a
zone of exclusion. Danish artist Jacob Kirkegaard's sound and video installation
AION features four sites that lie within the compass of this zone. For the accompanying CD release *4 Rooms*,[6] the track titles simply name the function of the lo-
cations: 'Church', 'Auditorium', 'Swimming Pool', 'Gymnasium'. Proper names
are silenced. Since no one remains to occupy these rooms—nearly all having
been evacuated following the accident—it is possible these names rest ineffable.
For who can articulate this space, if not those who me(e)t there?

In a sense, Kirkegaard is attempting this articulation with minimal intervention. By recording the room and feeding its audio back into the space, the
room begins to respond. Over time what emerges, as he states on his website,
is 'the voice of the room itself'.[7] The architecture (re)sounds. The space articu-
lates itself mediated by a microphone, recording equipment and speakers. The
process echoes Alvin Lucier's *I am sitting in a room* (1969) except in a more immediately de-humanized form. '[Kirkegaard] put up a microphone and a speaker,
started the recording and left. After ten minutes, he returned, stopped the recording and played it back into the same space'.[8] Kirkegaard leaves the room
to meditate. The empty room begins to make audible what could not be heard
prior: its structural mantra. No longer a dormant, internal potential, the space
awakens and is voiced. Yet, other inaudible processes radiate invisible. In the
words of Nietzsche scholar and sound theorist Christoph Cox,

> the drones that emerge from these rooms are, presumably, inflected by the
> radioactive particles and electromagnetic waves that still invisibly move
> within them. They are also haunted by the human beings that once in-
> habited them. Like sound, radiation doesn't die but only dissipates, di-
> lates, or loses energy.[9]

Human voices could be heard echoing in each of these four rooms prior
to the 26th of April 1986. On this day in Chernobyl, Ukraine a catastrophic

---

5. Richard E. Berg and David G. Stork, *The Physics of Sound*, 3rd ed, Upper Saddle River, Pearson
Prentice-Hall, 2005, p. 63.

6. Jacob Kirkegaard, *4 Rooms*, Touch, Tone 26, 2006, CD.

7. Jacob Kirkegaard, *AION*, available at: http://fonik.dk/works/aion.html (accessed 16 November
2014).

8. Ibid.

9. Christoph Cox, 'Sound Art and the Sonic Unconscious', *Organised Sound* 14.01, 2009, p. 25.

nuclear accident occurred. Afterward, so as to reduce the spread of contamination, a *zone of exclusion* was built, forcing the evacuation of tens of thousands. These are the absent voices of Kirkegaard's *AION* and *4 Rooms*, released
twenty years after the catastrophe. The *zone of exclusion*, also sometimes pronounced as the more ominous sounding *zone of alienation*, 'will remain uninhabitable for thousands of years'.[10] Uninhabitable, for the human security system cannot cope with the speed of decay this level of radiation here provokes.
The *zone of alienation* excludes human life as the remaindered millennial material endures. 'Kirkegaard's recordings, then, can be seen as an effort ... to
rescue sonic emissions that outlive those who produced them'.[11] But who is it
that produced these sonic emissions? Is it the rooms themselves, these nonhuman, decomposing architectures? Or, perhaps, it is Kirkegaard and his technological apparatuses?

Kirkegaard's attempt to erase traces of himself, and his cursory remarks of
the people excised from the area, form part of his self-consciously de-humanized process. Yet, each of the four rooms continue to point to their human architects, to human builders, and to their now-displaced human inhabitants—all of
whom we do not directly hear. In a passage from Seth Kim-Cohen's *In the Blink
of an Ear: Towards a Non-Cochlear Sonic Art*, he writes of Kirkegaard's *Four Rooms*:
'What we hear is haunted not by the actuality of the human beings who once
inhabited the rooms but by their histories and by history'.[12] What is required for
this aural haunting to take place is what he names 'the radioactive, electromagnetic *text*'.[13] If when listening to Kirkegaard's recordings we are *alienated* from
the radiant text illuminating these histories or if we are *excluded* from gaining
access to them, it is unlikely that human traces will be heard, even in the form
of a ghost.[14] Without the accompanying radioactive, electromagnetic text, these
apparitions fail to appear. For us to aurally meditate on these expelled voices and the inaudible radioactivity of the rooms they once inhabited, a textual
(non-cochlear) mediation is required.

SOUND-INFLICTED

> Sound on its own is as incomplete as visual images and lan-
> guage on their own.
> —Peter Cusack[15]

10. Kirkegaard, *AION*.

11. Cox, 'Sound Art and the Sonic Unconscious', p. 25.

12. Seth Kim-Cohen, *In the Blink of an Ear: Towards a Non-Cochlear Sonic Art*, New York, Continuum,
2009, p. 132.

13. Ibid.

14. Electronic voice phenomena (EVP) is the perception of sounds resembling speech in audio recordings that are purported to have been made in situations without the intentional physical presence
of someone speaking. The voices that emerge in recordings via EVP have been typically associated
with ghosts. The audio of Kirkegaard's *4 Rooms* and *AION* is such that one could perhaps hear—in a
pareidolic fashion—voices singing, yet to hear the traces of speech would be very unlikely. For two divergent accounts of EVP see Konstantin Raudive's *Breakthrough: An Amazing Experiment in Electronic Communication with the Dead*, trans. N. Fowler, Garrards Cross, Colin Smythe, 1971, and Joe Banks' *Rorschach
Audio: Art and Illusion for Sound*, London, Strange Attractor, 2012.

15. Peter Cusack, 'Field Recording as Sonic Journalism', *On Listening*, eds. Angus Carlyle and Cathy

The epigraph for this section was written on the 25th anniversary of the Chernobyl incident. Echoing Kim-Cohen, Peter Cusack observes that—in order to enter discursive regimes—sound requires another medium of articulation. This other medium inflects the sound, or at least the way one listens to it. An inflection by other media is common practice in what Cusack has coined *sonic-journalism*. He asserts that a sound recording can only be considered a piece of sonic-journalism if the 'original factual and emotional content' remain unaffected.[16] More specifically for him, it is imperative that one does not interfere with the recorded sounds once they have been captured. His approach is in direct opposition to Kirkegaard's, whom he might criticize for using the sounds from the *zone of exclusion* 'as source material for further work'.[17] Rather than implementing (Lucierian) processes to augment the sonic environment, Cusack's sonic-journalism seems to (pre)suppose that there can be *direct* recordings of the field of sound 'at hand.' But is not the selection of recording equipment already a mode of intervention, or—and perhaps more so—the decision of when and where to record? A sonic-journalist reports on current events. It is their assignment to aggregate, to assess importance, to find global relevance in the local and to relate the global to disparate locales—among other things. The question of bias looms.

Sounds From Dangerous Places is Peter Cusack's most recent publication of sonic-journalism.[18] It consists of two CDs with an accompanying eighty-page book of images and text. The first thing heard is a rapid, electronic pulse and Cusack articulating numbers '600...700...800...900...1000...1000...900...800...700'. Between these numbers the wind can be heard—though easily misheard as a passing car—and very quiet footsteps. The title provides more context, 'Radiometer, Kopachi', and the text from the book offers still more:

> A radioactive 'hot spot'. What remains of the village of Kopachi lies buried under rough mounds of grass-covered earth, now growing birch trees and marked by small yellow and red warning signs. Used tyres litter the ground. The readings are high and as I walk towards the mounds they increase. At 1000 microroentgens I turn around.[19]

An image is printed to the left of the text. It is clear that Cusack wants to provide the listener with an abundance of information so that s/he is able to be attentive to the situation 'at hand'. The sonification process[20] used in transforming the exposure levels of X-rays and gamma rays into audible pulses emitted by the radiometer is seemingly inadequate to convey the intensity of the force of radiation, so it is supplemented by Cusack's reading aloud. Cusack is right to as-

Lane, Axminster, Uniformbooks, 2013, p. 28.

16. Ibid.

17. Ibid, p. 26.

18. Peter Cusack, *Sounds from Dangerous Places*, Surrey, Rer Megacorp, 2012.

19. Ibid, p. 26.

20. For more on the process of sonification see Alexandra Supper's 'The Search for the "Killer Application": Drawing the Boundaries around the Sonification of Scientific Data' as well as Jonathan Sterne and Mitchell Akiyama's 'The Recording That Never Wanted to Be Heard and Other Stories of Sonification' both included in *The Oxford Handbook of Sound Studies*, eds. Trevor Pinch and Karin Bijsterveld, New York, Oxford, 2012.

sume the mapping of rapid pulses onto high levels of radiation is not a given, but such a convention has become habit. The short, high-pitched beeps of the Geiger counter—invented in 1908—are now quite familiar. Cusack's re-articulation of the abstract pulses reinforces the legible intensity of the radiation; instead of relying on the relative speed of the pulses in relation to one another alone, the listener hears the magnitude of the radiation doubled by a spoken supplement. This is could be an attempt to reinforce the factual and emotional content of the original site in concordance with the demands of Cusack's sonic-journalism as mentioned above.

Much of Cusack's project can perhaps be characterized by the notion of the supplement: text supplemented by audio supplemented by image supplemented by history, etc. He asserts:

> The interpretation of sound certainly benefits from a knowledge of context in the same way that captions and titles enhance photographs. However, field recordings convey far more than basic facts. Spectacular or not, they also transmit a powerful sense of spatiality, atmosphere and timing.[21]

Listening is locative and so the unadulterated field recordings of sonic-journalism should allow one to displace their ears into a semblance of the sonorous situation recorded by the journalist. This, of course, assumes that the listener has a sound system that can re-produce the 'spatiality, atmosphere and timing' of the initial situation. Any sound system is more or less able to accurately convey the sense of timing, but it can be argued that the sense of spatiality and atmosphere require at least as many channels as the original recording setup. Any re-production of the sonorous situation that fails to satisfy this minimal requirement will in some way skew the spatiality and atmosphere of the original sonic event. If, for example, the situation is recorded in stereo (two channels) and the listener's sound system is such that it has only one channel, much of the spatiality and atmosphere will be reduced. The lack of a one-to-one correspondence of channels cancels out the spatiality and atmosphere of the initial situation. The listener then is forced to interpret and speculate on the dimensionality of this site through a skewed audio re-production.

Yet, this is only one of the potential impasses that prevent the listener from being perceptually transplanted into a semblance of the sonic event. Echo and reverberation also play large roles in constructing auditory space—to name only two other contributing factors.[22] Furthermore, the re-production of space

---

21. Cusack, 'Field Recording as Sonic Journalism', p. 26.

22. There is an exhausting amount of literature on the question of a sound recording's fidelity to an original sonic event and the production of space in audio engineering. At the birth of audio recording, fidelity of sound was already a point at issue. With subsequent (radiophonic) experiments with the recording process, alien and artificial sonic spaces were beginning to be conjured. As fidelity to the original seemingly increased, so was there a proliferation of the artificial. A full engagement with this history and literature would take us too far afield, although the resonances between radiophony and the radioactive are suggestive. For a very detailed and informative account of the prehistory of sound recording see Jonathan Sterne, *The Audible Past: Cultural Origins of Sound Reproduction*, Durham, Duke University, 2003. To name only three other significant texts on audio production and sound's spatiality: Richard Blesser and Linda-Ruth Salter, *Spaces Speak, Are You Listening*, Cambridge, MIT, 2006, Peter Doyle, *Echo and Reverb: Fabricating Space in Popular Music Recording, 1900-1960*, Middletown, Wesley-

by stereo recordings is already an epiphenomenal illusion constructed by the 'relative difference in intensity between the two polarized sound-emitting loud-speakers'.[23] This differential relation results in each sound's perceived spatial distribution. Technosonic theorist David Cecchetto keenly points out:

> the sound is emphatically *not* where it sounds like it is. Indeed, the added twist is that it also isn't where it *appears* to be (i.e., coming from the loud-speakers) because it only comes to be at all through the differential act of hearing, which is the very act that would place it where it isn't.[24]

The location of a re-produced sound, then, is illusory (elusory), yet, as mentioned by Cusack above, we do inevitably get a sense of the initial sonorous event's spatiality. But perhaps when Cecchetto is indicating that the sound is *not* where it sounds like it is and not where it *appears* to be, he is noticing that, when we attend to a field recording, we as listeners are translocated into another soundscape. Because field recordings tend to emphasize spatiality and atmosphere, they have the capacity to inflect the space the listener is in with the original recorded soundscape. Although we might not be hearing a particularly accurate (sonic)image, there is still an interference pattern being created between the recorded site and the space the recording is played back into. In other words, *the initial sonic event is inflicted upon the listening environment.* The sound extracted from the *zone of exclusion* is diffused through another context. This diffusion, however, should not be heard as a major imposition: it is not yet the case that field recordings have become ubiquitous—we as listeners still tend to decide whether or not to inflict our listening environments with the audio recordings made by Cusack and Kirkegaard.

But as listeners, although we can sonically navigate the field recording as we desire, the unrecorded sound field—described above as the audio situation 'at hand'—is out of our hands, and thus outside our auditory horizon. The soundscape is manufactured by the decisions of the sonic-journalist and his or her recording apparatus. *Interpreting the Soundscape* is a CD compilation that supplements issue 16 of the *Leonardo Music Journal*.[25] Curated by Peter Cusack, it features a recording of one of the four rooms made by Kirkegaard. In the liner notes Kirkegaard seems keenly aware of the intervention performed by him and his equipment, 'no matter how careful I might have been not to interfere with [the recording process] during the recordings, there was an exchange taking place between the room and the microphone'.[26] He even goes on to explicitly state that he uses 'a Sanken CSS5 shotgun microphone' to make the recordings, ensuring *the radioactive, electromagnetic text* that accompanies Cusack's CD compilation betrays his decision to occlude details from the text appearing with his *4 Rooms*. It is as if Cusack has asked Kirkegaard to account for his sonic manipulation of the source material, so Kirkegaard writes:

an University, 2005, and Julian Henriques, *Sonic Bodies: Reggae Sound Systems, Performance Techniques, and Ways of Knowing*, New York, Continuum, 2011.

23. David Cecchetto, *Humanesis: Sound and Technological Posthumanism*, Minneapolis, Minnesota, 2013, p. 2.
24. Ibid.
25. Peter Cusack (cur.), *Interpreting the Soundscape*, Leonardo Music Journal, Vol. 16, 2006.
26. Ibid, p. 72.

'Concert Room' begins with the raw recording. After 3 minutes I start filtering the recording in order to bring forth the emerging tone that I heard. As the track moves on, I let this tone unfold and come out stronger, while at the same time the other sounds of the room begin to fade.[27]

DIGRESSION: ULTRA-RED AND THE (NOT A) SOUND FIELD (VIBRATIONAL CONTINUUM OR OSCILLATION-ORIENTED ONTOLOGIES)

> The bandwidth of human audibility is a fold on the vibratory continuum of matter.
> —Steve Goodman[28]

After having the participants of many of their projects listen to a sequence of organized sound material Ultra-red ask them: 'What did you hear?'.[29] This seemingly naive question serves as the underlying motor for the politico-aesthetic organization. Ultra-red's audio concept-space is outlined in their 2008 pamphlet *10 Preliminary Theses on Militant Sound Investigation*. This brief booklet begins with Ultra-red defining their grounding concept, 'the field of sound', as the undifferentiated sound mass that is both 'the site and means of Militant Sound Investigation'.[30] It is the sound world of unmediated real-time,[31] the *one* vibratory continuum of matter. *Militant Sound Investigation* operates on and via the field of sound because this site is the 'radically immanent' sound world from which we are inseparable. There is no way for us to step outside or parse the field of sound, while leaving it unfiltered and unchanged; we are altogether steeped in its sound. Any and all perception is already an act of differentiation. To acknowledge and organize the field of sound is to begin to delineate contours within its formless mass and transform it into a soundscape.[32] This is crystallized in Ultra-red's formula: 'SOUND FIELD + ORGANIZING = SOUNDSCAPE'.[33] The field of sound is undifferentiated until it is ordered—until it is recorded, perceived, filtered and/or manufactured. All operations on the sound field turn it into a soundscape, for even at the most minimal level these processes necessitate distinction and the field of sound is absolutely indistinct. Organization is 'an edit that differentiates between the terms within *a* sound field'.[34] Ul-

---

27. Ibid.

28. Steve Goodman, *Sonic Warfare: Sound, Affect and the Ecology of Fear*, Cambridge, MIT, 2010, p. 9.

29. Ultra-Red, *10 Preliminary Theses on Militant Sound Investigation*, New York, Printed Matter, 2008, available at: http://asounder.org/resources/ultrared_10_preliminary_theses_on.pdf (accessed 30 January 2015).

30. Ibid, p. 1.

31. Although 'real-time' often designates the mediated perception of a live event, Ultra-Red seem to use the term to denote the unmediated event of perception of sound. See especially ibid., pp. 1-2.'e work of hyperstitionalist and sterveld, New York, Oxford, 2012rsity,

32. For a radically politicized perspective on organization see the work of hyperstitionalist philosopher Nick Land. In an interview conducted in 1997 for *Wired UK* he states, 'organization involves subordinating low level units to some higher level functional program. ... Organization is suppression.' In relation to sound, auditory perception can be conceptualized as the higher functional program that organizes the lower level field of sound, modulating it into a 'soundscape' in the process.

33. Ultra-Red, *10 Preliminary Theses on Militant Sound Investigation*, p. 4.

34. Ibid, p. 1, my emphasis.

tra-Red's use of the indefinite article for the sound field, in the prior quotation, is misleading. If there is a multiplicity of sound fields, then the potential to distinguish one sound field from another arises. However, given that the sound field is defined as an undifferentiated sound mass, Ultra-Red are assuming that prior to any conceivable differentiation it is still possible to delineate differences. There are two ways to resolve this inconsistency, unless it is Ultra-Red's wish to remain self-contradictory and paradoxical: either (a) it is *not* possible to have complete disorganization—pure deterritorialization, without anterior territorialization or posterior reterritorialization—so coding takes place 'all the way down', and, even at the most minimal level possible, distinctions can be made ensuring that the sound field becomes an inexistent, unattainable ideal; or (b) there is only one field of sound and if another sound field is defined it can only appear as a misrecognized soundscape—i.e. this *other sound field* is not a field of sound at all. The first sonic ontology is that of discreteness, the second is one of continuity.[35] These two ontologies clash with one another and if sound investigation is really to be militant, more consistency is needed. With this in mind, Ultra-Red's phrase, 'any belief that the site is wholly organized prior to the investigation is liable to encounter crisis'[36] can be re-written 'any belief that the site is *in any way* organized prior to the investigation is *inconsistent, unless the site is a soundscape*'. The crisis invoked by Ultra-Red that follows from the belief in an anterior organization prior to any engagement with the sound field, is redoubled by inconsistently ramifying the presuppositions inherent in their own militant glossary. Rather than deciding between working with the precondition of *the* vibratory continuum or *a* discrete oscillation-oriented ontology, Ultra-Red's cursory indistinction unproductively borders the unintelligible, beckoning a paradox that leads their project towards ruination through misuse.[37]

THE EVERYDAY NUCLEAR SONIC

> Attentive listening on location can reveal sonic threads running through the narratives and issues under examination and suggest unexpected questions and directions to be pursued.
> —Peter Cusack[38]

---

35. See John L. Bell, *The Continuous and the Infinitesimal in Mathematics and Philosophy*, Milano, Polimetrica, 2005, available at: http://publish.uwo.ca/~jbell/The%20Continuous.pdf (accessed 26 October 2014), for a detailed historical account of this distinction. There is a sense in which a discrete sonic ontology is presupposed by the technique of additive sound synthesis, while subtractive sound synthesis entails a continuous sonic ontology. In the former, discrete sine waves are 'added' to each other in order to synthesize whatever sound is desired; in the later, undifferentiated noise is primary and the production of other sounds requires a process of filtration.

36. Ultra-Red, *10 Preliminary Theses on Militant Sound Investigation*, p. 9.

37. It is worth noting that contemporary mathematics and philosophy does offer abstract mechanisms for navigating the concept-spaces between the discrete and continuous. However, unlike Ultra-Red, the 'pendular movement' required in order to articulate such an operation is always rigorously defined and relies on an extremely technical formalization. For an introduction to this see Fernando Zalamea, *Synthetic Philosophy of Contemporary Mathematics*, trans. Zachary Luke Fraser, Falmouth, Urbanomic, 2012.

38. Cusack, 'Field Recording as Sonic Journalism', p. 27.

Listening to Jacob Kirkegaard's *4 Rooms* alongside Peter Cusack's *Sounds from Dangerous Places*, we hear a vast difference in the portrayal of Chernobyl. Although both use image and text to supplement their audio recordings, their approaches are radically divergent. In contrast to Kirkegaard, what is most striking in Cusack's work is the presence of people. In the notes on Cusack's website he states: 'The danger is not necessarily to a short-term visitor, but to the people of the area who have no option to leave or through the location's role in geopolitical power structures'.[39] In Kirkegaard's work the listener is led to believe that the *zone of exclusion* in Chernobyl is a desolate, unpopulated site. As mentioned above, nothing except his own presence in the initiation of the process informs the listener otherwise. The soothing, hypnotic sounds of the four empty rooms convey no sense of the active presence of humankind. All that is present—or made present—is their architecture, long-abandoned. Even in the accompanying images and text, there is no mention of people living within the *zone of exclusion*. *4 Rooms* conveys a post-apocalyptic bias of the *zone*.

Cusack, on the other hand, seems to privilege the human and the living. From his own voice in the opening track to the closing track of frogs croaking, the presence of a living, albeit devastated, ecosystem is constant. Along with the beeping of radiometers, the crackling of electric power cables and squeaky hinges, we hear birds, insects, a boar, a horse, poems and conversations. We even hear songs from people who still live in the *zone of exclusion*, something unthinkable in the portrait of the *zone* created by Kirkegaard. Given the title of his project is *Sounds from Dangerous Places*, Cusack is attempting to highlight the geopolitical struggles occurring throughout the region via his sonic-journalism. The crackling of wires 'was electricity flowing in the wrong direction, into Chernobyl rather than out, a sonic manifestation of the massive drain on Ukraine's resources that Chernobyl has become'.[40] The human voices heard are of those not given the choice to leave.[41] The (sonic) image we hear from Kirkegaard of the *zone of exclusion*, forecloses humankind's intervention. The contaminated areas are not to be entered, except via audiovisual proxy. 'Kirkegaard's recordings... point toward an elemental time the half-life of which dwarfs human history'.[42] For Cusack, this (sonic)image is inverted. The contaminated areas *must* be entered into or, at least, we must not portray them as static because the affected areas are still active, politically-charged conflict zones. Cusack's intervention is initiated so as to call attention—to ask for an attentive listening—to soundscapes that are in need of reorganization. 'Sonic-journalism occurs when field recordings are given adequate space and time to be heard in their own right'.[43] Thus, when listening to the field recordings made by Cusack of the *zone of exclusion*, we are asked us to attend to the devastatingly precarious condition that the people

39. Peter Cusack, *Sounds from dangerous places book and CDs* (web), available at: http://sounds-from-dangerous-places.org (accessed 16 November 2014).rin 05, ins U Pan,995. 221–235.
available at: he Chernobyl eken, Ghent, KASK/Wooruit, 2010, pp. 130-45, for an account
40. Cusack, 'Field Recording as Sonic Journalism', p. 27.
41. Cusack, *Sounds from dangerous places book and CDs* (web).
42. Cox, 'Sound Art and the Sonic Unconscious', p. 25.
43. Cusack, 'Field Recording as Sonic Journalism', p. 26.

who are forced to remain there continually face. Rather than portray an emptied 'elemental time' well beyond the human, Cusack zooms in to the scale of the everyday nuclear sonic: a slow decay. Fatally irradiated, it is after the end of the world, yet you—as someone who is safely listening to the *zone of exclusion*—know not to abandon the sense that this audio signals an apocalypse in process.

Both Kirkegaard and Cusack articulate a nuclear sonic that is life-threatening. For the former, the *zone of exclusion* presents a portrait of life that has already been annihilated, although human sonic architectures are still able to sound if provoked. The negation of life is here taken up as the immediate (death) threat of the nuclear sonic. Although Kirkegaard does not successfully remove himself from the recording process, it is clear that the radiant sounds will continue to resonate whether or not anyone attends to them. Structural mantras remain even in a de-humanized, post-apocalyptic soundscape where architecture and sound sculpture blur. Life has not only been threatened, but this threat has already been acted upon. For him, the *zone of exclusion* within Chernobyl is emptied of its former inhabitants whose voices have dissipated yet continue to haunt architectures that maintain their silence. When the nuclear sonic is scaled to the level of human decomposition, a different sense (tense) is invoked and the threat of death becomes one that continues to be lived out—a passing threat, not one that has already passed. The sonic-journalistic portrait Cusack makes of the *zone of exclusion* offers a soundscape that not only transports the listener to the alienated *zone* via field recordings—(sonic)images of the recent past—but also tunes the listener in to the notion that this *zone* is a region that continues to co-exist with the rest of the world. The *zone of alienation* is not one we must be alienated from. The plight of those who permanently live in the *zone of exclusion* foregrounds the life-threatening logics at the core of the global nuclear regime whose base matter is the radioactive, millennial materials that undo the human, however slowly.

EXTENDED DURATION

> It is art that at once forms the figure of a common humanity
> (man as homo faber), at the same time as the resistance and
> decay of art objects opens life and creation to temporalities
> beyond those of a self-legislating humanity.
> —Claire Colebrook[44]

The performance of Jem Finer's music composition, *Longplayer*, began January 1, 2000 and is set to continue without repetition for one thousand years. The score for the piece outlines detailed yet abstract instructions for the piece's realization. It provides a recipe for both an automated digital version as well as an analog one for six musicians. Simply described, *Longplayer* consists of six distinct loops that run at different timescales. The shortest of these takes approximately four days to complete and the longest returns to its initial state every thousand years. In consequence, as the piece progresses, markers—both abstract and ac-

---

44. Claire Colebrook, *Essays on Extinction. Vol. 1*, Ann Arbor, Open Humanities, 2014, p. 145, available at: http://quod.lib.umich.edu/cgi/p/pod/dod-idx/death-of-the-posthuman-essays-on-extinction-volume-one.pdf?c=ohp;idno=12329362.0001.001 (accessed 23 February 2014).

tual—indicate the position of each segment and the state of the composition as a whole. So long as there is a way to calculate the current position of each segment the piece can continue. If the music stops, one is to either begin from the position where it has stopped or determine where to reset the markers so the music can be in sync with the current date and time. In the latter instance, portions of the piece will remain silent. At the moment of this writing a computer situated in a lighthouse at Trinity Buoy Wharf located in London, England—the same site where the piece began sixteen years ago—continues to monitor the progress of the markers, diffusing *Longplayer* throughout the space while simultaneously streaming its sound online.[45] Although the lighthouse is only open to the public on Saturdays and Sundays from 11h to 17h, the online stream allows one to tune in at anytime.

Longplayer was composed over the course of five years from 1995 to 1999. Jem Finer's thought process and selected journals are documented in a large format book of the same name as the piece.[46] In it we also find three essays, images of the installation at Trinity Buoy Wharf, a score, a mind map and a record of locked grooves. The latter provides the source material necessary in order to realize the piece. What we hear when listening to the record, entering the lighthouse or streaming the work online is the sound of Tibetan singing bowls arranged into a tranquil composition. The actual recording used for the source material of *Longplayer* is only twenty minutes in length. To generate the complete, infra_perceptibly[47] slow-moving sound of *Longplayer*, a process that prolongs the duration of the original material is used. This is done by splitting the source material into distinct segments that loop around each other. The result is an extended duration: twenty minutes becoming a thousand years.

Another musical composition of extended duration is John Cage's *Organ²/As Slow As Possible*. Composed in 1987, *Organ²/As SLow aS Possible* is a piece of indeterminate length that is adapted from an earlier version scored for piano, *As SLow aS Possible*. Since pianos are unable to sustain notes—a note immediately decaying once it is struck—performances of this version can only last between twenty and seventy minutes long. Simply put, note lengths on a piano are generally determined by the velocity with which the note is struck: the faster one strikes a note the louder it is and the longer it sounds. In order not to introduce unscored silences into the piece, the performer would have to proceed to the next instruction before the present note fully decayed into imperceptibility. Unlike the piano, however, notes of an organ can be sustained indefinitely. By adapting *As SLow aS Possible* to organ the duration of performances could be significantly increased. Thus, a performance of *Organ²/As SLow aS Possible* was organized to occur in St. Burchardi church located in Halberstadt

45. Visit www.longplayer.org to stream the piece.

46. Jem Finer, *Longplayer*, London, Artangel, 2001.

47. The minute shift displacing the hyphen to an underscore makes the notion of this concept legible. See the work of xenaudial pragmèticist Marc Couroux, who coined the term, available at: http://www.couroux.org (accessed 28 April 2015), especially his 'Preemptive Glossary for a Technosonic Control Society (with lines of flight)', available at: https://www.academia.edu/4302532/Glossary_for_a_Techno-Sonic_Control_Society (accessed 10 July 2015).

that would last for 639 years, scheduled to begin in 2001 and end in the year 2640. This specific duration was chosen in order to commemorate the date of the first known permanent installation of an organ. Documentation can be found that traces this event back to Halberstadt in 1361, which is 639 years before the scheduled start of the piece. For this performance, 2001 acts as a durational mirror simultaneously extending into the historical past and projected future of the organ with the same magnitude. It is clear that the symbolic duration of this interpretation of *Organ²/As SLow aS Possible* is not a constraint that is inherent to Cage's composition. A version that lasts for one thousand years or longer can easily be imagined.

However, what is difficult is to actually organize and incarnate the performance of such extended durations. Since this length of time 'exceeds the memory of any one person and probably the memory of any one civilization and possibly the memory of an entire species'[48], it will be necessary to transmit all that is necessary for the continuation of the performance—and perhaps what is necessary for its reception too—in a manner that will still be meaningful in any alien future. In order for compositions of extended duration to endure they must be intelligible to whatever and/or whomever the future entails because the realization of these works rests on their interpretation. However, it is no guarantee that any of the systems of communication we currently employ will be intelligible in a thousand years. How is it that we can purport to have insight into the distant future's literacy? It is commonly stated, that the pronunciation of Latin is unknown today; the transmission of its specific phonetic register cannot be traced, although we continue to hear its mutations in all the Latinate languages that are derived from it. Given this, how can we assume that we have the capacity to transmit the instructions for the continued performance of a musical composition? Yet, even at a more proximate temporal distance to us, there are examples of the obsolescence of communicative codes: digital formats undergo such rapid changes that there are already many formats that are obsolete and unreadable.[49]

Of course, speculating about a population's investment into a musical composition a thousand years into the future is somewhat unfair. We are not yet transported directly from the present to an alien future. Our movement towards the distant future incrementally proceeds. Perhaps it is best to hear these distant futures from the perspective of our continuing approach; for even millennial materials count seconds. The preparations that were and are necessary in order to sustain the performances of both *Longplayer* and *Organ²/As SLow aS Possible* confront us with the challenge of how to ensure succeeding generations will be invested in the performance of such compositions. Put another way, the continuation of these performances are dependent on the investment of future generations. Not only this, but the initial decision to initiate these pieces of extended duration is also the possible future anterior constraint of generations (and spe-

48. Janna Levin, 'Time is Dead', in Jem Finer's *Longplayer*, London, Artangel, 2001, pp. 7-9.

49. An intuitive example of this is that of a program that is not coded to handle its legacy formats. If an application is substantially updated it is often the case that it can no longer open files created on the older version(s) of that program. These older file formats are legacy systems.

cies) to come. Future generations will have continued *Longplayer* and *Organ²/As SLow aS Possible*, or at least that is what seems to be desired by those that organize around these compositions. With *Organ²/As SLow aS Possible* it is already the case that we are sustaining a 'permanent installation' that will have lasted 1278 years (from 1361 to 2640).

Listening to these compositions as the incremental extension of a millennial material, we must not downplay the seriousness of imposing structures onto succeeding populations. If the concept of the Anthropocene allows us to attend to the ongoing impact that humanity has on the global environment, the *anthroposonic* tunes us in to its aural variant. For those involved in the maintenance of the performances, it is clear that future generations are to inherit the performance. In one of the articles included in the *Longplayer* book, 'Time is Dead' astro-physicist Janna Levin states that '*Longplayer* relies on a collective human memory' and goes on to suggest that 'instead of a mechanical object, maybe *Longplayer* should be passed on by word of mouth as a chant, a myth'.[50] For *Longplayer* to extend to its full length then, it must embed itself into aural tradition. The same logic can be applied to the case of *Organ²/As SLow aS Possible*. As part of its performance someone must change the notes at specifically determined times. The next change is set to occur on the 5th of September 2020. It is necessary that some kind of tradition be created in order for this change to actually occur, otherwise the commencement of this performance will have been in vain.

But is not the attempt to sustain such trans-generational performances already something done in vain? The idea that a composition made by a single person is to last beyond the confines of their own life reeks of self-importance and self-aggrandizing; most especially when the ramifications of sustaining the performance is *nothing but aesthetic*. The anthroposonic here is nothing but another form of anthropocentrism. One thousand years: 'although it is only around ten times the longest human life span, it can amount to more than seventy human generations'.[51] Jem Finer himself describes that with the composition of *Longplayer* he wanted 'to make something that made time, as a long and slow process, tangible'.[52] What is left unsaid is that this perceptual deceleration of time is laced with his own organizational process. Of course, there are many traditions—aural, oral and otherwise—that continue to be passed from one generation to another. The arbitrariness and contingency of Finer's organizational process is not specifically an issue. What is problematic is the apparent enforcement of the composition's prolongation. With John Cage's *Organ²/As SLow aS Possible* this troublesome ramification is subdued. Although Cage does indicate that the piece is to be played as slow as possible, he does not make any prescription that his piece should be trans-generational or even trans-individual. Extending the duration to 639 years was the decision of several musicologists at a conference five years after the death of John Cage.[53] If to hear these composi-

---

50. Levin, 'Time is Dead', p. 9.

51. Levin, 'Time is Dead', p. 7.

52. Finer, *Longplayer*, p. 13.

53. Being so strongly against fascistic and hierarchical structures, Cage was not of the type to want to impose on generations to come, yet—in a stroke of irony—his shadow continues to loom over music.

tions is solely, as sonic anachrofuturist Kodwo Eshun writes, to 'experience the vivid foresight of events that have yet to occur in the past tense'[54] then we risk neglecting the incremental duration that constitutes such performances and the ramifications resulting from constraining future generations to the maintenance of its continuation.

Common to both *Longplayer* and *Organ²/As SLow aS Possible* is the imposition of an external sound-organizing mechanism into the space of its performance. One cannot visit the lighthouse at Trinity Buoy Wharf or the St. Burchardi church in Halberstadt and hear the inherent soundscape. The sounds now present in these places are not native. In the words of Eshun, these are 'unidentified audio event[s]'[55] or alien sound smuggled into existing architectures: 'an event that disguises itself as music, using other media as a Trojan horse to infiltrate the landscape with disguised elements of untimeliness and atopia'.[56] Due to the extended durations of both pieces, the infiltrating matter will modulate existing soundscapes to contours of human design affording an anthroposonic that has the potential to significantly alter the field of sound. The world is transformed into something that needs to be tuned, a large-scale music composition.[57] The anthroposonic operates via implantation: sounds composed elsewhere are sown into another context. This is a very different register than that of the nuclear sonic discussed earlier. In the case of the nuclear sonic, sounds are extracted from their irradiated, native contexts to become *affective presentations of that context*. The original site continuously permeates the recorded sound through a supplementary radioactive, electromagnetic text. With the nuclear sonic, what we hear is consistently inflected by the original, threatening context. These 'sounds from dangerous places' translocate the listener while maintaining them at a safe distance. Sound recordings from Chernobyl will not harm you, although they are able to point to the *zone of exclusion* that, with extended exposure, will advance your decay.[58] Imminent danger is dislocated, at least for those not part of the audio extraction process. Within the context of the anthroposonic, the danger is no longer imminent. It is 'an acclimatization to millennial duration becoming affective'[59] for and by the human. By implanting sounds from elsewhere (elsewhen), composed to be heard by human listeners, these examples of the anthroposonic sustain aural architectures built within the niche of the human auditory bandwidth. But this is only a marginal range or fold of the vibra-

His 'silent' composition *4'33"* being a case in point.

54. Kodwo Eshun, 'An unidentified audio event arrives from the post-computer age', in Jem Finer's *Longplayer*, London, Artangel, 2001, pp. 10-11.

55. Ibid, p. 10.

56. Ibid, p. 11.

57. This, of course, is in reference to R. Murray Schafer's influential text *The Soundscape: Our Sonic Environment and the Tuning of the World*, Rochester, Destiny, 1994, which inaugurated the discipline of Acoustic Ecology.

58. For a terrifying yet insightful account of how the representation of the 'difficult weeks' following the explosion and meltdown of a nuclear reactor in Chernobyl *literally* became lethal—the material of the film itself became irradiated in the process—see Susan Schuppli, 'The Most Dangerous Film in the World', in *Tickle Your Catastrophe*, eds. Frederick Le Roy, Nele Wynants and Robrecht Vanderbecken, Ghent, KASK/Wooruit, 2010, pp. 130-45.

59. Eshun, 'An unidentified audio event arrives from the post-computer age', p. 10.

tory continuum. What extends the sense of these compositions is their duration. In both *Longplayer* and *Organ²/As SLow aS Possible* the question of human extinction is emphasized because of their extended durations, but what the listener of this anthroposonic will die from is nothing but age.

ANNIHILATED FUTURES

> The epoch of nuclear confrontation, which—contrary to superficial appearance—has scarcely begun, has facilitated the rigorous formalization of this macro-political incentive to the abandonment of limitation, all the way to Mutually Assured Destruction.
> —Nick Land[60]

The nuclear sonic, as mentioned before, cannot prepare us for what is to come, since what is to come will happen to us, we will be opened. But what if the nuclear sonic offers a way to strategize the provocation of the global regime? What if, via the infra_ and sub-sonic, we could accelerate our global interconnection? Or—and perhaps even more necessary—what if the nuclear sonic could allow us to hit the handbrake on capitalist and neoliberal acceleration? Full stop.

Yet, this can easily turn into the development of monotonic commitments that fascistically constrain populations to come. What might be necessary is the development of tactics for the provocation of a global regime that can be modified in step with unfolding contingencies. The future is volatile, so why would we assume that what we know today will continue to be tomorrow? This is not to suggest the Humean dilemma of the coming-sun, but it is a call to tune in to future sonic forces—whether of the unaffordable nuclear, of the anthropos or something beyond—that may in fact already be modulating us.

The Fukushima catastrophe began with an earthquake—a subsonic vibrational force. This force was so powerful as to be classed as 9.0 on the Richter scale, which is said to be the same intensity as the infamous Lisbon earthquake that provoked the Enlightenment. Shortly after, a tsunami overtook the East coast of Japan and caused major damage to the Fukushima Daiichi Power Plant.

> That [the atomic bomb] has to be secret makes it dull and meaningless. Sure it will destroy a lot and kill a lot, but it's the living that are interesting not the way of killing them, because if there were not a lot left living how could there be any interest in destruction.[61]

Whether military or domestic, the nuclear and its radioactivity establish the possibility for global catastrophe. The millennial half-lives of these materials, far outlast that of human life cycles. If our models of listening are circumscribed within the limits of an individual human being or even the human species as a whole, how is it they can become nuclear? What would it mean to take up a mil-

---

60. Nick Land, 'Philosophy in a War-zone', *Dissolution (6edfsdf4c7e7)*, 2013.

61. Gertrude Stein, *Reflection on the atomic bomb*, ed. Robert B. Haas, Los Angeles, Black Sparrow, 1973.

lennial listening? We have all listened to the radio but how can we listen *radioactively*? Perhaps with this preliminary investigation into different instances of listening to millennial materials, we can begin to attend to their murmurs. Yet, as always, a dark side looms: 'It is fair to say that between the mind's habitual standards and the atomic effect there remains a disproportion that makes one's head spin, leaving the imagination before the void'.[62]

62. Georges Bataille, 'Concerning the Accounts Given by Residents of Hiroshima', trans. Alan Keenan, in *Trauma: Explorations in Memory*, ed. Cathy Caruth, Baltimore, Johns Hopkins, 1995, 221-35.

5

Geology Without Geologists

Douglas Kahn

I was flying from Sydney to Amsterdam to speak at *The Geologic Imagination* conference. A book of the same name was published to accompany the event and,
because I was a contributor, I had an advanced copy that I proceeded to read
cover-to-cover on the flight. It is a gruelling, long trip but the theme had been
central to my research for over a decade and had informed my last book. For me
the term *geologic* seemed to capaciously accommodate the logics and logos of geo-
at the expansively finite scale of the earth, both real and imaginary, invoking the
eco-politics and aesthetics required not merely for species survival but also for
reasons to survive.

The geologic cannot be reduced to rocks, or just rocks. The geologic and geology are functionally inseparable but the geologic is a discursive site rather than
a science and, more importantly, geology is not just a science; geology includes
geologists. In the world of *geos* human populations have, as Michel Serres says,
become tectonic plates that weigh upon the earth. Seen from space these plates
glow at night, feebly mimicking day but radiating into the heavens nonetheless.
Although life passes into darkness daily almost all of earth's energy, all but one
part in four to five thousand, originates in the sun. Even what geologists in their
rocky dominion, in their abductive (as in abduction/kidnapping), extractive logic call *energy*, as in *energy resources*, is but an archive of the sun, and the geologic is
but a tiny dot in the heliologic.

Confusion is inevitable given that *geologic* and *geological* are interchangeable
in common usage. Still, questions need to be raised now that geology has risen
so precipitously in respectability. Theorists, academics, and artists who could
have cared less in the past are now raising the rubble and unleashing a virtual
avalanche of the inert. They have found a touchstone in geology, a bedrock of
materiality, and want to ride it as a rocky life raft into a world of rising sea levels. Their extrapolations from the dead zone, however, are only helping to sup-

port an already overpopulated and over-popularized world of geologists that it-self hastens the hothouse.

All sciences may appear equally deserving as a science *qua* science when in fact their fortunes rise and fall. Seismology, for example, was a relatively minor science until underground nuclear testing policy required its services for both monitoring and masking; Cold War geophysics became geopolitical as seismol-ogists registered tiny vibrations from afar and that was enough stimulation for them to madly reproduce. They flowed in great numbers into to the oil industry in Texas, the Middle East and offshore, as the oil fueling the Warm War flowed out. You may hear a few of them on the news rumbling on after big earthquakes, but there are not enough earthquakes to keep them gainfully employed.

Sciences are clearly unequal since nobody has reason to defer to seismology in discussions about massive threats to life on earth that presently inform and are informed by ecology. Seismologists have none of the eco-cachet of their un-derground colleagues in geology even though they work with one another day-to-day elbow-to-elbow. More recently you may hear seismologists commenting upon the artificial tremors set off by fracking, but this was the same gas explored through seismographic means. Being involved in both the cause and effect is a good way for a science to make news.

Seismology, like their adjacent science in the fossil fuel industry, likes rocks, albeit usually in larger formations. What brings them together in degrees of magnitude, what makes them meet at a common work site is the short-term wealth that can be drained from the commonwealth of the land. They depend upon one another and fossil fuel industries depend upon them. Where then are the seismologic imaginations of the fate and future of life on the planet? In fact, if geology is a science of the inert, why has it become relevant and at times ven-erated in an ecological discourse dedicated to keeping the species extant, when the seismological movements of the inert would seem to be one step closer to the vibratory actions of life?

The reason for this ascendancy of geology is not mysterious. It is attribut-able to its place in discussions of the Anthropocene. What is most immediate-ly a scientific proposal and process to determine a category within the Geologic Time Scale (there you go) has become generalized to mean a merger of nat-ural history and human history where a mutual indebtedness is amortized at the expense of both. Unmoored from science, the Anthropocene has become shorthand for the larger condition of anthropogenic climate change amid a vast range of other environmental violence, disasters, catastrophes, or whatever your preferences may be on a Calamity Scale.

Discussions of the Anthropocene have become so generalized that they of-ten occur where little or no mention is made of the geology underfoot. Indeed, this would be the preferable situation: geology provides the backstory then steps back so the plot can be developed with greenery. Geology has contributed to the confirmation of anthropogenic climate change and, along with other sciences, located causes and culprits; its further refinements should see it reduced to a bit part but instead it is cast as a protagonist.

Too many ecological imperatives, analyses and theories occurring under the auspices of the Anthropocene place geology in an inordinately important place, apparently by default. By comparison, the work of the Intergovernmental Panel on Climate Change (IPCC) is much more important than the International Commission on Stratigraphy (ICS), the organization assigned the task of determining whether the Anthropocene is a valid category and, if it is, locating an appropriate geological marker. The ICS mission is to meter whereas the IPCC mission is to survive. In fact, the ICS only presumes the survival of geologists far into the future, perhaps as a lost tribe, to read its yardsticks. It is a gift to their children's children's children but only if they take up the profession, and that would require either a strong genetic predisposition or a breeding program.

It is clear that the privileging of geology within ecological discussions is due to a compelling term—the Anthropocene—and thus to an act of branding rather than anything intrinsic to geology. If the problem ended there in accidents of language then there would be little issue. The more substantial problem is that the status of geology in the eco-politics of the Anthropocene requires that it be a geology without geologists. Actual geologists are integral to the fossil fuel industries at the crux of global destruction, so once the connection is made between geology (the study or discourse on the *earth*, so proscribed) and geologists (the people who do geology), then the geologic of the geological elicits a description of pure political deracination.

Geology has claimed a position to address the most crucial problem based upon its grasp of grand narratives of the past when in fact its practical role in an operational, destructive past is masked, while its continued role exacerbates the problem. Geological practice is yanked from its professional roots and thrown into an image of blue-sky research. Blue skies are a hopeful trajectory from the depths of winter and other inclemency and mass extinctions, so it is strange to see rocks claiming space. It defies the gravity of the situation. Floating a geology without geologists is the only way that that geology *per se* could be granted a pride of place within ecological debates. It is a bait-and-switch.

My own contribution to the book *The Geologic Imagination*, 'Reverse Icarus,' was delivered as a paper at the *Aesthetics After Finitude* conference in Sydney just before leaving for Amsterdam. It was a heliological examination of a geologic. Writing the essay provided me with an opportunity to revise the mythological structure of the actions of Icarus, Daedalus and Perdix in Ovid's *Metamorphoses* to fit with the historical reversal of the earth-sun relationship. Although revising a myth is a literary procedure, the role reversal was grounded in historical events.[1]

The sun coming down to earth was evident in the political discourses, artistic practices and anecdotal statements that accompanied the very first acts of the nuclear age: the Trinity test, the atomic bombing of the civilians of Hiroshima and Nagasaki by the United States, and the subsequent spectacle of nuclear weaponry. This relationship to the sun was amplified during the Cold War with the so-called hydrogen bomb. The atomic bomb used fission whereas the hydro-

---

1. See 'Black Sun, Black Rain', in ibid. pp.193-201

gen bomb used the fission of an atomic bomb to trigger fusion characteristic of the stellar nucleosynthesis that drives of the sun.

Although I use *Cold War* loosely as beginning with Hiroshima, more properly it was not the kiloton capacity of atomic weapons but the megatons of thermonuclear devices with the heightened prospect of global mass annihilation that underpinned the term. In any case, since the late-1980s the symbolism of the sun descending to Earth has been revivified with the realities of global warming and prospects of another annihilation, the sun setting upon humanity. This is what I call the Warm War.

Both nuclear weaponry and global warming are self-annihilating energy spasms where the *selves* are the human species. At first, instant incineration versus a slow burn appear to be on wildly different time scales, but from any perspective apart from a news cycle the temporal difference is insignificant and, from a geological one under consideration, nonexistent. In fact, each has a perfectly valid argument for preceding the other. So the sun descends in both the Cold War and the Warm War. *Reverse Icarus* reworked *Metamorphoses* through the latter.

The myth of Icarus needs to be reversed. Icarus does not fly into the Sun; the Sun descends onto him. His waxwings do not melt under the Sun's heat, casting him into the sea where he drowns; glaciers and polar ice caps melt and seas rise to engulf him where he stands. He has not ignored the instructions of his father, Daedalus; it was his father who broke the bond with the Earth that brought the Sun down and sent the seas washing onto land. Daedalus too will drown or succumb to the ills of overheating before water fills his lungs. The Sun indiscriminately passes judgment on everyone and everything, sets on the species and claims its full dominion over Earth.[2]

The revised myth does not have a happy ending, since my first obligation was to Greco-Roman myth as a genre, most of which never ends well, rather than catastrophism as a genre.[3] The latter upsets some science communicators who are more comfortable with crises and disasters as plot devices than catastrophes. They are afraid that people will warm to dying in a climate of nihilism sending people to stew in their own juices that will overflow and contribute in turn to sea level rise. Apparently, either they have a novel device that measures catastrophic events attributable to global warming or have a singular notion of an event.

There was plenty of geologic in this new myth but not much geology. More importantly, it was a geologic in light of the heliologic. If there is anything geological in it then it is in the exhumation of fossil fuels: what geologists do. Fossil fuels can be understood as old sun, their exhumation as a cycling of the sun, and global warming as retribution from the sun for presenting a burning corpse

---

2. 'Reverse Icarus', in *The Geologic Imagination*, edited by Arie Altena, Mirna Belina and Lucas van der Velden. Sonic Acts Press, Amsterdam, 2015, pp.41-52

3. My updating of the myth was in lesser part a reaction to how Bruno Latour capitulated to the cleverness of Daedalus as *technique*, when in fact he was a conniving, diabolical character (Daedalus that is; Latour is brilliant and charming). Bruno Latour, 'A Collective of Humans and Nonhumans: Following Daedalus's Labyrinth', *Pandora's Hope: Essays on the Reality of Science Studies*. Harvard University Press, Cambridge, 1999, pp.174-215.

within its body of live energy. So the heliologic is a good way to sort through rocks. It would be a way for geologists to tell which are the deadly ones, which ones not to disturb. It will keep separate too a study of the earth and the burning of the earth, i.e., geology and geologists.

And for people who use geology to extract the foundations of deep-time, they can extrapolate instead upon a larger cycling of the sun that does not separate them from the present. Their blue- sky would come from above, a less deadly energy source. If they continue to look down into the rocks they will become wedged into a geocentrism that itself is an iteration of a self-cancelling anthropocentrism, as long as a geology-without-geologists is still employed. Geologists employed in the fossil fuel industries will be economically and ecologically retrenched soon enough. Academic purveyors of deracinated geological discourses of the Anthropocene may wish to study the course catalogs from their own institutions if only in duty of care for the present students being fabricated for the industry.

The Geologic Imagination book was an incredibly pithy and relevant compendium; it is frankly rare to be schooled with such insight and creativity from page to page. But then came the opening sentences of an essay by the British geologist Michael Welland:

> Geologists and Australian Aboriginal peoples have much in common.
> They share an intimacy and a connectedness with the landscape, see in
> it stories that have to be understood and recounted, and enjoy a geolog-
> ic imagination.[4]

I had to stop because my disgust was visceral. There was no jet exhaust in the aircraft cabin so the waves of nausea must have come from these sentences. My reaction was no doubt amplified by the fact that the afternoon before I left Sydney I heard Aboriginal activists on the radio discussing in great detail the desecration and long-term debilitation of their land by mining. But I was already too familiar with the role that geologists play in the fossil fuel economy, and how international corporations and the Australian government continue to oppressively claw at Aboriginal land for uranium, coal and fracking, not to mention all else the land and people hold.

Still, I wanted to grant Welland the benefit of the doubt for his essay that he called *Poetry and Bookkeeping*. No one in their right mind could confuse geologists as a whole with being custodians of the land. He was, after all, a geologist at a non-academic conference at the core of an arts festival; it would be unfair to indict him for an awkward moment in what could be unfamiliar territory. Just as artists, writers and other non-scientists get their science wrong, perhaps he was a scientist who got his poetics wrong. When two-way streets narrow down people need to give way.

The case for bad poetry by a well-meaning scientist disappeared in learning he earns his living flying around the world in service of oil and gas exploration. He is known primarily for his book *Sand: the never-ending story*, a politically neutered pop-science book filled with fun facts.

4. Michael Welland, 'Poetry and Bookkeeping', in *The Geologic Imagination*, op. cit., pp.121-133.

The not-so-fun facts that might shine too much light on his day job were
conspicuously absent. Only in passing do we find out that "the world's largest
accumulations of oil and gas are found in the spaces between sand grains, 'or
mention of where sand is the name of the game: "the tar sands of the Orinoco
and of Canada'. These are, after all, 'the largest oil accumulations in the world',
even if they are the last throws of the fossil fuel industry.[5]

No mention is made of the geopolitical and eco-political issues arising from
the fact that Orinoco reserves in Venezuela are at the root of the United States'
attempts at political destabilization of that country or the Athabasca tar sands
in Alberta, Canada are the fountainhead for the hotly contested Keystone Pipeline that runs all the way to the Gulf Coast in Texas. Nothing about devastation
of the land, the desolation, displacement, habitat destruction, pollution, nothing
about global warming, as these images of *largest accumulations* appear and fade
away. Nothing about capital accumulation at the expense of the commons and
the future. Nothing about the smash and grab.

For a book on sand, missing are the specialist sands used in fracking for
which he is, according to his blog, an apologist.[6] Sand is also a critical component of the aquifers that oil, gas and extractive chemicals pollute and render toxic for consumption by humans (directly and indirectly) and other species, not just those humans ingest. To the working sand geologist both oil and
gas reserves and aquifers are, moreover, *reservoirs*. The voracious fossil fuel industry is putting its geologists on the frontlines of an oil-and-water confrontation
on a very large scale, even before global warming issues of the carbon released
into the atmosphere are tallied. As Welland puts it: 'Reservoir engineering—
the analysis, quantification, modeling, and prediction of the behavior of water
and hydrocarbon [oil, gas] reservoirs—is a whole science in itself, and it is critical for our way of life.'[7]

This *way of life* separates like oil and water between general notions of *life*
(regardless of whether particular humans grant that privilege to other biotic
forms), and a fossil fuel industry code for "standard of living" with its undercur-
rent of blackmail of impoverishment if they are obstructed in any way. *Our way
of life* introduces the possessive of a presumptive *we* connoting different socio-ge-
ological strata, those being us reservoir engineers, we in the employ of the fossil fuel industries, or we who have benefitted in our standard of living from fossil
fuel use and those who have not, the last fracturing along default lines revealing
valuable veins of socioeconomic class.

Fun fact: the Canadian tar sands were 'brought to the attention of the Hud-

5. Michael Welland, *Sand: the never-ending story*, University of California Press, Berkeley, 2009,
pp.264-265.

6. On his blog he stated, 'I should probably declare my general position: fracking is proven and reliable technology that presents problems only when regulations are loose, regulatory enforcement is deficient, and 'cowboy' operators are allowed to flagrantly disregard good engineering practice. The fact
that these issues can be, unfortunately, quite often the reality is a justifiable cause for concern—it's not
rocket science to fix but the media frenzy is arguably misdirected'.
http://throughthesandglass.typepad.com/through_the_sandglass/current_affairs/ (accessed 23 February 2015).

7. Op. cit., pp.264-265.

son's Bay Company three hundred years ago by local tribes who used the tar
to waterproof their canoes', which remains fun as long as it is a relic, because
too close to the present and First Nations and Native Americans wage protests
against the tar sands and pipeline.[8] What is not mentioned, therefore, should
give pause to indigenous people on all continents when geologists buddy up and
start smooth talking about a 'geologic imagination' and sharing 'an intimacy
and a connectedness with the landscape ...' Intimacy and connectedness ends
once resources are depleted or markets turn sour, then it is a matter of flying to
another land and getting all intimate and connected again. In a *poetry and bookkeeping* of fossil fuel geologists, the poetry fades once the corporate bookkeeping in place.

Here is a fantasy world of geology-without-geologists, a slick green-washed
fiction washing up on shore as an oil slick. Only under the auspices of the blue-
sky deep-time abstractions of geology could one feel licensed to explore for poetics by drilling into the longest of continuous cultures on the planet. The bottom line is that geologists in the fossil fuel industry do not develop custodial
relationships. Their devotion to deep-time is how much time it will take to drill
or bore or dig and how deep, and how quickly they can render the land obsolescent. Their *longue durée* is built atop earlier histories written by victors who have
ground people under their boot into a geological layer that can be economically and poetically mined and minted as required.

Geology is clearly in a conflicted position. As a science it has made defining contributions to earth systems knowledge and climate modeling, even if has
become disproportionately prominent in general ecological discourse. As a profession, geologists are complicit in the fossil fuel industry in the overheated core
of ecological conditions leading to meltdown, cornerstones without whom the
industry would crumble long before its inevitable market collapse. They need
to divest themselves of their own positions before financial violence visits their
own. Their prospects will soon drop dramatically and funds for future roles remediating the open cut scars they have left behind will magically disappear with
more bankruptcies and corporate shell games. They need to stop exploring and
explore other opportunities.

Conscientious geologists need to add minerals to a collective backbone and
prevent their colleagues who mine careers in *energy resources* from doing more
damage. It is not clear that this will happen any time soon. On 17 June 2015,
the Geological Society of London adopted the American Geosciences Institute Guidelines for Ethical Professional Conduct, most of which outline obvious
standards of scientific truthfulness, reporting and collegiality. Specific to geology we do find, 'Sample responsibly so that materials and sites are preserved for
future study', which might be difficult to maintain at an open cut mine.

Sifting through them for anything that may relate to global warming turns
up: 'Support responsible stewardship through an improved understanding and
interpretation of the Earth, and by communicating known and potential impacts
of human activities and natural processes'. It does not point to supporting *respon-*

---

8. Ibid, p.265.

sible stewardship by concrete action; it can thereby hide behind a condescending posture of *science communication* so as not to jeopardize, say, the Geological Society's publication of the journal *Petroleum Geoscience* or other instances of culpable Professional Conduct. Keep pointing to the blue sky, they say, so nobody looks at the earth. Distraction aids extraction. It buys time. The problem is that where the blue sky once was the weather has changed.

Those working in coal mining, oil drilling and gas extraction, it will be argued, are but grains of specialist sand in a much larger landscape; mere operatives following orders from their superiors, who themselves are but taking orders from market demand or a non-locatable malfeasance in the momentum from a darker side of mankind. Are they not but small fish destined to fry in an overheated climate of their own making? If they wash the soot from their hands, would not others quickly take their place? This is nothing but a professional nihilism, a death-drive that communicators would talk about if they were doing their job.

What other rationalizations are possible within a *geological imagination*? They should know that similar models of defense have had little success for other professions in the past. Most will no doubt stay around as long as they can before their pits spit them out or they have no more to explore, but they should back away now from their bores and tunnels and apply their skills elsewhere, somewhere less deadly. Keep carbon in the ground since waving pickaxes in the air does little good once it has been burned and released. Stop digging holes, seal them up, and begin remediating the massive damage already done.

6

Folding the Soundscape :: An ad hoc Account of Synthes\is

Adam Hulbert

One of the more successful manoeuvres of the Phonoegregore[1] has been to make space inaudible. That is, they frequently operate to produce specific outcomes by rendering the active material of the soundscape conceptually silent. This stratagem has allowed them to use various material technologies to enfold the communicating subject unnoticed, and has diverted attention from the manipulation of surfaces by attributing an illusory depth to the event of sound. The deliberate enfoldment the soundscape within the 'holding music'[2] of technologies of control has come to be known, by the Phonoegregore, as *synthes\is*. This approach has been used variously throughout history toward the purposes of actual control of human subjectivity.

Initially, the operation of synthes\is required a large-scale but also localised proxy for the soundscape. For this reason, early religiomaterialistic approaches frequently positioned the listening subject as enfolded within the technology of architecture. In response to sociotechnological *noise*[3] these strategies shifted to in-

---

1. The activities of this "spectral sonic cabal" of influencers came to light in the *Tuning Speculation* conference, Toronto, November 2013 where Marc Couroux presented 'Xenochronic Dispatches from the Domain of the Phonoegregore' in relation to the involvement of cybercapitalist interests in the earworm algorithm (see https://vimeo.com/81563854). The text for this talk was accessed 10 July 2015 at <https://www.academia.edu/5050613/Xenochronic_Dispatches_from_the_Domain_of_the_Phonoegregore>.

2. Perhaps apocryphally, Pythagoras has been attributed as describing a rock as 'music frozen in time': this was adopted in the 1800s by Schelling and Goethe (among others) in relation to architecture. This Pythagorean teaching is particularly notable given the later manipulations of materioacoustic space by the Phonoegregore. In 1917, Erik Satie—perhaps having encountered the technique through his gnostic connections—channeled this to different ends, with the concept of *furniture music* as a modulating influence within the soundscape. Although he composed only a small number of pieces under this rubric, he evidenced an ongoing interest in repurposing this Phonoegregoric strategy, and was later known to have secretly kept a cabinet that was filled with plans for imaginary buildings.

3. Jacques Attali understood music to be the articulation of a social order, and noise as an emergent set of relations that remain unrecognisable to existing orders: see Jaques Attali, *Noise: The Political Econo-*

corporate new understandings of materiality, particularly the invisible vibratory forces outside the acoustic spectrum, such as electromagnetism, which were less localised, and well-suited to conveying messages as though from an occluded (simulated) centre. As cybernetic models began to facilitate communication, the techne of synthes\is spread into these networks, eventually adopting the adaptive neuroformalistic models used in the present. The following is an ad hoc account of some previous plateaux of synthes\is stratagems: these provide some context for the developments of recent formulations.

FAUXREVELATORY DEPTH: A STRATAGEM OF ACTUAL CONTROL

Prior to touching on specific moments of synthes\is, however, it is perhaps useful to identify the operation of control in relation to the listening subject. Those initiated into the Phonoegregore and related interests share the goal of *actual control*. This should not be confused with *absolute control*, which is—despite the nomenclature—a weaker variant: the latter being unable to adjust to changes in interstitial spaces, and therefore with limited capacity to address issues of emergence and bifurcation. Actual control relies on the ability of any system to evoke a depth that lends significance to particular organisations of relation.

The Phonoegregore attach virally to the mechanisms of *fauxrevelatory depth* in a given system to enact widespread change that is incorporated as natural into the social fabric. The tenacity of Phonoegregoric stratagems is largely attributable to the ability of actual control, when effective, to turn the system against itself rather than against the vector. Thus, for example, the many criticisms of capitalism (to state just one instance of an infiltrated system) are generally directed at the actual operation of the co-opted system, rather than at the activities of the Phonoegregore themselves in manipulating a shared understanding of depth.

This fauxrevelatory depth is facilitated through the turning or folding of surfaces and flows. In the listening subject, this can be described in terms of *vortical semiosis*, a process that allows the sign/subject to emerge as separate to the soundscape.[4] Once perception is understood to be a material process, it is more straightforward to identify that significance in sound events will not arise from the interaction of depth with surface (such as psyche with sound), but rather the movement of the flowing forces of perception and sound at different speeds, as modulated by resonance with other materials. In the formation of a vortex, streaming water organises flow into a seemingly differentiated entity through a series of turns. This occurs, without any particular vitalist imperative, whenever rapidly-moving streams encounter slower-moving flows: note, for example, the differentiated vortex that may exist in relation to a stone in a rapidly moving stream, or when the fast moving river transitions to the slower moving ocean.[5]

---

my of Music, Trans. Brian Massumi, Minneapolis, University of Minnesota Press, 1985.

4. For discussion of this in relation to implosive listening see Adam Hulbert, *Turning and Returning: Composition in the Streaming Soundscape*, PhD diss., University of Western Sydney, 2010.

5. For further details on the model of fluid dynamics that informs this description, see Ernst-August Müller and Dietrich Rapp, 'Streaming: A Picture of the Etheric,' in *Towards a Phenomenology of the Etheric World*, edited by Jochen Bockemühl, New York, Anthroposophic Press, 1985.

The key to fauxrevelatory depth is to mask the process of turning by shifting attention to the implied centre.

The vortical sign/subject exists in relation to the semiosphere only insofar as the environmental conditions promote its emergence. Although an acoustic sign appears as a discrete entity, this identity through time is the result of a holding pattern that shapes the streaming movement of sound and perception to provide temporal and spatial consistency. This pattern could, at any moment, be otherwise; and removal of the conditions of emergence results in a return to turbulence.[6] In order to enact actual control of streaming (and therefore contingent) processes, synthes\is is involved with the processes of modulation that shape conditions of emergence, and does not attempt to shape streaming directly.

Actual control of the vortical sign/subject requires the ability to operate simultaneously at two speeds: shifts (or bifurcations) are inevitable, so actual power must incorporate both hegemony and resistance. One manifestation of this is the strategy of *obfuscation via interexteriority*: here both an idea and its passionate resistance are deliberately cultivated, such that each side, in their attempts to maintain absolute control, are unknowingly perpetuating a spectator class, which is the actual target for control. It is useful to note that the fractality of this system means that it operates through a range of levels of observation (or overhearing). Recent Phonoegregoric strategies have capitalised on this fractality, and are becoming increasingly molecular: although in the context of human subjectivity they all have in common a contestation of some surface of the body.

Eschewing the nano/pico regimes of the Phonoegregore's current strategy, the remainder of this discussion will examine a series of moments in the synthetic history of Phonoegreoric stratagems of control. The following are four plateaux in this account of the enspacement of the sign/subject through synthes\is.

NOTE ON THE VERACITY OF THE PRELIMINARY RESEARCH

This research is based on a folio of unmarked notes from a researcher with apparent sympathies to Phonoegregoric stratagems. The research notes were delivered anonymously to a colleague,[7] and the veracity of this historical account cannot be determined definitively. Most sources seem to be from existing scholarship, and where possible footnotes were added to identify the source of these and any further commentary that has been incorporated into the text.

The initial research is attributed to M. August Mountweazel. Although the legitimacy of the name cannot be ruled out entirely, it is probably a pseudonym, given the shared surname with the fictitious Lillian Virginia Mountweazel, whose fake biography was added to the 1975 edition of the New Columbia Encyclopedia to identify copied entries in cases of perceived copyright infringement from rival reference publications.[8] This name was likely to have been cho-

---

6. Perhaps it is worth noting, for clarity, that this primacy of turns and flow in the lifecycle of signs is more in line with Lucretian atomism than it is with more recent semiotic formulations: c.f Michel Serres *The Birth of Physics*, trans. Jack Hawkes, Manchester, Clinamen Press Ltd.

7. This colleague, for reasons of security (legitimate and/or paranoid) wishes to remain anonymous.

8. Henry Alford, 'Not a Word', *The New Yorker*, August 29, 2005, accessed 10 July 2015 at http://www.

sen for its evocation of the simulacrum as the replicating process for hyper-stition. (Even treating this as a speculative account assembled for dubious or paranoid reasons, there are some interesting links with known Phonoegregoric stratagems as identified in accounts by researchers in the field of occultural, and specifically phonoccultural, studies.[9])

The rough notes that are available at present have been organised chron-ologically according to subject and are provided, in a slightly expanded form, below.

SEVERAL PLATEAUX OF SYNTHES\IS

Croton, Magna Graecia / 530 BC

An early innovation in actual control through synthes\is was the understand-ing of silence as synthetic material: as an architecture rather than an absolute. Among their many systematic methods for approaching divine mathematics, the Pythagorean sect developed the techne of *echemythia* (also, *ekhemuthia*; silence). Con-trary to more recent religious formations, silence was, for the Pythagoreans, not a quality of the infinite divine. Instead, echemythia was an embodied techne. That is, silence contained specific rules for gesture and subjugation that were introduced in order to facilitate instruction between initiate and master, with the latter as the proxy for the authenticating religious centre. Echemythia proscribed specific em-bodied postures rather than conceptual abstractions, and the ability to maintain this difficult bodily discipline acted as a test for initiates.[10] Here, an enforced bodi-ly stillness set up a tropic relation to the flow of sound, diverting it toward an ideo-logical enfoldment. The most conscientious believers moved from the outer forms of the *acoustickoi* into the initiate class of the *mathematikoi*. For the successful initi-ates, periods of silence supposedly made celestial harmony audible. This cosmic expansion of the listening subject marked a transformation from silence to reso-nant sounding, and provided the framework for participation in the soundscape at all levels with a synechdochic relation to a perceived harmonic centre.

However, there were those among the *acoustikoi* who, without being initi-ated into the more precise religiodogmatic exposition of the inner teachings, identified the impact of spatial organisation on religious revelation and subjec-tivity and separated the process from any inevitable outcome. This heretical subclass can be considered to be a nascent form of the modern Phonoegregore. They understood that the power of religious dogma did not originate in the au-thenticity of revelation, but rather stemmed from the ability—through physi-cal or dogmatic means—to enfold the body into the form of a specific listening subjectivity.

According to their more pragmatic understanding of echemythia, this sets up a recursive self-authenticating loop: the revelations from this religiodogmatic

---

newyorker.com/magazine/2005/08/29/not-a-word.

9. See http://www.theocculture.net for current research.

10. This discussion seems to refer to Book 1 of Aulus Gellius' *Attic Nights*, as quoted at length in Michel Foucault, *The Hermeneutics of the Subject: Lectures at the College de France, 1981-82*, trans. Graham Burchell, New York, Palgrave, 2005, pp. 413-416.

entrapment are isolated from their emergence through materiality, and are authenticated as metaphysical and eternal by the process of tropic enspacement. This is the originary deception of the various feints enacted by the Phonogregore: to use any method—be it religious, architectural or psychotropic—to situate the body in such a way as to ensure receptivity to fauxrevelation. The actual revelation experienced by the subject is, in this context, largely irrelevant, except insofar as it continues to act as an internalised guarantor for the system of relations suggested by the architect of the initial experience.

Yucatán, Mexico / circa 800-1200 CE

One of the important findings of archeoacoustics is that the largely forgotten tradition of architectural synthes\is played a significant role in producing subjectivity prior to the era of cybernetic communication. Notably, although significant scholarly attention has been paid to Jeremy Bentham's proposed method of ocular control in his outline of the Panopticon in the late 18th century,[11] the relation of this architecture of entrapment to a much older tradition of acoustic control is frequently neglected. Richard Burger details, for example, an intricate architectural 'tradition-based convincing system' for shamanic traditions in the 3000-year-old complex of Chavín in Peru.[12] Among various methods, this temple exploits a variety of materials to either reflect or absorb sound. This is based on manipulation of the *precedence effect*: a perceptual auditory effect that conflates directionality with the earliest arrival of sound energy.[13] Such misdirection of perception would have been quite effective in reliably reproducing the experience of a relation with an occulted centre. This would then be supported by directional authenticity: the structure and materiality of the plaza served to forcibly silence the speech of the listeners while emphasising the audibility of the line of speech of the oracle.

While the displacement of perception clearly served useful ways to control subjectivity in the context of Chavín, this still required the presence of a figure of authority to enunciate. An early example of truly synthes\ic enfoldment based on materiality alone can be found in the Mayan temple complex of Chichén Itzá. At structure 5B18 (the pyramid of El Castillo), the staircase folds the sound of an initial event (a clap or a drum) and through acoustic dispersal and resonance cumulatively emphasises some frequencies while using a material filtering to suppress others. Here the complicity of space in transforming event is particularly evident. A different initial sound may vary the acoustic effect, and the various sounds made possible through interface with the body have been attributed to sundry deities among the polytheistic regime. The pyramid of El Castillo is primarily known to transform a handclap event into the chirp of the

11. Jeremy Bentham, *The Works of Jeremy Bentham, vol. 4 (Panopticon Constitution, Colonies, Codification)* , John Bowring .ed., New York, Russell and Russell Inc. accessed online < http://oll.libertyfund.org/titles/1925#lf0872-04_head_004>.

12. Cited in Miriam Kolar, 'Tuned to the Senses: An Archaeoacoustic Perspective on Ancient Chavín' July 22, 2013, accessed July 10, 2015 <http://theappendix.net/issues/2013/7/tuned-to-the-senses-an-archaeoacoustic-perspective-on-ancient-chavin >

13. Kolar, 'Tuned to the Senses', para 18.

resplendent Quetzal, a bird associated with the god Quetzalcoatl/Kukulcán, while many footsteps ascending the steps produce the sound of rain, congruent with the mask of the rain god Chaac found at its summit. Anecdotally, a nearby temple produces the sound of a snake, which blends with the chirp to evoke the feathered serpent Quetzalcoatl/Kukulcán in its chimeric glory.

At the base or ascension of the pyramid, the listening subject finds the echo of their acoustic events wrenched from them, co-opted into the evocation of a god or other guarantor of authenticity. Meanwhile, the veracity of the referent is confirmed in the visual landscape during each equinox when the perfect balance of light and shade enables the seven diamond scales of Quetzalcoatl/Kukulcán to descend as a shadow from the heavens. This *fauxrevelatory event* serves to justify the ongoing occlusion elsewhere in the complex, and by 'observing listening' guarantees the presence of the listening subject as unified and knowable.

Here, a careful application of mathematics has synthesised a complex narrative of deity by transforming surfaces only: a stratagem that can be found in a more refined form in the age of algorithmic synthesis. The spiritual realm is evoked through the primacy of the operation of echo diffraction and shadow over their usually more dominant correlates. This is the pretence to depth, created by an algorithmic abduction of time into the Mayan calendar and space into human-material technological pairing. This fauxrevelatory depth perpetuates the centre by co-opting the machinery of enspacement to entrap the social subject into reproducing an institutionalised religiocultural experience.

Washington, USA / 1896 CE

The initial plateaux showed dogma as a code to shape the listening subject through bodily positioning. This was then expanded, in the previous plateau, into a larger architectural machine, which effectively stole the sounds of the human body to replace them with synthetic experiences. While religious tradition and sacred sites were, for several millennia, sufficient for synthes\is of subjectivity, the increasing sprawl of cities required an equivalent expansion of the materials of actual control. Along with this was the increasing importance of capital in relation to Phonoegregoric stratagems.

A model fitting to the project of actual control in this latter communication era may be found in the first patented electronic additive synthesiser in the 1890s, Thaddeus Cahill's *Telharmonium*. Cahill's US patent (000580035-001) was for: "Art of and Apparatus for Generating and Distributing Music Electrically."[14] This was the first patent to use "synthesizer" to describe the device, and was proposed prior to the advent of amplification. Loosely, we can define the early *synthesiser* (this term is likely to have been adopted in common use a corruption of the Phonoegregoric word, *synthes\is.R*: a word for the technology for production of simulacra)[15] as a connected series of various materials (physical

14. For a detailed discussion of the history of this instrument, see Reynold Weidenaar, *Magic Music from the Telharmonium*, Lanham, M. D., The Scarecrow Press, 1995.

15. Here, *.R* probably refers to 'the encoding of the real': although no existing sources verify this in earlier contexts, similar algebraic stand-ins have been found from reverse-engineering existing algo-

or conceptual) placed in such a way as to virtually produce significant acoustic experience.

The Telharmonium operated within a dedicated wired network, initially using cables provided and laid by the New York Telephone Company, which were designed for carrying human voice over distance. Technology to extend the voice was, therefore, co-opted with modulated tones, provided by a machine that took 30 railroad cars to carry and operated from a basement under the city. This networked synthesiser replaced two-way communication with co-opted cybernetics. Here is an early instance of the 'held' subject of the spectator class: the silenced individual trapped in a network suspended by holding musak. The held subject was, from the onset, a class situated within the interests of the bourgeoisie: at various times, this network of the telharmonium connected a dinner club, a casino theatre, the museum of natural history, a fine-dining restaurant (the first paid subscriber), and a small number of very wealthy individuals.[16]

During the era of the telharmonium, the effective silencing of the consumer was in its initial stages, and was not without hitches. Specifically, the generated signal resonated the interstitial space afforded by physical proximity to the telephonic wires that were laid adjacent. The resultant crosstalk lost the nascent New York Electric Music Company the contract with the telephone company for physical infrastructure, but has afforded one of the more effective strategies of Phonoegregoric vector, wherein earworms are distributed via resonance through discrete but adjacent networks.

Osaka, Japan / 1982-84 CE

The miniaturisation of the architecture of synthes\is, alongside the accelerated potential of mass-production towards the close of the 20th Century threatened to impact the control regimes of the Phonoegregore by making technologies of entrapment accessible to divergent interests. Though eventually quite successful in co-opting subcultural dissonances (the *iTuning effect* of platform coercion and sound laundering), the implications of synthes\is in relation to neuroplasticity were initially underheard until their emergence *en masse* through underground parties.

A classic example of this, of course, is the Roland Corporation's TB-303 Bass Line 'transistor bass', created under the supervision of Tadao Kikumoto (developer of the equally notorious TR-909 drum machine). The bait-and-switch of supposed bass guitar synthesis was one of the few times that Phonoegregore themselves were deceived: the simulacra of the TB-303 as an inferior copy (in a Platonic sense) obscured its virtuality when introduced into existing networks. The founder of the Roland Corporation, Ikutaru Kakehashi, left a clue for oc-

rithms. Note that this finding is based on a personal communication from the researcher who provided the original text, and cannot be verified further due to the classified nature of the materials of research.

16. Once the role of audio as holding became widely acknowledged (in the form of 'being on hold' within a bureaucracy or corporation), this overt strategy was abandoned by the Phonogregore.

cultural scholars when he employed Burrough's method of cut-up's[17] by random-
ly selecting the name Roland from a telephone directory.

Japan was the ideal nursery for this new form of machinic unfolding, as the
nation was—perhaps uniquely—positioned in the 1980s to recognise the value
of technocratic stratagems without being convinced of the necessity of fauxrev-
elationary depth that accompanied such revelations in much of the west. After
visiting Tokyo during the era of the TB-303, Gilles Guattari described Japan as
a place where:

> Externalized interiorities and rebel exteriorities with univocal signifying re-
> ductions populate the surfaces and engender new depths of the sort where inside
> and outside no longer maintain the mutually exclusive relationship of opposition
> to which Westerners are accustomed.[18]

Thus, prior to its co-option, the dancefloor became—with the use of the
TB-303—a potent force for deactivating previous gestural priming through
capital-driven spaces.

We know from current research that the latter rogue synthes\is accelerated
what Félix Guattari has termed Japan's *machinic eros*, and briefly situated contemporary subjectivity outside actual control. Globally, pockets of machinic becoming emerged; at the close of the millennium these extended into, for example,
the synthe-driven afrofuturism of Detroit techno[19] and the deliberate stratagems
of embodied derevelation experimented by Nick Land and the Cybernetic Culture Research Unit (Ccru) in the context of post-rave jungle.[20] The efficacy of
this form of resistance partially arose from the deliberate enspacement in the interstices between networks.

AFTER/WARED: FORAYS INTO *XENOCRACY*

After this point, the various fragments of source material become largely in-
decipherable, and ongoing efforts at decryption are yet to yield results. The use-
fulness of examining the above tropic shifts in the enfoldment of subjectivity is
perhaps questionable, given that these manoeuvres have long since been abandoned in favour of a much more complex neuroformalistic turn. Nevertheless,
they do allow the occultural researcher some limited awareness of the foundational mechanisms of actual control. Moreover, they allow for the possibility of a
xenocratic alternative: xenocracy describes a multimodal articulation of the flows

---

17. William Burroughs, 'The Cut Up Method' in Leroi Jones, ed. *The Moderns: An Anthology of New Writing in America*, New York, Corinth Books, 1963, accessed online, July 10, 2015 at < http://www.writ-ing.upenn.edu/~afilreis/88v/burroughs-cutup.html>. In this passage Burroughs also describes *the fold in method*, where a page is folded to create new relationships using the surface of linguistic signifiers. A type of cultural disruption is implied with the connection of cut-ups with the Hashisheen assassins, as described by Burroughs in Bill Laswell, *Hashisheen: End of the Law* (audio recording: Sub Rosa, 1999). Further discussion of the relation of the cut up method to the Hashisheen is at <http://www.subrosa.net/en/catalogue/soundworks/bill-laswell_03.html>.

18. Félix Guattari, 'Tokyo, the Proud', *Delezue Studies* Vol 1, No 2, 2007, p.97

19. Benjamin Noys, 'Techno-Phuturism' in *Malign Velocities: Accelerationism and Capitalism*, Winchester, Zero Books, 2014.

20. Nick Land, 'No Future' in *Fanged Nouema: Collected Writings 1987-2007*, New York, Sequence Press, 2013.

of power through the soundscape.[21] Toward this end, it is perhaps useful at this stage to briefly outline later developments of synthes\is technology (to the extent that they are known), and to identify some of the implications of these ad hoc plateaux in understanding these developments.

As an addendum to the discussion above, the effectiveness of the rogue synthes\is of the TB-303 was relatively short-lived. The priming of specific individuals with perfect pitch to the phonoegregoric earworm, as noted in Marc Couroux's seminal writing on the subject,[22] meant that a number of the more accomplished synthesiser users began unwittingly replicating mathematical relations that again triggered individuals to reproduce Phonoegregoric synthes\is. Furthermore, commercial networks and platform-based distribution were effectively used to co-opt rather than repress the early experiments in xenocracy by reframing the conditions of emergence to suit actual control.

Nevertheless, xenocratic societies may continue to operate in the dark web. Some research[23] posits that various strands of AI spectreware, based on the infamous IREX2 code,[24] have begun to adapt convolution impulses to recode torrented audio files in order to propagate the tools of enspacement among the increasingly active spectator class.[25] This is not without precedent: a similar manoeuvre of priming was presciently identified by Philip K Dick in *Radio Free Albemuth*, where encrypted messages originating from an alien satellite were copied into popular music and then distributed over radio to prime the population to rebel against a neo-fascist US government.[26]

From the initial Pythagorean heresy, the entrapment of subjectivity has occurred according to an enfoldment of the soundscape. The entrapped subject then does the work of erasing the enfolded becoming, with the traceless and empty centre remaining as a seemingly eternal and inevitable occluded guarantor for this self-authenticating system (and its corresponding semiotic framework): this is the mythopoesis of the *always already* listener.

The work of occultural studies seems to be moving towards rediscovering the fragments and surfaces of becoming-sound. These provide lines-of-flight

---

21. For further discussion on xenocracy, see Adam Hulbert, 'Without Latency: Cathode Immersions and the Neglected Practice of Xenocasting for Television and Radio', VIEW: Journal of European Television History and Culture, Vol. 3, No. 7 (http://journal.euscreen.eu/index.php/view/article/view/JETHC086/188).

22. Couroux, 'Domain'.

23. In much of the frontier studies of Phonoegregoric strategies, researchers are reluctant to submit preliminary findings for publication, and generally prefer to remain anonymous. The speculation here was provided anonymously, as based on a 'verified but undisclosed' source. Given the widespread disinformation and obfuscation surrounding this topic, such information should, of course, be considered to be potentially unreliable.

24. For further discussion on the IREX2 code, see Marc Couroux, 'Internal: AUDiNT (Phonoccultural Studies)', *Un Tune Magazine*, accompanying the 2005 CTM Festival, pp. 81-84.

25. *Torrenting*, of course, is a variation of streaming.

26. Interestingly, the protagonist of this story acts as a diversion by enacting a similar but unsuccessful embedding. The failure of this 'bad copy' diverted the attention of the government, playing a key role in potentially undermining absolute control. See Philip K. Dick, *Radio Free Albemuth*, New York, Harper Collins, 2008. Dick himself heard narrowcast messages of seemingly extra-terrestrial origin through his radio. He also had a number of encounters with the FBI, and through them, potentially, came across the various guises of the Phonoegregore.

from actual control and in so doing further earlier experiments in xenocracy that sought to reconfigure synthes\is. This approach allows for synthes\is to act as part of the material activity of the soundscape; rather than as a techne for replicating culturally-occluded technoarchitectural mechanisms of fauxrevelatory depth. It is too early, of course, to tell how effective these new synthes\ic modes of listening will be in avoiding the entrapment of actual control.

7

Transfinite Fiction and the case of Jorge Luis Borges

Baylee Brits

> There is a concept which corrupts and upsets all others. I re-
> fer not to Evil, whose limited realm is that of ethics; I refer to
> the infinite.
> Borges, 'Avatars of the Tortoise'

The great Argentine miniaturist, Jorge Luis Borges, held numbers to be essential to the reconstitution of both poetry and prose, after what he saw as a saturation and loss of vitality in both forms at the outset of the twentieth century. Here
I will contend that it is the connection between numeracy and artistic form 'in
Borges; short fiction that will push his prose past this perceived aesthetic stagna-
tion, which revolves around the preeminence of finitude in the novel form. Borges' 'aesthetics after finitude' entails revolutionizing prose so that it is capable of a
transfinite aesthetic, one common to other proto-modernists and modernists, including Stephané Mallarmé and Samuel Beckett. Here I will outline a provisional theory of the *transfinite aesthetic*, which in Borges' work is achieved through
"transfinite allegory." This new literary technique, an "aesthetics after finitude"
for the twentieth century, seeks to formally exceed the bounds of the novel, specifically the borders that define and enclose the territory of the novel: the tran-
sience of experience, the influence of locality, the possibility of transformations
in consciousness. The Kantian regime that privileges the shifts and torsions in
consciousness and hence finite experience, as influential in literary form as it is
in philosophy, is only one governing mode of prose composition: the other is the
transfinite aesthetic.

MODERNISM AND THE TRANSFINITE

Borges' perspective on late nineteenth-century poetry, and the failings of this
form, are apparent in the manifestos and experiments that came out of his participation in avant-garde groups in Spain the early 1920's. Whilst he and his fam-

ily were stranded in Europe during World War One, the young Borges became
involved with the *ultraists* in Seville and Madrid, returning to Argentina in the
early 1920's convinced that primordial metaphor would rescue verse from poetic ornamentation. Borges eventually disowned this "ultraist" enterprise, but
it would provide the foundations for his lifelong preoccupation with fictional
worlds created without rigid or naïve symbolism, and his commitment to the
construction of fictional worlds through systems of abstraction, suggestion and
a mathematized order or imagination. The young Borges found his inherited
forms to be "saturated", an idea made explicit many years later in an essay on
the novel published in 1954, entitled "A Defense of *Bouvard and Pécuchet*." In this
essay Borges argues that Flaubert, creator of the realist novel, is also the first to
"shatter" it.[1] Within this discussion of Flaubert, Borges makes a significant aside
about numerals in *Ulysses* and the death of the novel:

> Flaubert instinctively sensed that death [of the novel], which is indeed tak-
> ing place (is not *Ulysses*, with its maps and timetables and exactitudes the
> magnificent death throes of a genre?), and in the fifth chapter of the work,
> he condemned the 'statistical or ethnographic' novels of Balzac and, by
> extension, Zola.[2]

Numbers, here, are the harbingers of the death of a genre. The statistical
quality of Balzac and Zola's narratives (an *enumeration* or *account* of a reality) perhaps give a sense of the death of the genre, but it is in Joyce's self conscious inclusion of these statistics in *Ulysses* that we see this most clearly. James Ramey,
in a study of Borges and Joyce, agrees with Cesar Augusto Sagado that Borges' relationship to the novel is "eschatological": Borges writes in (and of) an end-
time of this prose form.[3] And, above all in Borges' short essay, he associates these
death throes with number. Borges claims that these death throes, the performance and drama of the death of the genre, are exemplified in *Ulysses*, a book
that Borges had, elsewhere, called a "miracle."[4] In Borges' eyes Joyce is attuned
to the failure of that novelistic relation to the "actual" instituted by Defoe, Field-
ing and others, whose prose numeracy grounded characters as subjects of their
world, facilitating the drama and immediacy that would make the novel such
a cultural force over the following centuries. Borges needed a new relation between prose and number: one that does not enumerate the reality it sets out to
describe or reduce realism to the staid presence of what Flaubert recognizes, in
Bouvard and Pécuchet, as the "statistical" or "ethnographic" novels of Balzac. The
tendency towards versions of verisimilitude inherent in the novel is here—after two centuries of vigorous development—an inhibiting rather than enabling
force, and numbers, as statistics, are the signal form that indicates this, for Borges. And yet, it will be on these very terms that Borges will revolutionize the form:

---

1. Jorge Luis Borges, 'A Defense of Bouvard and Pécuchet,' in *Selected Non-Fictions*, ed. Eliot Weinberger, trans. Esther Allen, New York: Penguin, 1999, p. 389.

2. Ibid.

3. James Ramey, 'Synecdoche and Literary Parasitism in Borges and Joyce,' *Comparative Literature* 61,
no. 2 (2009), p. 142.

4. Borges reviewed *Ulysses* in superlative terms in 1925. See: Jorge Luis Borges, 'Joyce's 'Ulysses," in
Selected Non-Fictions, ed. Eliot Weinberger, trans. Suzanne Jill Levine, New York: Penguin, 1999, p. 13.

through numbers, but not finite, probabilistic numbers. Instead, Borges will re-place the finite counting inherent to prose form with a transfinite count.

A TRANSFINITE FICTION?

Perhaps the most important mathematical event of the last 150 years is Georg Cantor's discovery of multiple, measurable "infinite sets". In other words, Cantor posited and made sense of the strange idea that there are multiple in-finities and that some infinities are bigger than others. Cantor's "infinite sets" are represented by transfinite numbers. A transfinite number is an *actual* infin-ity, without being the *absolute* infinity (and, hence, is measurable and has a rel-ative size). Cantor represented the transfinite cardinal numbers with aleph let-ters, which linked the finite numbers that we use to count with their infinite potentialities, "fix[ing] the infinite" as Quentin Meillassoux would say.[5] In Mor-ris Kline's words, "Cantor's greatness lies in his perception of the importance of the one-to-one correspondence principle and in his courage to pursue its conse-quences. *If two infinite classes can be put into one-to-one correspondence then*, according to Cantor, *they have the same Number of objects in them.*"[6] By establishing a one to one correspondence between two sets (matching the objects of one set to the objects of another), one can tell whether one set has a greater or lesser number of objects in it that another. For instance (in an example used by Kline) the set:

1 2 3 4 5 6 7 ...

Can be said to have the same number of objects as the set:

b) 6 7 8 9 10 11 12 ...

simply because one can show that there is a 1-1 correspondence between these sets. By showing that some sets of numbers do not have a 1-1 correspondence Cantor can prove that some sets are "larger" than others. For instance, com-pletely counter-intuitively, the number of squares and the number of natural numbers is the same, because for each natural number there is a square and hence both sets have a cardinality of $\aleph^0$, but ordinal numbers, which cannot be put in a one-to-one correspondence with natural numbers or squares become $\aleph^1$. Thus Cantor demonstrates the existence of two different sizes of infinities, there-after extrapolating the possibility of not one infinite, but *infinite* countable *infini-ties*, of different "sizes."

Borges had an explicit and sustained engagement with Georg Cantor's transfinite numbers. He was a reader of mathematical texts, including Russell and Whitehead's *Principia Mathematica* and Kasner and Newman's *Mathematics and the Imagination,* and in his essays and stories he engaged directly with the is-sue of an actual infinity. This engagement would shape many of his short stories, not only those that he collected in the volume named for Cantor's choice of sym-bol for his transfinite numbers, *The Aleph.*[7] Indeed, Borges took a broad interest

---

5. Meillassoux, *The Number and the Siren: A Decipherment of Mallarmé's 'Coup de Dés,'* Translated by Rob-in Mackay. Falmouth: Urbanomic, 2012, p. 99.

6. Morris Kline, *Mathematical Thought From Ancient to Modern Times,* vol. 1, Oxford and New York: Ox-ford University Press, 1990, p. 398.

7. Floyd Merrell suggests that there is a crucial difference between Borges and Cantor: Cantor hoped

and enjoyment in mathematics. In his 1940 book review of *Mathematics and the Imagination*, he predicts that, in addition to "Mauthner's *Dictionary of Philosophy*, Lewes' *Biographical History of Philosophy*, Liddell Hart's *History of the War of 1914-1918*, Boswell's *Life of Samuel Johnson*, and Gustav Spiller's psychological study *The Mind of Man*" this volume was likely to become one of the works that he has "most reread and scribbled with notes."[8] Borges was particularly well versed in the consequences of Cantor's theory of the infinite, and its differentiation from vague, non-mathematical visions like Nietzsche's "Eternal Return." In an essay entitled "The Doctrine of Cycles," Borges engages with Cantor's work on infinity in order to disprove the ideas of Eternal Recurrence of Nietzsche's Zarathustra. "[Cantor] asserts the perfect infinity of the number of points in the universe, and even in one meter of the universe, or a fraction of that meter. The operation of counting is, for him, nothing else than that of comparing two series,"[9] Borges explains. His illustration, as ever, is vivid:

> For example, if the first-born sons of all the houses of Egypt were killed by the Angel, except for those who lived in a house that had a red mark on the door, it is clear that as many sons were saved as there were red marks, and an enumeration of precisely how many of these there were does not matter. [...] The set of natural numbers is infinite, but it is possible to demonstrate that, within it, there are as many off numbers as even.[10]

In Borges' argument, Nietzsche's eternal return (or "eternal recurrence") is impoverished because it falls into the trap of assuming that an infinite number of particles cannot be presented an infinite number of ways by virtue of finite force. What is attractive for Borges in Cantor's theories of the infinite is the profusion of forms of counting that negate Nietzsche's single count. In Cantor's vision, the infinity of natural numbers and the infinity of points in space belong to different sets and are incommensurable. These counts give way, for Borges, to an infinite generation; an intellectual prospect that Nietzsche's theory is devoid of by virtue of the fact that there is only *one* infinity, not multiple infinities of different sizes. This modern vision of infinite generation is more than simply an intellectual intrigue for Borges: it goes to the heart of the construction of fictional worlds.

In an echo of Borges' own claims in "A Defense of *Bouvard et Pécuchet*," Anthony Cascardi claims that Borges' modernism relies on the rejection of literature as a repetition of the world. Instead, Borges' approach would be to *create* worlds. "The work of art," Cascardi writes, can "reassert its claim to be something more or other than a mimesis of the world, in part by reflecting on the

that the paradoxes of his set theory would be resolved, making a total system. Borges, on the other hand, had no such hope, and reveled in the paradoxes. Floyd Merrell, *Unthinking Thinking: Jorge Luis Borges, Mathematics and the New Physics*, West Lafayette, Indiana: Purdue University Press, 1991, p. 61.

8. In this review Borges also refers to Bertrand Russell's classic *Principia Mathematica*, which he took copious notes from. See: Jorge Luis Borges, 'From Allegories to Novels,' in *Selected Non-Fictions*, ed. Eliot Weinberger, trans. Esther Allen, New York: Penguin Books, 1999, p. 337.

9. Jorge Luis Borges, 'The Doctrine of the Cycles,' in *Selected Non-Fictions*, ed. Eliot Weinberger, trans. Esther Allen, New York: Penguin, 1999, p. 116.

10. Ibid. pp. 116-117.

impossibility of it ever being a full and complete mimesis of the world."[11] In this vein, Cascardi claims that the "imperfections" worked in to Borges' worlds "suggest how art remembers what it was like to *be* a world, not just to *be like* the world."[12] This is a kind of refusal to "clone" the world through description, one that entails a refusal of broader representational completion. These imperfections, in Cascardi's argument, speak to art's "memory" of the time in which it did create a world: the time of myth and epic that preceded the Romance and novel. This mimesis, in Borges' hands, becomes the product of another mimesis: a world contingently created from another. This is an act not of linear progression but "permutations and combinations."[13] These worlds do rely on permutations, combinations, axioms and, as I hope to prove here, transfinite numbers. Floyd Merrell links "the demise of totalizing narratives" that Cascardi is speaking of directly to Cantor's infinities, citing Cantor's remark that "the least particle contains a world full of an infinity of creations."[14] There are two problems, here: a literary one and a mathematical one. The first is the problem of the literary creation of novelty and the state of Barthesian "exhaustion" that Cascardi cites: the state of cultural saturation whereby literature comes to take other literature as its subject matter. The second is the mathematical paradox of completing the "set of all sets." Merell puts this perfectly in his gloss of Cantor: "everything is contained in everything else."[15] Looking at this through the combined perspective of literature and mathematics, Borges' vision of an "infinity of creations" appears, then, not as recollection of a lost mimesis (as Cascardi feels it does) so much as a *mathesis* of literature; this is not a restitution of a descriptive totality, so much as a modern awareness of the mathematical presence of multiple totalities, each of different measure. In each case what is required is the transfinite operation upon the totality of writing, or, to follow Cantor, the totality of sets.

THE LIBRARY OF BABEL

Borges' most famous short work, *The Library of Babel*, is our path into understanding the formal achievement of this transfinite operation on writing. The volume entitled *Labyrinths*, home of *The Library of Babel*, contains a series of stories that revolve in some way around a labyrinthine structure. In Emir Rodriguez Monegal's words, labyrinths are "according to tradition, the representation of ordered chaos, a chaos submitted to human intelligence, a deliberate disorder that contains its own code."[16] The "code," here, is also the "clue", a word that originates with the Greek term for the thread given to Daedelus by Ariadne, to help him find his way out of the labyrinth that he had built to house the Mino-

---

11. Anthony Cascardi, 'Mimesis and Modernism: The Case of Jorge Luis Borges,' in *Literary Philosophers: Borges, Calvino, Eco*, ed. Jorge J.E. Garcia, Carolyn Korsmeyer, and Rodolphe Gasché, New York and London: Routledge, 2002, p. 116.

12. Ibid. p. 116.

13. Ibid. p. 113.

14. Merrell, *Unthinking Thinking: Jorge Luis Borges, Mathematics and the New Physics*, p. 61.

15. Ibid.

16. Emir Rodriguez Monegal, *Jorge Luis Borges: A Literary Biography*, New York: Paragon House Publishers, 1988, p. 42.

taur. Borges, of course, is obsessed with the labyrinth as a combination of both order and disorder, and as a predicament that requires some mysterious key to unlock. Borges' most famous "labyrinth" is "The Library of Babel," which is a narrative account of a universe that takes the form of a library ordered by regular geometric cells. "The Library of Babel" is a labyrinth insofar as it is infinite and thus contains all possible books and, most importantly, the "book of Books" that forms the code for all others. The existence of this book is a rumour: it has not been found by any of the "librarians" but provides the most important justification of the Library for the librarians, as well as an impetus for their search through the books. This rumour is derived from speculation that emerges from the logic of the library itself; the speculation that the library contains every possible permutation of the alphabet of Babel.

This book in many ways stands in for the mythological minotaur, here: it is both the source of the Library and that which the Library keeps hidden. The Library is thus a labyrinth in the sense that its nature presents a conundrum: on the one hand a quest to find this essential book, and on the other hand a metaphysical problem concerning the order and contents of the library and the lives lived in the library. In both of these cases we are dealing with the mystery of the *thought* of the library, an unspoken divine that drives the questions of the narrator or a clue that unravels the being of the library, that shows up its pattern. The labyrinth is thus a double bind in the sense that the appearance of the question is also the grain, the method, of the search.

The Library of Babel houses the books that the inhabitants—who are referred to as the librarians—spend their lives combing. The narrator is an ageing inhabitant of the Library, whose sight is failing and who seems to be reaching the end of his or her life: "now that my eyes can hardly decipher what I write, I am preparing to die just a few leagues from the hexagon in which I was born."[17] The narrator's brief and strange account seems to be at once an outline of the only world in which he has lived his life, as well as an explanation of the world for one who lives outside the Library. In this sense, the short story is fundamentally contradictory: the representative account of a total universe is presented as if for the foreigner (the various details of the uniform structure of the library are noted) or, in other words, a world that supposedly contains no outside is presented *for an outside*. The story opens with the essential structures of the Library:

> The universe (which others call the Library) is composed of an indefinite and perhaps infinite number of hexagonal galleries, with vast air shafts between, surrounded by very low railings. From any of the hexagons one can see, interminably, the upper and lower floors. The distribution of the galleries is invariable. Twenty shelves, five long shelves per side, cover all the sides except two; their height, which is the distance from floor to ceiling, scarcely exceeds that of a normal bookcase.[18]

17. Jorge Luis Borges, 'The Library of Babel,' in *Collected Fictions*, trans. Andrew Hurley, New York: Penguin Books, 1998, p. 112.
18. Ibid.

How the narrator knows the height of a "normal bookcase" is a mystery: he has lived his whole life in the Library. The self-conscious estrangement that occurs here is carried right through the story and is particularly significant given that the production of texts has such consequences for the constitution of the Library. The "significance" of this is a kind of anti-significance: this discrepancy in the form of the narrative signals the contradiction in positing any totality at the same time that it constructs the "total" Library.

The epigraph to "The Library" is taken from Robert Burton's *Anatomy of Melancholy* (Pt 2., Sec. II, Mem. IV) and foregrounds the issue of textual production as a process of combinatorics: "By this art you may contemplate the variation of the 23 letters...."[19] Though Borges only provides a snippet of this section from Burton's masterpiece, the passage that it falls within is fascinating in terms of its use of numbers. Burton sets out, here, to make the point that through the simple variant combinations of twenty-three letters of the alphabet (during Burton's time the Classical Latin alphabet contained twenty-three letters, not yet including j, u and w) one is afforded an exceptional imaginative range. Within a wider section on the value of literature and discourse as a solution to melancholy, Burton cites numerical combinations of the letters of the alphabet to give a sense of the vast possibility that emerges from language alone. What is intriguing is Burton's exact delineation of this realm of possibility:

> ten words may be varied 40,320 several ways: by this art you may examine how many men may stand one by another in the whole superficies of the earth, some say 148,456,800,000,000, *assignando singulis passum quadratum* (assigning a square foot to each), how many men, supposing all the world as habitable as France, as fruitful and so long-lived, may be born in 60,000 years, and so may you demonstrate with Archimedes how many sands the mass of the whole world might contain if all sandy, if you did but first know how much a small cube as big as a mustard-seed might hold, with infinite such.[20]

Here, in order to give a sense of the full range afforded by the humble alphabet, Burton in fact defaults away from the alphabet and starts listing very large numerical figures. Numbers are given the power to ascribe the further reaches of the expressive capacity of the alphabet. What is notable about the epigraph to "The Library of Babel" is the wider numerical import of the passage from which that sentence is extracted: the contemplation of the variation of the twenty-three letters leads to the contemplation of a condensation and extensity of these letters, and of course Burton expresses this condensation through numbers rather than letters. Of the very large numbers in the theory of eternal recurrence, Borges writes: "This chaste, painless squandering of enormous numbers undoubtedly yields the peculiar pleasure of all excesses."[21] Burton seems to be applying this very technique, here. There would, conceivably, be a number to describe the extent of variation of the twenty-three letters: a number that sits

19. Ibid.
20. Robert Burton, *The Anatomy of Melancholy*, New York: The New York Review of Books, 2001, p. 95.
21. Borges, 'The Doctrine of the Cycles,' p. 116.

outside of the alphabetic universe that Burton opens for his reader. The task of
the librarians, the contemplation of the books, the limits of their universe, and
the chances of their finding a "book of books," happens in the context of just the
sort of numbers that Burton deploys. One might say, in other words, that the
capacities of language to describe and imagine vast possibilities—even the simple, random combinatorial possibilities of the alphabet—are undergirded by a
number. Indeed, here, the "truth" of the alphabet, and so of literature, appears
numerical.

The narrator carefully and systematically describes the Library and the
means by which the librarians understand its potential totality. The only departure from the essential function of the Library—housing books—is in the literally narrow provisions—two small spaces in the cells—in which the librarians
may sleep or relieve themselves. The books in the Library do not necessarily make sense: rather, they are arrangements of letters that do not necessarily produce words, sentences or meaning of any kind and, in fact, statistically
will not do so. The "meaning" is instead produced in instantiation or permutation: each book another possible arrangement of the letters or characters of the
twenty-five letter alphabet, even if it is only the most minimal change, of just
one character. Thus there must necessarily exist a "written" account of every
life, and of all future events in the Library. The Library thus appears as infinite
to its inhabitants, in the sense that it expresses, in its very form, all possibility.[22]
The random arrangement of letters means that "for every rational line or forth-
right statement, there are leagues of senseless cacophony, verbal nonsense, and
incoherency."[23]

Upon introducing the Library, our ageing librarian relates the basic axioms
of his world: the first principle being that "The Library has existed ab aeterni-
tate."[24] The narrator repeats what he or she calls "the classic dictum," supposedly a common belief about the nature of the library, which is in fact a rephras-
ing of Giordano Bruno's description of God: "The Library is a sphere whose
exact centre is any hexagon and whose circumference is unattainable."[25] This
is, of course, also a version of infinity severed from the number line, the version
reflected in Cantor's uncountability proofs (where, as Borges himself notes, all
you need is a 1-1 correspondence to construct a measure of infinity). This "classic dictum" is less a statement about a cosmic distribution impossible to imagine

22. The number for all possible combinations of the 25 orthographic symbols in the library is of
course not infinite. It is merely, as William Goldbloom Bloch points out, 'unimaginably vast.' The number that Bloch comes up with is 251,312,000. This of course, pertains only to a *sense* of the infinite rather than the infinite as such. It also pertains, however, to some certainty that the library never repeats a
volume: a fact which is necessarily unverifiable because any full index of the library would be an entire
replication of the library. As such, the safest 'size' to posit for the Library of Babel is somewhere in between 251,312,000 and ∞. This number, however, does not include the possible arrangements of letters
on the spines of the books. Current research, as Bloch notes, posits the size of our observable universe
as 1.5×10^{26} meters across. Bloch calculates this in terms of cubic meters, and demonstrates—aston-
ishingly—that our universe 'doesn't make the slightest dent in the Library' in terms of cubic size. See:
Bloch, *The Unimaginable Mathematics of Borges' Library of Babel*, p. 18-19.

23. Borges,'The Library of Babel,'p. 114.

24. Ibid. p. 113.

25. Ibid.

than a claim about the Library as instantiation. Reminiscent of Asimov's *Nine Billion Names of God*, the "meaning" of the Library is the inclusion of every possible arrangement of letters, and in this inclusion the Library is complete and is manifest as a labyrinth. The Library presents the form and limits of everything the librarians can know, and it is precisely these limits that form the basis for theories of the being of the library. The second principle of the Library stipulates the number of letters:

> *There are twenty-five orthographic symbols.* That discovery enabled mankind, three hundred years ago, to formulate a general theory of the Library and thereby satisfactorily solve the riddle that no conjecture had been able to divine—the formless and chaotic nature of virtually all books.[26]

The librarian relates an instance where a book his father "saw in a hexagon in circuit 15-94, consisted of the letters M C V perversely repeated from the first line to the last. Another (much consulted in this zone) is a mere labyrinth of letters whose penultimate page contains the phrase *O Time thy pyramids*."[27] The M C Vs demonstrate this "chaotic nature of all books," and the significance of this text is precisely the absence rather than presence of any semiotic import.[28] The MCV's demonstrate that this alphabet and the dialects, languages and various forms of meaning that it produces, also contain their antithesis: the capacity for meaninglessness. What is deeply unsettling, regarding this story, is the presence of a footnote that implies that the work we are reading is a copy: "the original manuscript has neither numbers nor capital letters."[29] The version of "The Library of Babel" that we are reading does include numbers—for instance, it refers to a hexagon in circuit "15-94"—and so there must be an "original" copy, then, where this would have been spelt out: fifteen-ninety four. Once again, what is behind the distribution of the hexagons are numbers, and what signals the status of the text as a copy is the supervenience of numeracy in a universe totalized by an alphabet.

Regardless of the limit of the orthographic symbols, we know that if the number line is potentially infinite, then so too are the books of the Library. The conditions for being and the conditions for knowing both revolve around the number of letters and the possible combinations of these letters. The twenty-five orthographic symbols are also a notation for an unimaginably large number of combinations. It is in the number twenty-five that we see the simultaneity of the ontic and the epistemic (the being of the universe, and the limits of what can be known in that universe), but, curiously, without the implication of a totality. This is not "god" or some other secular philosophical absolute (consciousness, perhaps) but simply the number twenty-five.[30] But, in so far as these letters can be combined to form number words, any calculation of combinations becomes redundant, precisely insofar as numbers can continue infinitely. All one

---

26. Ibid. p. 113.
27. Ibid. p. 113-114.
28. Ibid.
29. Ibid. p. 113.
30. Ibid.

could produce is a key for an endless creative process: those simple twenty-five orthographic symbols that are vastly more generative of permutational combinations than the decimal system.

The narrator details the various superstitions that have prevailed, from time to time, in regions of the library: the Vindications, the Crimson Hexagon, the Man of the Book. The notion that the Library contains all possible narratives, including those that will occur in the future and those that have occurred in the past ("the archangel's autobiographies"), inspires religious fervour:

> When it was announced that the Library contained all books, the first re-action was unbounded joy. [...] There was no personal, no world prob-lem, whose eloquent solution did not exist—somewhere in some hexagon. [...] At that period there was much talk of The Vindications—books of *apologiæ* and prophecies that would vindicate for all time the actions of every person in the universe and that held wondrous arcana for men's fu-tures. Thousands of the greedy individuals abandoned their sweet native hexagons and rushed downstairs, upstairs, spurred by the vain desire to find their Vindication.[31]

This fervour comes from the most interesting (and horrifying) possibility that the Library (literally) materializes, which is validation simply through existence: the realm of possibility is already delimited through the record of all possibility. Each vindication is an individual manifestation of the necessity and reason for existence. This fervour is reversed in another superstition held at one time by the inhabitants of the Library (or a certain susceptible set of them): "the Book-Man. On some shelf in some hexagon, it was argued, there must exist a book that is the cipher and perfect compendium *of all other books*, and some librarian must have examined that book; this librarian is analogous to a god."[32] Anoth-er form of this speculation is the presence of a total book with a circular spine: "Mystics claim that their ecstasies reveal to them a circular chamber contain-ing an enormous circular book with a continuous spine that goes completely around the walls. But their testimony is suspect, their words obscure. That cy-clical book is God."[33] The Library is the measure of time and life because it con-tains all possibility *at once*, already rolled out and specified, and the Vindications or the great circular book are merely the most explicit, extended version of this. The simple possibility of an essential book that provides the key to the unrave-ling of the rest of the Library, the codex for the universe that proceeds from it, is the most condensed version of the same impulse. This labyrinthine morphol-ogy is distinctive because it posits a conflation of ontology and epistemology at its core: the key that lets Daedalus escape his labyrinth. The possibilities for the 'art' of twenty five orthographic symbols is at once the scope of all knowledge of the library (epistemology), insofar as it is mediated by language, but equally the conditions for being in the library, insofar as the world exists for housing the books and, more minimally, the librarians who attend to the books (ontology).

---

31. Ibid. p. 115.
32. Ibid. p. 116.
33. Ibid. p. 113.

Alfred North Whitehead theorizes the distinction between the modern and the pre- or non-modern on the basis of a conflation, or severing, of the link between ontology and epistemology. For Whitehead, the modern severing between ontology and epistemology contradicts the foundations from which modern science developed. To Whitehead, these foundations are found in medieval Christianity as much as Ancient Greek science.[34] For Whitehead, Greek "science" was never truly a science, but a necessary extension of metaphysics. Rather, Whitehead contends that it is "scholastic divinity" that forms the necessary ground for the Enlightenment flowering of empiricism.[35] Crucially, the innovations within science that emerged from scholastic divinity relied on what Whitehead calls the "instinctive belief" in the "secret" and the metaphysical consistency behind natural order: "I mean the inexpugnable belief that every detailed occurrence can be correlated with its antecedents in a perfectly definite manner, exemplifying general principles."[36] The forgotten foundation of modern science is in the presumption of completion (the presumption of a total rationality in the universe) and, by virtue of this completion, the presumption of consistency. In other words, the flowering of naturalism emerged from the medieval Christian requirement for an invisible order (a secret), that underlies and generalizes the most minute natural phenomena, creating a necessary link between ontology and epistemology. The Library mirrors this connection between order, secret, ontology and epistemology perfectly.

In Whitehead's history and theory of the Enlightenment the connection between representation and presentation are severed by the secularization of modern science, the disavowal of the foundational connection (the Christian connection that is also the Parmenidean connection) between ontology and epistemology that produces the conditions for modern science in the first place. There are two points regarding "The Library of Babel" that are significant here: the first concerns a mode of formal allegory that emerges from this conflation of ontology and epistemology, and the second regards the consequence of this, which is the production of an "in-significant totality" or, in other words, a "transfinite aesthetic." The Library revolves around a book that provides a locus in which ontology and epistemology are conflated: it is the key for the labyrinth, providing the source and extent of possibility of the material universe of the Library. The Library revolves around a moment of pure presentation, not yet an instantiation or permutation, and not a re-presentation of the twenty-five orthographic symbols. This "book" would be entirely future-oriented: not refer-

34. Murray Code provides an excellent summary of Whitehead's perspective on the conflation of ontology and epistemology. Even more significantly, he frames this modern 'denial' of its foundations in terms of a failure to be properly modern: '[...] it would be better to describe Whitehead as attempting to frame a thoroughly nonmodern naturalism in the sense outlined by Bruno Latour, who charges the moderns with never having been truly modern since they never tried to bring all the explanatory resources of nature, culture and discourse under one roof. They instead opened up a chasm between epistemology and ontology by trying the former to a sensationalist theory of perception and the latter to the doctrine of mechanistic materialism.' See: Murray Code, *Process, Reality and the Power of Symbols: Thinking with A.N. Whitehead*, Hampshire and New York: Palgrave MacMillan, 2007, p. 62.

35. Alfred North Whitehead, *Science and the Modern World* (New York: The Free Press, 1925), p. 12.
36. Ibid. p. 15.

ring to or representing anything, but providing the molecular form of the world that will surround it. This book provides the same function for the librarians as what Whitehead calls the "secret" that animated the Christian scholastics, and conflates the ontic and the epistemic in the same way. However, there are two levels to this observation: the first regarding the nature of the Library and the lives of the librarians, the second regarding *The Library* as a story, and how it relates to a version of the "total book" envisaged by Mallarmé as a part of his development of an infinite art. Just as the Library revolves around some necessary microcosm that is the total book, *The Library* is reciprocally constructed around a total book: the universe of Babel, and all of its contents. *The Library* is only an allegory of a total world, and the extensity of language and the function of presentation in our world insofar as the Library occupies a similar distance to its potential "total book." The short story here revolves around an imagined total book that justifies and provides the reason for the universe that the narrator lives in, just as the world that this narrator tells us about orbits around the same structure (which provides a rationale for the estranging contradictions of the story, whereby the narrator explains his world as if to someone from another world, as if there were an outside). In the case of *The Library* (the story) the total book is of course "The Library of Babel," in The Library (the world) the total book is of course The Golden Book, the Vindications, the circular book or whatever other figure of an essential or total book the librarians might formulate. This reciprocity allows this story to become a curious formal allegory, whereby the contents of the story reflect the narrative's own creation and explanation of a total universe.

To make this effect of "The Library of Babel" clearer, it is useful to turn to a story that also presents a kind of total book, albeit one that retains a "significance" and has vastly different effect as a result. This story is entitled "The Book of Sand". This title refers to the name of a book that is sold to the narrator of the tale, a book that seems to be of infinite length. "The Book of Sand" starts with a reflection upon the problem of infinity and verifiability:

> The line consists of an infinite number of points; the plane, of an infinite number of lines; the volume, of an infinite number of planes; the hypervolume, of an infinite number of volumes... No—this, *more geometrico*, is decidedly not the best way to begin my tale. To say that the story is true is by now a convention of every fantastic tale; mine, nevertheless *is* true.[37]

In this story the (again unnamed) narrator recounts how he came to own "The Book of Sand" and how he would eventually dispose of the menacing volume. The narrator acquires the book from a man who arrives at his home claiming that he sells Bibles, but actually offering another "sacred book" that he found in "northern India, in Bikaner."[38] This book is unusually heavy and possesses other strange traits:

> At the upper corner of each page were Arabic numerals. I was struck by an odd fact: the even-numbered page would carry the number 40, 514, let us say, while the odd-numbered page that followed it would be 999. I

---

37. Jorge Luis Borges, 'The Book of Sand,' in *Collected Fictions*, New York: Penguin, 1998, p. 480.
38. Ibid.

turned the page; the next page bore an eight-digit number. It also bore a small illustration, like those one sees in dictionaries: an anchor drawn in pen and ink, as though by the unskilled hand of a child.[39]

The book was named the "Book of Sand," by the former owner, an illiterate man of the lowest class in India, who named it thus because "neither sand nor this book has a beginning or an end," a suspicion that is affirmed by the narrator's attempts to locate the first or last pages of the book.[40] Eventually, our narrator's life becomes contorted by his possession of the book, he is subject to a form of paralysis: "I began noting [the illustrations] down in an alphabetized notebook, which was very soon filled. They never repeated themselves. At night, during the rare intervals spared me by insomnia, I dreamed of the book."[41] In order to free himself he must lose the book, and, appropriately, he chooses to deposit it in what he considers to be an innumerable place: "I remembered reading once that the best place to hide a leaf is in the forest. Before my retirement I had worked in the National Library, which contained nine hundred thousand books... I took advantage of the librarians' distraction to hide the Book of Sand on one of the library's damp shelves."[42]

The Book of Sand is a total book, but one that has no relation to the world or a world: it is not generative in the least. The book here is pure substance (in the sense in which substance is described above, as the material substrate of the "secret" that scholastic divinity sought in the world). It is horrific because it contains *everything*, rather than the code or key for the *potentiality for everything*. The difference between the Golden Book or total book in "The Library of Babel" and "The Book of Sand" can be summarized in the discrepancy between a "significant totality" (a totality that describes or contains all possibilities), which describes the latter, and an "in-significant" totality (one that produces the conditions for all potential materiality), which describes the former.

The idea of an insignificant totality emerges from the formulation of an insignificant or "ontic" mark, recently theorized by French philosopher Quentin Meillassoux. Each of the superstitions in the Library centre around the notion that one of the books holds a code from which the world of the Library proceeds. As I argued above, this is formalized as a conflation between the ontic and the epistemic, albeit a conflation that never leads to a totality; that never reveals the "secret" that Whitehead understands the medieval Christian scientists to be pursuing. There is no complete science behind the Library. Regardless of their semiotic meaning, regardless of whether the marks form words or sentences, the librarians pore over the works which may or may not have semiotic meaning: the cause for attention is not only this type of meaning but rather the fact that the marks constitute portions of the sequence of possibility, and indeed the book could form the codex to wider sequences, even, ultimately, the codex to all the Library. This book that the Library revolves around is thus an instance of "on-

---

39. Ibid. p. 481.
40. Ibid.
41. Ibid. p. 483.
42. Ibid.

tic" writing: a mark, or a text, or some form of writing in those books that inscribes the possible infinite destiny of the inhabitants (rather than representing
such possibility). "Ontic signification" refers to the mark used in mathematics,
and differentiates it from representational writing. Meillassoux arrives at the
term through investigating the status of mathematics as a science of ontology:

> In order to resolve the problem of the absolute scope of mathematics, I be-
> gan by trying to identify a minimum requirement of any formal writing—
> logical or mathematical—that distinguishes it from natural languages
> [langues naturelles]. I tried to reach a precise and determinative point of
> difference, capable of distinguishing a symbolic, or formal, language from
> a natural language.[43]

Here, Meillassoux theorizes the way that mathematics uses signs in an exceptional form, articulating the difference between the writing of mathematics and
of "natural" language in terms of a minimal difference: "This minimum requirement actually seems to me to consist in a remarkable usage— a systematic
and precise usage—of the sign devoid of significance [dépourvu de sense (sic)]."
[44] This curious description of mathematical presentation indicates a form of
mathematical signification that is separated from semiotic signification; a mark
is not "significant" because it is self-contained. These criteria lead Meillassoux
to assert ontic signification as a distinct form of signification: the placeholder
or mark that mathematics uses to demarcate the real. Meillassoux's contention
that the "writing of mathematics" is the use of signifiers without significance
describes a form of sign that technically could be substituted for any other sign,
and which obeys operational protocols rather than hermeneutic ones.

What is distinctive in the total book of the Library of Babel is its status as
an ontic mark: it obeys these operational protocols; it is a self-contained text
that provides the "key" to the Babelian universe. If indeed the Library is a total book, it is a totality by virtue of its pure, meaningless production. This total
book does not catalogue all aspects of the world, like the Book of Sand, but inscribes the potentiality of the world: it is a totality that is generative without being prescriptive. There are two possibilities regarding the total book: in the first
instance, it could be a book hidden somewhere in the Library, perhaps an unusual form of book, like the imagined circular book or golden book. The other
"total book" is the world that the story presents: it is world within *The Library of
Babel* as opposed to the world within The Library of Babel which provides the
vision for the Library without describing or representing all its contents. Here
the formal allegory of the work and the ontic signification come together: the
story itself mirrors the problem faced by the librarians of Babel, with the reciprocity of the two worlds functioning to posit a generative but unseen ontic
"book."

---

43. This excerpt comes from a conference paper given by Quentin Meillassoux: Quentin Meillassoux, 'Contingence et Absolutisation de l'Un,' in *Conférence Donnée À La Sorbonne, Lors D'un Colloque Or-
ganisé Par Paris-I Sur 'Métaphysique, Ontologie, Hénologie'*, Paris, 2008. This translation is by Fabio Gironi,
and is currently only published at: http://afterxnature.blogspot.com.au/2011/10/translation-of-meil-
lassouxs-contingence.html#more. All parenthetical notes are Gironi's.

44. Ibid. (Gironi trans.)

This is speculative literature, or literature "after finitude" at its finest. A properly infinite book, here, is a *transfinite* book, constructed as a kind of measurable infinity by virtue of the distance between two points: form and content. What form, then, must be forged from the death of the novel? I would like to suggest that it is this unusual formal allegory that Borges so masterfully constructs, here; one that does not require a belief in any abstraction or divinity. Many of Borges' most successful stories revolve around the capacities of fiction to suggest worlds beyond itself, and the source and meaning of the extensity of fiction. But to look at this only at the level of content misses precisely the mode in which the "other world" comes into being, which is through number. Like Mallarmé, Borges is interested in a "total book": an essential structure or principle that underlies the possibilities available to fiction. I have argued above that Borges creates a kind of "in-significant totality" to produce a genuinely *generative* fiction.

Borges' stories allegorize their own processes of composition by bringing into relief their own "enigma": an infinite presentation rather than a finite representation. The double forms of number for the story allegorize the organization of expression and tropological movement of the very fictional work. However, we are not dealing exclusively with a traditional, de Manian formal allegory, as the presence of number in the texts suggests something beyond this. The autonomous and material aspects of language that necessarily defy both the formalist critics and any pretension to unified poetic works are rendered in Borges' work as the essential collapse of ontology and epistemology in substance: "The Library of Babel" must posit the Library in order to posit, within that world, the superstition of a "Golden Book," for instance. In other words, what we have with Borges is the replacement of a stable relationship between language and the world with number. Number here comes to stand in for the link between sign and referent, and fascinatingly the restitution of a foundation for language in Borges work is not found in natural language at all, but the other form of language: mathematical writing or the ontic mark. This relies not on any spiritual foundation for allegory, but nor is it limited to an awkward science of the symbol (though it replicates this form closely). This allegorical form is not rooted in individual experience either, and takes no coherent subject-sensorium as its point of origin. This new form rests not on divinity but on $\aleph_0$ and can be called "transfinite aesthetic": it produces the measure of a certain infinity, rather than reproducing the immediacy of uncontainable experience.

8

Picture that Cyclone

Stephen Muecke

'All day and night the wind played ancestor music' writes Alexis Wright in *Carpentaria* as she crafts a syntax whose agency is designed to keep an indigenous cosmos alive.[1] The wind is an agent who plays, and the music belongs to the spirits of ancestors, not to humans. Such syntax, and such *cosmoi*, have accompanied human imagination for ever. Europeans revere their classical traditions and gods, those divine and semi-divine beings of Mt Olympus and the Underworld. Every household has its god, every notable river, tree, cave and spring. Today, perhaps in a more secular fashion, they revere and keep alive this sacred cosmos as the very origin of contemporary European cultures. These ancestors, these fictional beings, says Bruno Latour 'possess a particular type of reality that it is appropriate to cherish and respect. We have never ceased, at least in our own tradition, to develop, recognize, celebrate, and analyze the specific character of that reality.'[2] And yet, another side of us Moderns is only too eager to relinquish these characters as *merely* fictional, obviously lacking in any truth-value: 'They have been valued to an extreme, while too hastily denied any objectivity'.[3] So where does that leave them, Latour asks, these 'creatures of the imagination'? Where do they come from? Well, the 'human mind' of course, 'that famous interiority, that artifact of Bifurcation, the bookend paired with exteriority'.[4]

We know this is not true because we meet fictional beings socially. We might meet Cinderella as a bedtime story, then later at school we are more elaborately introduced to King Lear and Emma Bovary. Far from them being the products of our imagination, they are out there in the world and when we talk of 'internalizing' them what we mean is there are meetings that create aspects of our subjectivities:

---

1. Alexis Wright, *Carpentaria*, Sydney, Giramondo, 2006, p. 458.
2. Bruno Latour, *An Inquiry into Modes of Existence: An Anthropology of the Moderns*, trans. C. Porter, Cambridge, Harvard University Press, 2013, p. 239.
3. *Idem.*
4. *Ibid.* p. 240.

We find ourselves on their trajectory; we are part of their trajectory, but their continuous creation is distributed all along their path of life, so much so that we can never really tell whether it is the artist or the audience that is creating the work. ... In other words, they too make networks.[5]

In indigenous Australia, ancestor beings are talked about all the time too, but they have different kinds of networks, different modes of appearance and disappearance, different modes of interacting with humans. And, the same as in any other set of cultures, these 'fictional beings' have full ontological weight, they are real, but in a different way from other kinds of reality.

Which brings me back to my titular statement, an injunction to 'picture that cyclone'. My questions concern cyclone imaginaries, interrogating them in ways not so different from the phenomenology of a Gaston Bachelard talking of the poetics of space[6]: what do they look like? What causes them? And what kind of objects are they? But if I want to give 'full ontological weight' to *speculative cyclone imaginaries*, to what they *might be*, then it might be a mistake to close the argument too quickly around the idea that the answers to such questions are 'obviously' *grounded in science*. Science is in charge here; stand aside ye gods of thunder and lightening!

Paintings and photographs of cyclones can make them look sublime, like a Turner painting, but science will tell you they look like this, which is just one way of picturing them[7]:

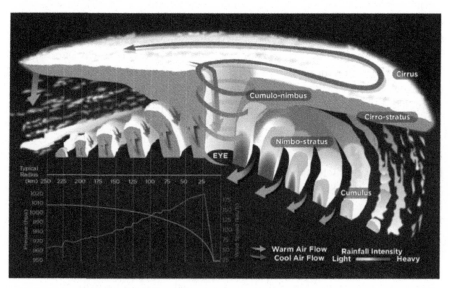

I can also find a completely different set of answers in Aboriginal Australia. It is a different picture. And it is not *grounded* in the same way, in fact, we might have to use Ben Woodard to question the 'long tradition' of the 'earth-anchoring

5. *Ibid.* pp. 242-43

6. Gaston Bachelard, trans. M. Jolas, *The Poetics of Space*, Boston, Beacon Press, 1969 [1958].

7. Anatomy of a cyclone. Updated 27 Feb 2013, 11:41am. ABC News Online looks inside a cyclone. Data: BOM/NOAA/Wikipedia Images: BOM/NOAA

of thought.'[8] A European thought that is in the habit of 'settling' itself around concepts of *patria, heimat,* enclosure and possession that 'reduces nature to a collection of objects' (I would say *all dead in the same way,* as opposed to all sorts of things *being alive in their own kinds of ways).* I shall talk below about tropical cyclones in Broome, Western Australia, where they are quite common, perhaps becoming more common. The Goolarabooloo people from there talk of 'living country'; all sorts of non-animate things are talked of as having lively trajectories through the world. But let Woodard continue:

It is such images of Earth as both dead body and mute cradle that we set out to destroy with digging machines, massive energy weapons, and total ecological collapse. These images perform a dual criminal function: one, to stabilize thinking, and two, to give gravity to anthropocentric thinking and being. [9]

The critique of a singular Nature, as carried out by Latour, Philippe Descola, Tim Morton and so many other contemporary philosophers and anthropologists, is something I shall take as read.[10] Released from this *terra firma,* our philosophies can now be shaken loose by cyclonic disturbances at the extremities of which the laws of physics start fraying and calling for new chaos theory-based algorithms in the data-crunching networks of climate-forecasting supercomputers.

All day and night the wind played ancestor music.

And Alexis Wright continues to describe the cyclone that will wipe away the fictional town of Desperance:

He became conscious of what the sea ahead was doing once more, and although he knew it was kilometres away, he heard the spirit waves being rolled in by the sea water creatures of the currents, and conspiring with the spirits of the sky and winds to crash into the land as though it was exploding. The earth murmured, the underground serpent, living in the underground river that was kilometers wide, responded with hostile growls. This was the old war of the ancestors making cyclones grow to use against one another.[11]

Bearing in mind this suggestion that cyclones might be caused by ancestors making war on each other, let's consider Dennis Daniels', account of a famous Australian cyclone as reported by anthropologist Basil Sansom:

CYCLONE STORY

There was this old fellow who took his wife from Borroloola to see the city of Darwin. In Darwin, the old fellow and his woman stayed in the Aboriginal settlement at Bagot. There the wife met a Darwin man. She went

8. Ben Woodard, *On an Ungrounded Earth: Towards a New Geophilosophy,* New York, Punctum Books, 2013, p. 6.

9. *Ibid.*

10. Philippe Descola, *Beyond Nature and Culture,* Trans. J. Lloyd, Chicago, University of Chicago Press, 2013; Timothy Morton, *Ecology Without Nature: Rethinking. Environmental Aesthetics,* Cambridge, Harvard University Press, 2007.

11. Wright, p. 470.

off with this man, joined him in his house at Bagot and said she had become a 'Darwin girl'. She would not return with her husband to Borroloola. Only magic does this to a woman, making her change over suddenly like that. The husband went back home. He was very angry. He was angry for that woman and that man. One day he sat down and began to sing up that Whirlywind. He was going to kill both of them, kill them both finally. He sang and sang. (He used clapsticks to give the beat for his singing.) He sang the Whirlywind down the river over from Borroloola and out into the sea (off the South-Western portion of the Gulf of Carpentaria). He turned the wind and made it go upward over the sea towards the North. He sang the wind past Groote Eyland. He went on singing. He sang the wind past the Gove Peninsula and there he made the wind turn West. He sang the wind on towards Croker Island. He was holding the wind, holding onto the wind all the time as he sang. Then the wind, that Whirlywind, said: 'Oh, what's that?' Whirlywind had smelt another wind coming from somewhere roundabout. This was a Young Girl Wind and the first wind smelt her underarm smell. The Young Girl Wind was coming from the West. Whirlywind started to chase after her. Smelling that smell, he went really mad. Chasing, chasing after the Young Girl Wind, the oldfella Whirlywind caught up with her. They stayed together in one place; they were over Darwin that whole night.

And that's the way you got all these houses smashed up and those people killed, what whitefellas are calling that Cyclone Tracy.

But the whitefellas got the wrong name; wrong name really! Two wind! And all the time the whitefellas were thinking 'One wind' and got the wrong name, that Tracy.

That wasn't Tracy. That was the oldfella Whirlywind that was sung up from Borroloola and the Young Girl. Two wind!

The narrator brings his story to its close with expressions of great glee interspersed with repetitions of: 'Two wind, that was two wind really!' He went on to laugh the more. Then he mentioned tee shirts. In the aftermath of the cyclone that devastated Darwin on Christmas Eve 1974, lines of tee shirts were produced for survivors and rescuers ruefully to wear. One carried the legend: **Darwin - Gone with the Wind**. But Dennis Daniels, narrator of the true Cyclone Story, cited another inscription: **What a Night I Spent with Tracy**. 'This one was half right, half right. Some whitefella got it half right. But, really, there were two winds: oldfella Whirlywind and the Young Girl.' After the laughing, he says: 'Darwin really got wasted. Wasted. I've been looking round. And all those fellas were killed!'[12]

This story by Dennis Daniels might 'just be a story', but Sansom calls it a Dreaming, having no doubts about how it is carefully articulated around Top End politics and religion. Maybe we can call it an *historical dreaming*, about *that* Whirly-

---

12. Basil Sansom, "Irruptions of the Dreamings in Post-Colonial Australia," *Oceania*, Vol. 72, No. 1 Sep., 2001, pp. 1-32, p. 19.

wind, about *that* Cyclone Tracy, where the demonstrative pronoun signals the kind of specificity that cannot be designated by general 'Laws of Nature'. 'Picture *that* cyclone', not 'generate laws for cyclones in the abstract' :

> The proper Cyclone Story [says Sansom] gives Dreamings as still those terrible and willful Powers who, moved by their own priorities and their private, self-centred calculii of desire, would often do enormous things. An eternal attribute of Dreamings is that, disdaining the presence of humankind, they may be wholly driven by their endogenous Dreaming relationships and concerns.[13]

Dreamings with endogenous powers that disdain 'the presence of humankind'. Curious. The Laws of Nature are supposed to do that too. Maybe the Economy as well, to the extent that it has become 'second nature' for the western Moderns.[14]

Let me be clear about the problem for this chapter. In juxtaposing 'explanations' —whatever they are—for where cyclones come from: a scientific account with an Aboriginal dreaming account, I am asking why reliance on the western scientific account might not be able to be universized without a bit of effort. Common sense, which people can always fall back on, tells us that the best explanation for a cyclone is a colourful cross-section mushroom cloud diagram, while the dreaming account should be firmly lodged in the category of strange beliefs and intriguing stories. There is an ontological separation; they are different ways of going through the world. They belong to different institutions. The scientific institution does its reliable work (thank goodness, we *do* want those weather forecasts to be quite accurate!) while the other can entertain us in the museum of past curiosities. We are used to saying that mumbo-jumbo has no future, the very definition of science being purification by classification and progressive isolation from past superstition.

But if you think that, then you haven't done your anthropology of the Moderns thoroughly enough. If you think that Science or the Economy can make their interventions in Aboriginal county as isolated tentacles of the Modern, that is, behave only as pure institutions that do their work efficiently, profitably and rationally, then you have forgotten that they bring their gods with them, that efficiency, profitability and rationality can't come on their own, as it were, but are already accompanied by transcendentalisms large and small.[15] These are costs that reappear on the balance sheet once we conceive of the world *ecologically*. But if we continue to think of it in a *modernist* fashion, the world looks

---

13. Sansom, p. 21.

14. Latour, *AIME*, Ch. 14 on the Economy and: 'But how can we approach The Economy with sufficient dexterity without giving it too much or too little credit? Because The Economy offers the analyst such a powerful metalanguage, its investigation might have been concluded at once, as if everyone, from one end of the planet to the other, were now using the same terms to define the value of all things. Not only would it offer no handhold to anthropology, since it would have become the second nature of an already unified and globalized world, but it would have achieved at the outset all the goals taken on by our projected diplomacy, by allowing all peoples to benefit from the same measuring instrument made explicit everywhere in the same idiom. With The Economy, there would always be mutual understanding, because it would suffice to calculate.' (p. 383.)

15. Bruno Latour, trans. S. Muecke, 'The Recall of Modernity: Anthropological Approaches,' *Cultural Studies Review*, March, 2007, pp. 11-30, p. 13.

open-ended. An institution arrives somewhere and says it is behaving efficiently, at the same time as it places centre stage its own gods (its cherished hopes and dreams), it buries its own mistakes and collateral damage, while also pushing aside other worlds constituted by their networks of institutions.

So have the Moderns successfully sequestered their divinities in church and their fictional characters in literature classes, where they can't get up to any mischief? Is a cyclone—or more pointedly, the increased incidence of cyclones with global warming now that we have entered the Anthropocene—a purely scientific issue? Human agency is playing a part in climate change, but climate still has massive 'endogenous powers' that 'we' can't control. This takes me to Tim Morton's designation of such massive things as 'hyperobjects'. The hyperobject is a catchy concept—that is, it catches you while you can't quite catch it. Morton first established it in *The Ecological Thought* in 2010.[16] His more recent book, *Hyperobjects: Philosophy and Ecology after the End of the World* explains why everyone is affected by hyperobjects, even if they strive to deny their existence.[17] Climate, natural oil reserves, the English language are all hyperobjects in that they cannot be grasped as 'simple' objects. Have you ever met 'English'? No, but what you experience every day are groping attempts to make meaning with words. Whispered lovers' words and words digitized and zapped across the internet are materially quite different things, but both belong to the hyperobject we call the English language. Here's another example: you feel the existence of global oil reserves each time you check, while pumping petrol, how much the price has gone up; and you sense there is something to do with oil in the Middle East conflicts, and how it makes you want to debate the burqa.

Hyperobjects are pervasive and don't allow you to rationally divide and resolve them within our institutions of Science, Politics or Art. This is why it doesn't work to say the facts are in on global warming as a purely scientific issue and we should therefore all be persuaded into action, the kind of tone used by Al Gore in the 2006 documentary *An Inconvenient Truth*. For such imperative deployments of science the issues are 'obviously' not related in any important way to ideologies or voting patterns, nor, indeed, related to aesthetics and philosophy. But no amount of science or human willpower can make that happen, because it is *already in there*, says Morton, infiltrating every aspect of existence. And of course we doubt the power of science to accumulate proof towards any real 100 per cent account, of causal connections. This gives skeptics and fossil fuel industries the same 'lack of certainty' arguments that big tobacco exploited in earlier debates.

Morton asks how people will react to the end of the modern world and to the new hyperobjective cosmos. 'You are walking out of the supermarket,' he narrates casually, and, 'As you approach your car, a stranger calls out, "Hey, funny weather today!" With a due sense of caution—is she a global warming denier or not?—you reply yes.'[18] We have all experienced this kind of hesitation and ap-

---

16. Timothy Morton, *The Ecological Thought*, Cambridge, Harvard University Press, 2010.

17. Timothy Morton, *Hyperobjects: Philosophy and Ecology after the End of the World*, Minneapolis, University of Minnesota Press, 2013.

18. Morton, p. 99

prehension about the weather. Innocent conversations about it seem to be no longer possible. Worries about the weather are a mere symptom of something huge, foreboding, and ungraspable in its entirety: climate is a hyperobject, and global warming is its apocalyptic avatar.

Morton is able to say that 'the world,' in the old sense, is over because the weather—like Nature—is no longer the neutral backdrop we can rely on to stay put, while we play out our little human dramas in front of it. If the hyperobject of global warming is imposing itself radically, and I am convinced that it is because even the deniers can't stop talking about it, then that old modernist world of human foreground and natural background is gone. And it hasn't been around for very long, certainly it would look like a very artificial construction to Indigenous Australian philosophers who never speak of Nature, but who constantly stress the inalienable connections that humans and non-humans have with each other.

You are right to get a sense of the ridiculous when you see, on TV, a skeptical captain of industry debating a greenie minister of religion, as if their opinions really mattered. It is not the absent scientist on the panel that is the real concern, it is that the conceptual architecture of the world they share is the same as it was at the time of the Industrial Revolution, that they still share the same language of human mastery, hope, and redemptive adjustment. They occupy the same clichéd world that would picture cyclones as beautiful landscape paintings, one which has forgotten all the violence that went into its creation—not just the painting, but the whole conceptual architecture.

I am thinking about the contrast between the usual photos of cyclonic weather, with their Turneresque sublime, and the Yukultji Napangati painting (fig. 2, 'Untitled') that captured Tim Morton when he was in Sydney, Australia. Morton looks at the 2011 work by the Pintupi painter, and he sees it 'surge toward me, locking onto my optic nerve and holding me in its force field.' He was thus captured by the Dreaming, 'the Aboriginal hyperobject,' finding it 'impossible to leave the painting. Hairs standing up on my body, tears streaming down my face, slowly I tear myself away...'[19]

---

19. Morton, p. 69

For Morton, the Napangati is a portal onto the 'Aboriginal hyperobject' that almost sucks him down into its vortex. This 'Aboriginal hyperobject' is just his gloss on the Dreaming, or what they call the *bugarrigarra* up in Broome. I could summon the most powerful concept-mashing and poetics that I could write in English to give you my gloss on the Dreaming, and still never get close. It exceeds description, which is why it is hyper, and why it can't be destroyed or even trivialized successfully.

> *It is waiting underneath the country.*
> *It persists through the county.*
> 'You people try and dig little bit more deep,' [said Paddy Roe about the country north of Broome]
> 'You bin digging only white soil,
> try and find the black soil inside.'[20]

And he was deeply concerned about the activities of mining companies who dig without asking:

> 'Well somebody musta made a mess of this one —
> You know these oil people didn't ask nobody —
> They just went in they own ways —
> Never worry about, any Aborigines —
> Looma people'[21]

And Paddy continues his story about an unusual cloud that emerges out to sea over the reef. It tells him something has gone wrong in *that* Looma country, where the oil company is, 200 kms away, so he heads down there to find his countrymen:

> 'So they musta knock some stone over —
> 'cos some stones, that snake you know
> [and laughs because he can only speak obliquely about sacred/magic business]—
> stone —
> outside you can see it — [22]

'This is living country!' is what any Aboriginal person from around Broome will tell you if they are anti-gas or anti-fracking. Reminding us of a character in Reza Negarestani's, cosmo-fiction, *Cyclonopedia: Complicity with Anonymous Materials,* weird Iranian archaeologist Dr. Hamid Parsani, who announced 'The Middle East is a sentient entity—it is alive!' before disappearing under mysterious circumstances. The disordered notes he leaves behind testify to an increasingly deranged preoccupation with oil as rotting corpse of the Sun, and the 'lubricant' of historical and political narratives:[23]

Once oil reaches its destination, the crusading war machines, whose first

20. Krim Benterrak, Stephen Muecke, and Paddy Roe, *Reading the Country*, 3rd edition, Melbourne, Re.Press, 2014, p. 189.

21. Benterrak, p. 217.

22. Benterrak, p. 219.

23. Reza Negarestani, *Cyclonopedia*. Melbourne, Re.Press, 2010. Part of the back cover blurb paraphrased here.

disposition is to be dynamic, will fuel up and assemble themselves with the oil and its derivatives. As the machines of the western enlightenment consume oil either by burning the blob or fattening up on the blob, the smuggled war machines start to activate and are chemically unbound. The nervous system and the chemistry of war machines smuggled through oil infuse with the western machines feasting on oil unnoticed, as petroleum has already dissolved or refinedly emulsified them in itself, as its chemical elements or its essential derivatives (Islamic ideologies, ambitions, implicit policies, socio-religious entities and formations, etc.).[24]

Global subterranean oil (as hyperobject) is alive and changing history. It's out of control, calling the shots, telling the stories, even extending its influence to remote Australia and getting Woodside Petroleum and Buru Energy to go out finding more, on the Dampier peninsula, the Fitzroy River valley or out in the Western Desert. Make sure you call it 'natural resources' they are told, as if it comes for free, as if humans are distant from these resources, as if they are not at all complicit, to use Negarestani's concept. Calling material 'natural' is modernity's way of idealizing matter. It's all just stuff made of carbon atoms, the same anywhere in the world, so human attachments to it make no sense in this hyper-rationalization for exploitability. But capitalists are canny, they know *exactly* which land they want to grab because the 'free' stuff is there; on the other side indigenous peoples of the world have sacred things in the county that attaches them *exactly* to places. But in the middle is a floating population of middle class greenies with free-floating concepts of Hope, Nature and Beauty, which are of no use or used wrongly, and a free-floating population of fly-in fly-out workers. These are the people of the Holocene, not yet of the Anthropocene. They think they are free agents buoyed by concepts of transcendence. They dream of heavens above, and of new planetary homes, should this world run out of resources. They have not yet come down to earth, 'earthbound' is what Bruno Latour calls it, people who's awareness comes from the knowledge of loosing places, unquantifiable territory, places where they live and belong.[25]

With the Anthropocene, the atmosphere has changed, as we try to debate something we can't fully grasp, yet we fear is changing things forever. The atmosphere of fear is what is held in common—by the so-called left and right wings of politics alike—and it means that we no longer are at all comfortable in that 'Modern World' so successfully critiqued by Latour, who caught the atmosphere. Postmodernity has returned with a vengeance, this time with an ecological motor driving it. And it is having serious effects in our academic disciplines as their most fundamental base concepts crumble away. What we used to call 'social reality' can no longer be taken for granted, 'nature' has been shown to be a European invention, set up as a uniform backdrop to the interesting varieties of 'cultures' we have been happily studying as variations within the equally dubious—now less centralized—concept of 'the human'. History can no longer be

---

24. Negarestani, p.71

25. Bruno Latour, War of the Worlds: Humans against Earthbound. Gifford lecture No. 5. 26th of February 2013. https://www.youtube.com/watch?v=gsZCS5Zicx4.

imagined unfolding on a time line from the past towards the utopian unknown. Now there is a serious twist in time. Time is what comes crashing back towards us from the *known future*, as opposed to unfolding of past scenarios. So now the issue is not to have one final attempt to sustain the utopian narrative, or assume reliable projections based on past experience, but to best prepare for the most probable eventuality.

This is why I think we have to be both speculative and realistic in our re-casting of an *anti*-modernist or *a*modernist survival story. *Picture that cyclone* is supposed to capture the syntax of that story: it is an imperative verb without a subject, whose content is speculation; the demonstrative pronoun 'that' is specific, relational and deictic; the object is a hyperobject. Thanks to the philosopher Quentin Meillassoux, we have been able to remove the tyranny of subject-object relations from the story, and move to (what he calls) the 'great outdoors'[26] where real things exist without waiting for human scrutiny to bring them into being; things like cyclones loaded with energy flows and endogenous powers. 'There's a cyclone coming!' It is anticipated by a shock wave of public feeling, where the public is totally democratized by the threat of being totally flattened. Flat ontology, indeed: the hyperobject creates a new society of swirling trees, animals, building materials and Dorothy's red shoes.

What better place than Australia to move to this great outdoors of speculative realism in order to philosophize all the better! And wonder where we are in this precarious age. I have engaged the problem of predicting and understanding actual cyclones by juxtaposing institutional ways of knowing as process ontologies. Cyclones gather strength as they move through the world, this is what I mean by process ontology, in parallel to knowledge of cyclones, or public feeling about cyclones both also gathering strength as they take their different specific paths through the world. Thus meteorological science, striving for reliability with a whole array of radar picturing technologies, number-crunching statistics and hunches based on prior experience. Well and good, where would we be without radar and statistics and beautiful colourful cross-section pictures of cyclones which try to grasp what this thing we can't grasp looks like?

And there is another aesthetic that has existed for millennia in Aboriginal Australia, one that seems to do less violence to the country than landscapes, with a diminishing perspective, seen from a masterful point of view. As 'all day and night the wind [plays] ancestor music' we anticipate the coming storm. In cyclone season up in Broome, you never know when one will come, or how it will start to form off the coast. Cyclones form when the conditions are right, but what causes them? How are cause and effect supposed to relate to each other, anyway?

And who will tell this story of preparedness for survival, now that the world of the industrial revolution has ended and, with the Anthropocene, we face up to the reality of being earthbound? In Negarestani's dystopian planetary novel, we found that it was the hyperobject oil that told (is still telling) a powerful story

---

26. Quentin Meillassoux, *After Finitude: An Essay on the Necessity of Contingency*, London, Bloomsbury, 2008, p. 7.

that is as frighteningly real as it is science-fiction: 'Outlines for a Science Fiction of the Earth as Narrated from a Nethermost Point of View,' is how that project was summarized on the way to completion.[27]

And in Australia, I prefer to listen to, feel, be in attendance upon, the *bugarrigarra*. I suspect that the *bugarrigarra* had something to do with saving a powerful site called Walmadany (James Prince Point). *Bugarrigarra* is another hyperobject narrated from a nethermost point of view, or at least immanently in country. Indigenous being-in-country does not have utopian designs of the future, because time is not working like that. Yet somehow—in April 2013 the announcement was made—an alliance of Indigenous peoples and greenies and others managed to resist Woodside Petroleum, made things so uncomfortable for them on Goolarabooloo country, that (for business reasons as well) they packed up and left. A small battle won in an on-going war.

The county must have been telling the story that united the people, the bilbies, the dinosaur footprints, a spiritual being called Marala, the *irrgili* trees, the *darial* birds, black cockies. And if the *bugarrigarra* was doing the narrating, maybe Woodside Petroleum, Buru Energy, the WA Govt. and the Murdoch press are becoming bit players in the story it has to tell about survival. 'The country narrates...' is a sentence without an object, an intransitive sentence, because the object is immaterial, contingent, complicit, but earthbound... as Alexis Wright reminds us, the snake has something to do with it:

> This is where the giant serpent continues to live deep down under the ground in a vast network of limestone aquifers. They say its being is porous; it permeates everything. It is all around in the atmosphere and is attached to the lives of the river people like skin.[28]

But speaking of survival, since I started with an image of an approaching cyclone, I want to get quite practical—none of this airy-fairy conceptual stuff—and tell you what to do to survive. You have to dig into the earth. Build yourselves a *mirdibalang* cyclone shelter, as instructed by Paddy Roe, big enough for five or six people, with a little fire for warmth and cooking (fig. 3).[29]

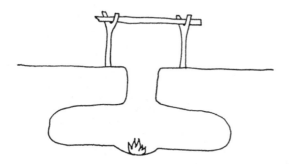

27. China Miéville, Introduction, 'Fiction by Reza Negarestani', *World Literature Today*, Vol. 84, No. 3, May/June 2010, pp. 12-13.

28. Wright, p. 2

29. Benterrak, p. 112-113.

9

Enter the Black Box: Aesthetic Speculations in the General Economy of Being[1]

Laura Lotti

The market was by now a pure abstraction.[2]

As markets become increasingly evanescent—due to the flickering materiality of layers and layers of code blindly interacting with each other—it has become more difficult, if not impossible, to formulate an intelligible image of the financial ecosystem. This is arguably due to the sheer complexity of the algorithmic infrastructure upon which contemporary financial operations are executed, which has been at the centre of much discussion since the eruption of the Global Financial Crisis (GFC) and the infamous Flash Crash of 6 May 2010.[3] Yet, in spite of the thorough analyses of the present politico-economic juncture, financial neoliberalism has escaped any effective critique and survived the crisis it created.[4]

In light of these premises, this paper proposes to look at contemporary neoliberalism as a primarily aesthetic mode of control; one that extends beyond and below the finitude of the human sensorium by operating directly in the realm of potentialities rather than in the statistical prediction of possibilities—in short, as

---

1. Many thanks to Andrew Murphie and Christian Gelder for their comments on early versions of this paper, and to Conor Hannan for his invaluable input throughout the writing process. Obviously, any errors or misinterpretations found in this paper are only mine.

2. Michael Lewis, *Flash Boys*, W. W. Norton & Company, New York, 2014, p.52.

3. The Flash Crash of 6 May 2010 famously raised awareness of the use and magnitude of high-frequency trading algorithms in share trading. However, the use of automated decision-making software may have contributed to the 2007 subprime mortgage crisis too, as some commentators highlight. In 2007 automated mortgage underwriting encompassed for 40% of all subprime loans in the US. Lynnley Browning, 'The Subprime Loan Machine,' *The New York Times*, March 23, 2007, sec. Business, http://www.nytimes.com/2007/03/23/business/23speed.html.

4. This thesis is maintained by Mirowski. Philip Mirowski, *Never Let a Serious Crisis Go to Waste: How Neoliberalism Survived the Financial Meltdown*, Verso, London, 2014.

an aesthetics after finitude. Informed by Luciana Parisi's work,[5] this paper specifically suggests that the ingression of computation into culture has instantiated a shift through which aesthetics becomes immanent to the becoming of the 'general economy of being'.[6] This concept was formulated by François Laruelle in his doctoral thesis, following Jacques Derrida, to indicate the interplay and synthesis of different processes, effects, and modes of being. My argument is that this move inaugurates a mode of control that relies on the 'creordering', evaluation, and economic exploitation of perceptions according to algo-financial logic, in a way that is not directly sensed, but that instead constitutes the foundations of sense perceptions in the living. By 'creordering' Jonathan Nitzan and Shimshon Bichler understand 'the paradoxical fusion of being and becoming, state and process, stasis and dynamism'[7] caused by the limitless force of capitalization, which not only allows for capitalists to retain their power, but also increases capitalist power through differential accumulation. While Nitzan and Bichler limit their claim to the 'gravitational force' of capitalization, I suggest that such an operatory mode may well extend beyond flows of capital to encompass desire, sense perceptions and cognition.

Whereas contemporary critiques of political economy tend to conceptualize markets and the economic sphere in opposition to the social—or even more so, as utterly alien to the vicissitudes of the collective—the GFC has pointed to the immanence of economic dynamics to modes of individuation and subjectivation. Specifically, in light of the social and affective capture by algorithmic platforms, François Laruelle's concept of an **économie générale** des effets d'être allows us to grasp the multiple operations involved in the production of the diversity of being, 'both in its real and possible terms'.[8] Summarising Laruelle's thesis in a few paragraphs is beyond the scope of this essay—and would be highly impractical, if not impossible, as Ray Brassier aptly remarks.[9] What is important to note, however, is that it provides a productive starting point for a conceptualisation of markets as constituted by operations of individuation unfolding across different planes—physical, living, and technical.

This concept has been taken up again by Laruelle in his subsequent text, *Au-delà du Principe de Pouvoir*, which is precisely concerned with going beyond the principle of individuation of power and the 'onto-theo-politics'[10] that have crys-

---

5. Luciana Parisi, *Contagious Architecture: Computation, Aesthetics, and Space*, Technologies of Lived Abstraction, The MIT Press, Cambridge, 2013. Chapter title in single quote marks, then book title in italics...

6. François Laruelle, *Au-delà du Principe de Pouvoir*, Payot, Paris, 1978; François Laruelle, "Économie générale des effets d'être", [s.n.], 1975. Translations from French are mine throughout the paper unless otherwise stated in the bibliography.

7. Jonathan Nitzan and Shimshon Bichler, *Capital as Power*, RIPE Series in Global Political Economy, London: Routledge, 2009, p.18.

8. Laruelle, "Économie générale des effets d'être." The page numbers of the manuscript are not always available in the copy I sourced.

9. Referring to Économie générale des effets d'être, and *Matière et phénomène* (1976), Ray Brassier quipped that they 'remain unpublished or perhaps unpublishable, given their gargantuan heft (both are over six hundred pages long) and hair-raising conceptual severity'. Brassier in François Laruelle, "What Can Non-Philosophy Do?," *Angelaki* 8, no. 2 (2003): 169.

10. Laruelle, *Au-delà du Principe de Pouvoir*, p.15.

tallised the conception of power into its existing forms of domination. In order to do so, Laruelle identifies three syntheses of the beyond of power: an aesthetic synthesis of power, corresponding to the production of the processes of production and the reason why power becomes a principle; an analytic synthesis, that is, the reproduction of power and of its principle according to internal rules; lastly, an economic synthesis, which relates to the consummation of the power relations and closes the cycle of the general economy.[11] To Laruelle, aesthetics is the force that triggers movement beyond the principle of power. The implications of aesthetics in the current power formation, and its role in overthrowing it, will be discussed in the following sections with the support of Gilbert Simondon's philosophy. Before delving into that, I start with an overview of the contemporary financial ecosystem, highlighting the function that algorithms play in the individuation of the contemporary 'sense of power'.[12]

BLACK BOX TRADING: FROM GAMBLING TO WARFARE

Today more than half of the entire US share trading volume is algorithmic. Algorithmic, or automated, trading traditionally consists in the use of electronic platforms by big investors (i.e. investment banks, pension funds, mutual funds) in order to split their buy-orders and lower their impact on stock prices and risk. By contrast, its subset, high-frequency trading (HFT), follows entirely different strategies that are essentially based on the speed by which algorithms access information in the market, and on noise-making, in order to confuse competitors.[13] Clearly, HFT and algo-trading in general, raise concerns about the transparency of markets, the equal access to information, and last but not least, the ontology of algorithmic trading agents. Moreover, they radically challenge foundational concepts of financial trading such as liquidity.[14]

Algorithmic trading is remarkably opaque. Trading algorithms are often referred to as 'black box'—in the sense that they are proprietary software, of which one knows the input and the output, but the operations that allow for such transformations are obscured.[15] Interestingly, the New York Stock Exchange's

---

11. Ibid., pp.35–36.

12. I recently wrote about the relation between Simondon and Laruelle, technics, sense, and power in: Laura Lotti, "Making Sense of Power': Repurposing Gilbert Simondon's Philosophy of Individuation for a Mechanist Approach to Capitalism (by Way of François Laruelle)', *Platform: Journal of Media and Communication* 6, 2015, pp. 22–33.

13. For an excellent review of the current HFT scenario, see: Nick Srnicek and Alex Williams, 'On Cunning Automata: Financial Acceleration at the Limits of the Dromological', in *Collapse: Casino Real*, vol. VIII, Urbanomic, Falmouth, 2014, pp. 463–468. Donald Mackenzie's recent work is also remarkable: Donald MacKenzie, 'How to Make Money in Microseconds,', *London Review of Books*, May 19, 2011; Donald MacKenzie, 'A Sociology of Algorithms: High-Frequency Trading and the Shaping of Markets', (Draft, Edinburgh, June 2014), http://www.sps.ed.ac.uk/__data/assets/pdf_file/0004/156298/Algorithms25.pdf; Donald MacKenzie, 'Be Grateful for Drizzle', *London Review of Books*, September 11, 2014.

14. The rhetorical argument for HFT is that it makes markets more fluid by providing the conditions for cheap and quick trades, thereby also making them less volatile. Yet, it has been proved that high-frequency algorithms are market neutral, in that they exploit differences in stock prices in a single sector thereby achieving superior returns without contributing to the liquidity of that market. For additional information, see MacKenzie, 'How to Make Money in Microseconds'.

15. The Problem of the Black Box is one of the foundational issues of cybernetics and is extensively

data centre in Mahawah, New Jersey, also looks like a giant black box—which already gives a sense of the aesthetics involved in algo-trading.[16] Moreover, because each player in the market doesn't know the extent and capacities of other players' algorithms, the increasing complexity makes it so that *no one knows why things happen.*[17] This is because, while the main types of algorithms are known—i.e. execution, volume participation, statistical arbitrage and market making algorithms—there is no precise information about the formal methods used by such algorithms to perform their functions in the market. In other words, one knows *what* they do but doesn't know *how* they do it. This is an instance of what historian of economics Philip Mirowski calls 'agnotology'[18]—the deliberate manufacture of ignorance and doubt by neoliberal contingents for specific political-economic purposes.[19] For this reason, Mirowski argues, neoliberalism manages to answer market crises with more financialization. But is neoliberalism simply an epistemic problem? It is frequently argued that contemporary power works affectively.[20] However, as it will be clear in the following paragraphs, my argument is that there exists a precise relation between the aesthetic and the affective and, in order to understand that, one needs to turn to a concept of technicity as the interface that not only makes the invisible visible but also operationable.[21]

For these reasons, a detour into the second post-war period is needed to uncover the origins of computational finance. These lie at the juncture of a peculiar set of relations that contribute to the individuation of what Mirowski calls

---

discussed by Ross Ashby in *Introduction to Cybernetics;* W. Ross Ashby, *An Introduction to Cybernetics,* Chapman & Hall, London, 1957, pp. 86–117.

16. In this regard, one should also mention dark pools—that is, private exchanges, generally owned by investment banks, in which participants can buy or sell shares without those transactions being visible to the public. For more information see: Donald MacKenzie, 'Dark Markets', *London Review of Books,* June 4, 2015; Scott Patterson, *Dark Pools: The Rise of the Machine Traders and the Rigging of the U.S. Stock Market,* Crown Business, New York, 2013; 'Shining a Light on Dark Pools', *The Economist,* August 18, 2011, http://www.economist.com/blogs/schumpeter/2011/08/exchange-share-trading.

17. I am referring here to events such as the Flash Crash. In spite of the years-long research in the event there are still doubts whether the crash was caused by an algorithm or by human intervention. For contrasting voices in the field see: Silla Brush, Tom Schoenberg, and Suzi Ring, 'How a Mystery Trader With an Algorithm May Have Caused the Flash Crash', *Bloomberg.com,* April 22, 2015, http://www.bloomberg.com/news/articles/2015-04-22/mystery-trader-armed-with-algorithms-rewrites-flash-crash-story; 'Findings Regarding the Market Events of May 6, 2010' (Securities and Exchange Commission, September 30, 2010); Donald MacKenzie, 'On 'Spoofing', *London Review of Books,* May 21, 2015.

18. The concept of agnotology is taken up by Frank Pasquale in *The Black Box Society* to describe the 'knowledge problem' intrinsic to the neoliberal operatory mode: Frank Pasquale, *The Black Box Society: The Secret Algorithms That Control Money and Information* (Cambridge: Harvard University Press, 2015). Added the and a colon here…

19. Mirowski, *Never Let a Serious Crisis Go to Waste,* pp.226–230.

20. See, for instance: Melissa Gregg and Gregory J. Seigworth, eds., *The Affect Theory Reader,* Duke University Press Books, Durham, 2010; Michael Hardt, 'Affective Labor', *Boundary 2* 26, no. 2 (July 1, 1999): 89–100. See also the issue 'The Effect of Affect', *Ephemera* 11, no. 3 (2011), http://www.ephemerajournal.org/issue/effect-affect.

21. To Gilbert Simondon, technicity is a mode of relation between man and world—it is a 'partial and transitory reality, both a result and a principle of genesis'. Gilbert Simondon, *Du mode d'existence des objets techniques,* Aubier, Paris, 1989, p.157.

'cyborg economics',[22] born out of the encounter between cybernetics and the new political ideas that emerged as a reaction to the war period. Although the intertwinement between economics and computation can be dated back to the influence of Adam Smith on Charles Babbage's analytical engine,[23] here I would like to focus on one major event that marked a turning point in the development of economics, which had important consequences for the contemporary political-economic landscape—a sort of Deleuzian abstract machine. I am referring to the formulation, in 1946, of the Monte Carlo simulations method, the first electronic method of automated statistical sampling.[24]

Formulated by Stanislaw Ulam—a physicist passionate about solitaire and poker—the Monte Carlo simulations method is a class of computational algorithms that relies on repeatedly random samplings to obtain the distribution of an unknown probabilistic entity. Ulam's question was: 'what are the chances that a Canfield solitaire laid out with 52 cards will come out successfully?'[25] In order to answer it, he posited that 'if electronic circuits could count, they could do arithmetic ... at almost incredible speed'[26] and therefore solve complex differential equations for the resolution of statistical problems. This was made possible by the first electronic computer—the ENIAC. The Monte Carlo method and the ENIAC were parallel discoveries originally conceived to solve problems in a thermonuclear reaction for the development of nuclear weapons. Nicholas Metropolis, one of the members of the Manhattan Project research team—together with John Von Neumann and Enrico Fermi—named this new method due the fact that Ulam's uncle liked to borrow money from relatives because he 'just had to go to Monte Carlo'—alluding to his passion for gambling.[27]

With the development of parallel processing in software and hardware technology, the potentialities of the Monte Carlo method have increased exponentially. Today Monte Carlo simulations have become endemic not only to the sciences, but more importantly and perhaps not surprisingly, to the functioning of contemporary planetary computation—being used also in engineering, robotics, computational biology, statistics, design and architecture and, with Phelim Boyle's seminal contribution, in mathematical finance for the pricing of options.[28] Even more so, with the accelerated speed of technological devel-

22. Philip Mirowski, *Machine Dreams: Economics Becomes a Cyborg Science*, Cambridge University Press, Cambridge, 2002.

23. As economist and AI-pioneer Herbert Simon observed: 'Physicists and electrical engineers had little to do with the invention of the digital computer ... the real inventor was the economist Adam Smith'. Herbert A. Simon and Allen Newell, 'Heuristic Problem Solving: The Next Advance in Operations Research', *Operations Research* 6, no. 1 (February 1, 1958): 2.

24. Other mathematical concepts underlie Monte Carlo simulations, such as Brownian motion and Kolgomorov's probability theory. Monte Carlo can be considered the key implementation of these previous mathematical discoveries.

25. Roger Eckhardt, 'Stan Ulam, John Von Neumann, and the Monte Carlo Method', *Los Alamos Science*, no. Special Issue (1987): 131–43.

26. N. Metropolis, 'The Beginning of the Monte Carlo Method', *Los Alamos Science*, no. Special Issue (1987): 125.

27. Metropolis, 'The Beginning of the Monte Carlo Method', p.127.

28. Boyle proved that applying the Monte Carlo method to the pricing of option could give the same results as the Black-Scholes equation. Phelim P. Boyle, 'Options: A Monte Carlo Approach', *Journal of*

opment, Monte Carlo simulations have set the blueprint for evolutionary programming, multi-agent systems, and genetic algorithms that today constitute
the foundations for much of the research in AI and neural networks.[29]

In short, there seems to be a clear relation between gambling, weapons of
mass destruction, modern finance, and conceptualization of 'intelligence'. In
this we can read the genealogy of neoliberalism, which was developing in those
years and which stands in mutual presupposition with the techno-scientific developments of the first half of the twentieth century. As a matter of fact, just one
year after Ulam's invention, in 1947 a group of intellectuals gathered around the
central figure of Friedrich von Hayek met in the Swiss resort of Mont Pelerin
for the first time with the aim to found a new politico-economic movement that
would overcome the limitations of the previous liberal doctrine—this movement became known as neoliberalism.[30] Mirowski defines the neoliberal project
as 'a scale-free Theory of Everything'.[31] This may be partially due to Hayek's interest in cybernetics and complex systems—disciplines that are responsible for
some of the most important discoveries of the twentieth century, and indeed for
the contemporary socio-political, economic, and cultural order.[32]

From this standpoint, it is clear how the development of digital technology
is intimately related to transformations in modes of subjectivation that are inherently economical and neoliberal. As Michel Foucault presciently noted, the
neoliberal model consists in the 'generalization of the "enterprise" form ... so to
make it a model of social relations and of existence itself'.[33] In fact, digital networked platforms have allowed for the neoliberal project to flourish, consoli-
dating the tendency toward total financialization on the basis of a hybrid paradigm between strategic war-thinking and speculative mode of thinking-feeling
indebted to gambling. Even more so, the preemptive mode of control of the neoliberal schema anticipates most of the features of contemporary object-oriented
programming and network design.[34] As Katerina Kolozova notes, capitalism, in

Financial Economics 4, no. 3 (May 1977): 323–38.

29. Genetic algorithms and multi-agent systems are largely used in the financial ecosystem too. For
more detailed information, see Yuan Luo, Kecheng Liu, and D.N. Davis, 'A Multi-Agent Decision Support System for Stock Trading', *IEEE Network* 16, no. 1 (January 2002): 20–27; René Carmona et al.,
'An Introduction to Particle Methods with Financial Applications', in *Numerical Methods in Finance*, ed.
René A. Carmona et al., Springer Proceedings in Mathematics 12 (Springer Berlin Heidelberg, 2012),
3–49; Pierre Del Moral, Gareth William Peters, and Christelle Vergé, 'An Introduction to Particle Integration Methods: With Applications to Risk and Insurance', *arXiv:1210.3851 [math, Q-Fin, Stat]*, October 14, 2012, http://arxiv.org/abs/1210.3851.

30. For an account of the development of the Mont Pelerin Society (MPS) see: Philip Mirowski and
Dieter Plehwe, eds., *The Road from Mont Pelerin: The Making of the Neoliberal Thought Collective* Harvard University Press, Cambridge, 2009.

31. Mirowski, *Never Let a Serious Crisis Go to Waste*, p.59.

32. Hayek himself outlined his own theory of the mind as early as 1952 in *The Sensory Order*, whose
main argument is precisely that of the necessity of constitutional constraints on government, since individuals, according to him, are epistemically unable to intervene effectively in spontaneously emergent
institutions. Friedrich A. Von Hayek, *The Sensory Order: An Inquiry Into the Foundations of Theoretical Psychology* (Martino Fine Books, 2014).

33. Michel Foucault, *The Birth of Biopolitics: Lectures at the College De France, 1978-1979*, Palgrave Macmillan, New York, 2008, p.242.

34. Neoliberalism's main features can be summarized as: computational view of the market; general, multi-purpose program; modularity; control through emergence; ubiquity. For an extensive discus-

its neoliberal phase, has entered the 'universe of speculation in the philosophical sense, but also in the sense of the speculative mind of gaming'.[35] This is evident in the functioning of the financial apparatus, which not only aims to bring the future into the present through complex models for the leveraging of risk and volatility but, by doing so, annihilates the very possibility of a future 'because all possibilities had already been used and bound by past operations'.[36] The consequences of this tendency for the collective sphere, of which markets are an integral component, will be dealt with in the following sections.

AESTHETIC SPECULATIONS

In order to attempt some kind of understanding of the modes of power and control at work in the global algorithmic ecosystem—a vectoral, abstract, speculative mode of power[37]—a speculative move of equal magnitude and opposite direction is required, in order to divorce thought from the naturalized form of neoliberal logic. Here I present two tendencies in financial mathematics and computation to illustrate the operations of contemporary financial markets, both derived from further developments in the Monte Carlo simulations method.

Although the black box of algorithmic trading is hardly penetrable, an extensive amount of research points to the use of genetic algorithms (GA) in financial mathematics.[38] GA is a heuristic methodology of search optimization based on metaphors with the natural science, such as inheritance, mutation, selection, and crossover. Essentially, GA is a simulation of organic evolution, in which a population of candidate solutions—creatures, phenotypes, individuals—is evolved for the optimization of a decisional problem, modelled upon data taken from the physical world. GA base their decisions on the 'survival of the fittest', mirroring the gene-centric game-theoretical evolutionary theory according to which each gene aims to maximize its own success either through co-operation or through selfishness, in accordance with the behaviour of the majority of the population in the organism.[39]

This view reflects the neoliberal conceptualization of the market first proposed by Friedrich von Hayek—a computational view, which blurs the differ-

sion see Mirowski, *Never Let a Serious Crisis Go to Waste*, pp.53–67.

35. Katerina Kolozova, 'Metaphysics of Finance Economy Of Its Radicalization as the Method of Revoking Real Economy', *Identities* 11, no. 1–2 (2015): 26.

36. Rosa Esposito, 'Using the Future in the Present: Risk and Surprise in Financial Markets', *Economic Sociology_the European Electronic Newsletter* 12, no. 3 (July 2011): 16.

37. I draw these features of contemporary power from the early François Laruelle (Laruelle, *Au-delà du Principe de Pouvoir.*) and Katerina Kolozova's Laruellian critique of capitalism (Kolozova, 'Metaphysics of Finance Economy Of Its Radicalization as the Method of Revoking Real Economy'.)

38. For instance, Calypso Technology, one of the most renowned OTC derivatives risk-management platforms, avails of the Galapagos distributed parallel genetic algorithm for its risk analysis and hedging applications. For more information see: Adam Honeysett-Watts, 'Calypso Acquires Galapagos', *Reuters*, February 26, 2009, http://www.reuters.com/article/2009/02/26/idUS193198+26-Feb-2009+BW20090226; Greg MacSweeney, 'Calypso Acquires Galapagos Portfolio Platform', *Wall Street & Technology*, February 26, 2009, http://www.wallstreetandtech.com/trading-technology/calypso-acquires-galapagos-portfolio-pla/214600176.

39. Richard Dawkins, *The Selfish Gene* (Oxford: Oxford University Press, 2006); Richard Dawkins, *The Extended Phenotype: The Long Reach of the Gene.* Oxford Paperbacks, Oxford, 1999.

ence between the natural and the artificial. Under neoliberalism the market is conceived as a huge information system that contains perfect information, whose knowledge and operations are more efficient than any human attempt, and therefore can offer solutions to any crisis. This is because the market is viewed as a natural state of mankind, whose 'naturalness', however, needs to be constantly constructed via political reforms aimed to preserve the 'freedom of exchange',—that is, the freedom for capital to naturally flow across national boundaries. From this standpoint, if the market is 'Nature', as the neoliberals would have it, GA are the evolving organisms inhabiting it, whose life-like-ness and evolutionary logic surpasses human existence.[40]

In addition to this, the operative logic of trading algorithms is linked to the ubiquitous role of smart and sentient algorithms in the contemporary media ecology, coupled with the potentialities of semantic search and facilitated by the pseudo-rhizomatic form of contemporary networks—a non-hierarchical, seemingly spontaneous, emergent structure, which is precisely Hayek's idea of social order. Algorithms read news, know about climate conditions and geopolitical scenarios, monitor behaviours, and so on, and in the span of few seconds or even milliseconds construct models to price goods that we, in the physical world, use daily—for instance, energy, metals, etc.[41] Interestingly, Google's trading algorithm seems to make decisions based on its search terms—a thesis confirmed by independent quants but not by Google itself.[42] By incessantly making correlations among events, algorithms also create new information, which may in turn manipulate markets in ways not accessible to us from outside the black box. Together, these two features of algorithmic trading—its genetic behaviour and its ubiquitous, imperceptible sentience—make of the neoliberal virtual machine a powerful apparatus of capture. Therefore the question becomes: how is the imperceptible—the black boxed—felt without being sensed? And how does this impact the evolution (and survival) of humanity in the face of evolutionary financial warfare?

---

40. This view mirrors the contemporary research in computational evolutionary economics, according to which markets themselves can be considered as formal automata. See: Philip Mirowski, "Inherent Vice: Minsky, Markomata, and the Tendency of Markets to Undermine Themselves," *Journal of Institutional Economics* 6, no. 04 (2010): 415–43; Philip Mirowski, 'Markets Come to Bits: Evolution, Computation and Markomata in Economic Science', *Journal of Economic Behavior & Organization*, Markets as Evolving Algorithms, 63, no. 2 (June 2007): 209–42.

41. The case of the 'hack crash' is emblematic in this respect. In 2013 a fake tweet from the Associated Press account announced that an explosion at the White House injured US President Barack Obama causing $136 billion to be wiped out from the Standard & Poor Index in less than 3 minutes before rebounding. For more information see: Tero Karppi and Kate Crawford, 'Social Media, Financial Algorithms and the Hack Crash', *Theory, Culture & Society*, May 4, 2015; Edmund Lee, 'AP Twitter Account Hacked in Market-Moving Attack', *Bloomberg Business*, April 24, 2013, http://www.bloomberg.com/news/articles/2013-04-23/dow-jones-drops-recovers-after-false-report-on-ap-twitter-page; Heidi Moore and Dan Roberts, 'AP Twitter Hack Causes Panic on Wall Street and Sends Dow Plunging', *The Guardian*, April 23, 2013, http://www.theguardian.com/business/2013/apr/23/ap-tweet-hack-wall-street-freefall.

42. *Money & Speed: Inside the Black Box (Marije Meerman, VPRO)*, 2012, http://www.youtube.com/watch?v=aq1Ln1UCoEU&feature=youtube_gdata_player; Tobias Preis, Helen Susannah Moat, and H. Eugene Stanley, 'Quantifying Trading Behavior in Financial Markets Using Google Trends', *Scientific Reports* 3 (April 25, 2013).

In order to answer these questions, Gilbert Simondon's philosophy offers fruitful conceptual tools to uncover the relation between the technical (in this case, digital networked algorithms) and the aesthetic (i.e. that which relates to sense perceptions)—in other words, a techno-aesthetics. To Simondon 'it is perhaps not true that every aesthetic object has technical value, but every technical object has, from a certain perspective, an aesthetic tenor'.[43] As Yves Michaud observes, Simondon's aesthetic theory radically challenges any previous approach to aesthetics, since it concerns: 'aesthetic impression (rather than the aesthetic object), techno-aesthetics (rather than natural aesthetics) and aesthetic attractors (rather than masterpieces)'.[44] Further, to Simondon, aesthetics not only relates to sense perceptions but it is a mode of thought in its own right. Aesthetic thought precisely serves the purpose of 'preserving the unity of thought … because it is the one to grasp being in its unity'.[45] Importantly, aesthetics is in close relation—a 'continuous transition'[46]—with the technical object. Even more so, 'the techno-aesthetic feeling seems to be a category that is more primitive than the aesthetic feeling alone, or than the technical aspect considered from the angle of functionality alone (which is an impoverishing perspective)'.[47] In other words, this reformulation points towards the radical immanence of the aesthetic to the technical, whose role is to orient human in the world through the creation of sense perceptions afforded by technical objects.

According to this techno-aesthetic view, aesthetics is not necessarily related to the sensible world, but in fact constitutes it via the insertion of 'key points' or seeds (as in the case of the process of crystallization),[48] that orient the individuation of the living. The claim of this paper is that, in the present algorithmic environment, this may indeed inaugurate a mode of control that directly relies on the 'creordering', evaluation, and economic exploitation of the senses according to algo-financial logic. In other words, contra Félix Guattari's argument for an ethico-aesthetic paradigm to be reached in the post-media era,[49] this paper advances the hypothesis that the neoliberal diagram of power has already entered an aesthetic paradigm, precisely thanks to the open, evolving axiomatic of post-mass media technology. As Michael Lewis puts it in Flash Boys: 'what had once been the world's most public, most democratic, financial market had become, in spirit, something like a private viewing of a stolen work of art'.[50] As will be clear in the following section, I suggest that it is precisely this inaccessibility that constitutes a new aesthetic feeling; however, it is also through an aesthetic synthesis, as Laruelle remarks, that one can advance beyond the onto-theo-political 'truth' of neoliberal power.

43. Gilbert Simondon, 'On Techno-Aesthetics', *Parrhesia* 14 (2012): 3.

44. Michaud in Arne De Boever et al., eds., *Gilbert Simondon: Being and Technology* (Edinburgh: Edinburgh University Press, 2012), p.131.

45. Simondon, *Du mode d'existence des objets techniques*, p.191.

46. Ibid., p.184.

47. Simondon, 'On Techno-Aesthetics', p.6.

48. Gilbert Simondon, *L'individuation À La Lumiere Des Notions de Forme et D'information*, Millon, Grenoble, 2013, pp.85–92.

49. Félix Guattari, *Chaosmosis: An Ethico-Aesthetic Paradigm*, Indiana University Press, 1995.

50. Lewis, *Flash Boys*, p.69.

BEYOND FINITUDE: OPEN AXIOMATIC

This reformulation of aesthetics in techno-logical terms resonates with the work of theorist and computer engineer Yuk Hui:

> Each epoch is characterized by certain technical aesthetics. The use of different media of production and operation introduces various forms of experience that renew our perception of the world ... Media aesthetics and its potential are closely related to, and conditioned by, the logic of technologies, which is concretised by new materialities.[51]

This conceptualization challenges the traditional understanding of aesthetics indebted to eighteenth century German philosophy, which emerged as 'an extension of the rationalist worldview'[52] initiated by Descartes' and Leibniz's metaphysics. According to this view, aesthetics is born against the infinite, as an attempt to tame the irrational realm of sensations.[53] Conversely, before the philosophical formulation of aesthetics as a finite, rational concept, aesthetics was ubiquitous, everywhere, unnoticed, corresponding to the continual flow of potential energy. Following a techno-aesthetic approach, the immanent relation between aesthetics and technicity today demands a shift in the philosophical conceptualization of aesthetics, precisely due to the peculiar ontology of algorithmic objects. As Luciana Parisi argues, computational aesthetics refers to the 'the ingression of incomputable information at the edge of each cognitive act of perception.'[54] In other words, it corresponds to the experience of discrete infinite datasets within finite algorithmic instructions that extend beyond the finitude of the biophysical world, and cannot be reduced to the ideal formalism of mathematics.

Whereas aesthetics has been traditionally linked to the sensual, these discrete infinities correspond to the 'key points'—the aesthetic attractors—that together constitute the abstract architecture, the groundless ground, upon which sense perceptions emerge. Simondon discusses this in terms of the event of the discovery of a chrono-topological axiomatic from which the individuation in the living emerges.[55] To Simondon, individuation happens through dephasing, which is also a doubling as it gives rise to a 'remarkable point'—that is, 'a turning point that resolves, momentarily, into this or that singular event or discrete occasion of experience'[56]—and a milieu. These points and milieus mark the axiomatic of signification of the living—an abstract, open infrastructure that doesn't concern language or meaning, but instead corresponds to a morphogen-

---

51. Yuk Hui, 'Induction, Deduction and Transduction: On the Aesthetics and Logic of Digital Objects', *Networking Knowledge: Journal of the MeCCSA Postgraduate Network* 8, no. 3 (June 3, 2015): 2, http://ojs.meccsa.org.uk/index.php/netknow/article/view/376.

52. Kai Hammermeister, *The German Aesthetic Tradition*. Cambridge University Press, Cambridge, 2002, p.4. See also Monroe C. Beardsley, *Aesthetics from Classical Greece to the Present*, The Macmillan Company, New York, 1966, pp.141–163.

53. I am greatly indebted to Justin Clemens' brilliant presentation at the *Aesthetics After Finitude Conference* for these insights.

54. Parisi, *Contagious Architecture: Computation, Aesthetics, and Space*, p. 69.

55. Simondon, *L'individuation À La Lumiere Des Notions de Forme et D'information*, pp.223–228.

56. Erin Manning, 'Always More than One', in *Always More than One: Individuation's Dance* (Durham, NC: Duke University Press, 2013), p.18.

esis of being. 'Topology and chronology are not a priori forms of sensibility, but the very dimensionality of individuating being'.[57]

Following this lead, trading algorithms introduce new chrono-topological coordinates, or key points, that add up to the open axiomatic of individuation. In terms of temporality, algorithms trade below the speed of human perception in registering a stimulus (e.g. while the human threshold is about 140 milliseconds, it takes about 8 milliseconds to send a message from Chicago to New York and back via microwave signal; furthermore, the fastest trades on the Nasdaq happen in microseconds, that is 1/1,000,000 of a second). Spatially, trading algorithms shift the focus, and economic value, on properties of materials and on distances once considered trivial (e.g. colocation[58] services in the Mahawah data centre can cost trading companies up to 10000$ a month). The fact that these types of algorithms operate below the threshold of human perception doesn't mean that they don't exist. These novel chrono-topological coordinates add new remarkable points, new occasions of experience, from which perceptions, sensibility, and affectivity are constituted by way of an operation of taking-consistency—of in-formation, as it were—both internal and external to the individual. In other words, the techno-aesthetic feel persists in experience without being necessarily sensed, precisely by entering the potential dimension of preindividual ontogenesis.

This resonates with Félix Guattari's discussion of 'energetic-spatio-temporal (EST) coordinates'. As Guattari puts it in Schizoanalytic Cartographies:

> Everywhere, in every register, in the form of barriers, moulds, modules, punctual, circular, strange (fractal) attractors, catalyzers, enzymes, genetic coding, gestaltist perceptions, mnemotechnical props, poetic constraints, cognitive procedures, but also financial institutions, institutions of publicity, etc, filters are constituted as interfaces between: 1) the virulent virtualities of chaos, stochastic proliferations; and 2) actual potentialities that can be listed and consolidated.[59]

In the contemporary financial world, ubiquitous, interactive algorithms precisely constitute these 'mutational filters',[60] that quantify and discretize qualitative relational dynamics (for instance, values, 'feels', beliefs) in real time, and conversely, transduce these abstract quantities into key points that contribute to the ontogenesis of new perceptions of the physical world. Further, in the moment in which algorithms compete against each other to shave milliseconds, the real-time-ness upon which financial engineering is predicated loses its traditional meaning and temporal consequentiality gives way to a topological, intensive surface that extends to more and more aspects of the world. That is to say, trading algorithms impact not only the 'intensive pricing surface of the market'[61]

---

57. Simondon, *L'individuation À La Lumière Des Notions de Forme et D'information*, p.227.

58. Colocation consists in placing trading companies' servers in the stock exchange's data centre to be as close as possible to the exchange's servers.

59. Félix Guattari, *Schizoanalytic Cartographies*, trans. Andrew Goffey, Bloomsbury Academic, New York, 2013, p.109.

60. Ibid., p.114.

61. Jon Roffe, *Abstract Market Theory*, Palgrave Macmillan, New York, 2015.

but, through pricing and affect modify the sensible world in an emergent fashion. Or, to put it differently, they construct real-time models of the world from the bottom up, in which technology becomes an integral part of the human sensorium, while at the same time humans become an incidental element in the sensing of machines.[62]

Further, as Gilbert Simondon explains, technical objects possess a power of amplification and 'irradiation of values'[63] that progressively extend from the psychic, to the collective and individual realms. When these machines were born out of 'Universes of value',[64] to use Guattari's vocabulary, involving gambling, mass destruction, constant surveillance, and ruthless capitalization to preserve economic freedom, as in the case of Monte Carlo simulation, the contemporary axiology of power becomes clear. This may also help explain how the 'black box' aesthetics operates at different scales of reality and how it is capitalized upon by apparatuses of control—from abstract, but concrete, algorithmic environments, to physical spaces such as stock exchanges' data centres, to the 'pervasive sense of dark foreboding'[65] that has invested the collective sphere that markets are an integral component of. When the feel of the market is automated, what is left to the human is the sense of displacement in front of the impenetrable black box.

This is close to what Luciana Parisi has recently warned us against in the field of urban design. To her, it is precisely the ontogenetic character of real-time algorithms that inaugurates a new mode of control—'postcybernetic control'—by concretising new spatio-temporal actualities in accordance with algorithmic speculative reasoning. Or in her words: 'the question of control is now as follows: how can that which relates to itself become? To put it crudely, postcybernetic control is now concerned with the programming of events'.[66] This is because advanced algorithms have introduced an invariant function in computation, which operates by establishing axioms over axioms, thus subsuming all possible scenarios into a given set. This has endowed software with the capacity to account for qualitative relational changes among parameters and to be affected by external contingencies in real time, thereby turning the Euclidean matrix of computation into a topological surface of spatio-temporal relations.[67] This logic initiates a mode of preemptive control that functions by calculating potentialities, rather than possibilities, thus 'flattening control and novelty (or event) onto

---

62. As Parisi notes, however, one should not conflate algorithmic evolutionary dynamics with the emergent properties of matter. Instead, one needs to consider the extraspace of entropic data that doesn't corresponds to the dynamic continuum of the biophysical plane but instead 'infects (or irreversibly reprograms) all levels of matter'. This will be dealt with in more details in the following paragraphs. Parisi, *Contagious Architecture: Computation, Aesthetics, and Space*, 9.

63. Simondon, *L'individuation À La Lumiere Des Notions de Forme et D'information*, p.342.

64. Guattari, *Schizoanalytic Cartographies*.

65. Matthew Fuller and Andrew Goffey, *Evil Media*, MIT Press, 2012, p.3.

66. Parisi, *Contagious Architecture: Computation, Aesthetics, and Space*, p.79.

67. Celia Lury, Luciana Parisi, and Tiziana Terranova, 'Introduction: The Becoming Topological of Culture', *Theory, Culture & Society* 29, no. 4/5 (2012): 3–35; Luciana Parisi, 'Digital Design and Topological Control', *Theory, Culture & Society* 29, no. 4–5 (July 1, 2012): 165–92.

a topological matrix of continual co-evolution'.[68] This mode of control, which operates not only in urban design but also in relational databases, interactive models and real-time simulations is immediately aesthetic, because it organizes perceptions according to its own functioning, in a way that is not humanly sensed; instead it 'creates the perception of space as a relational field of emergence'.[69] The form of aesthetic control that Parisi uncovers in the field of architecture can be true for market structures too. While parametrically-designed buildings create alien urban spaces, algorithmic financial markets create geo and socio-political scenarios that are always already foreign to us.

BEYOND HUMAN: ONTOGENESIS

In other words, the chrono-topological coordinates introduced by trading algorithms mark the vanishing point of the human, the *façade* beyond which the Anthropocenic perspective ends and the true, obscene (as in: off-scene) Electrocenic axiomatic weaves itself autonomously from human intervention.[70] However, one need not conflate the 'Electrocene' with neoliberal logic. This is because the values of technicity 'surpass utility'[71] and instead come to constitute the 'regulatory normativity'[72] of technics. As Muriel Combes put it: 'When all is said and done, it is technics and technics alone, considered from the point of view of its genesis, that contains an intrinsic normativity capable of regulating the social itself, and the role of culture is to make humans recognize this virtual normativity in order for it to become effective'.[73] The point is that *this* culture—a culture based on 'agnotological' practices—hasn't been able to make this normativity manifest; it is up to the 'inventors' of our times, in alliance with contemporary technology, to make this happen.

Simondon's study of technical objects insists on this point. Although he never witnessed the concretization of the cybernetic model into the Internet, he presciently advanced the hypothesis that the former may inaugurate a new era of technological development, due to the instantiation of a 'movement of thought'[74] that would contribute to the development of a technical mentality—a thought-network, that is 'the material and conceptual synthesis of particularity and concentration, individuality and collectivity'.[75] To Simondon cybernetics furnished the model for the invention of post-industrial technical objects—that is, technical objects, such as information and telecommunication networks, that eschew the foreclosing industrial regime of functioning.[76] Post-industrial technical objects consist in the unity of two layers of reality: one stable and permanent,

68. Parisi, 'Digital Design and Topological Control', p.171.

69. Ibid., p.167.

70. Dan Mellamphy and Nandita Biswas Mellamphy, 'Welcome to the Electrocene, an Algorithmic Agartha', *Culture Machine* 16 (2015).

71. Simondon, *Du mode d'existence des objets techniques*, 222.

72. Ibid., 227.

73. Muriel Combes, *Gilbert Simondon and the philosophy of the transindividual*, trans. Thomas LaMarre, MIT Press, Cambridge, Mass., 2013, p.63.

74. Gilbert Simondon, *Sur la technique: 1953-1983*, Paris: Presses Universitaires de France, 2014, p.302.

75. Ibid., 307.

76. Ibid., p.303.

which adheres to the user, and the other modular, impersonal, mass-produced by industry and distributed by all the networks of exchange.[77] Their reticular, distributed, structure makes them open and participatory. While Simondon was mainly referring to communication networks constituted by phone cables and antennas, contemporary algorithms epitomize post-industrial technical individuals. Indeed, the process of transduction that occurs from mathematical formalization to digital concretization (i.e. the fact that electronic circuits 'can count', as in the implementation of the Monte Carlo method) opens algorithms to the incomputable dimension of a preindividual reality, thereby creating infinite occasions to produce novelty.

This is clearly demonstrated by Parisi, for whom the evolutionary dynamics of advanced algorithms are not simple simulations. This is because algorithms undergo a process of ontogenesis, which implies the radical immanence of incomputability in their becoming—as Kurt Gödel, Alan Turing, and more recently Gregory Chaitin have demonstrated. In the context of financial markets, this means that trading algorithms incorporate contingency in the very fabrics of their being—a thesis already supported, following a slightly different lead, by Elie Ayache in *The Blank Swan*.[78] This instils a more open character to algorithms in complex environments, and may help explain black swans events such as the Flash Crash of 6 May 2010 and the thousands of mini-crashes that have been occurring in the markets since the mid 2000s. Further, it challenges the efficient market hypothesis upon which contemporary financial engineering is predicated, and the figure of the rational agent in market modelling. Moreover, it turns the market, and culture at large, into an unintended consequence of this open formalism. This is precisely the effect of the surplus value of code[79]—the metastability immanent to algorithmic objects that constitutes the trigger of ontogenetic processes. In truth, this already testifies to an economy of excess, rather than scarcity, that is immanent to the general economy of the modes of being.

This new mode of computation calls into question the rational logic of the numbered number, and instead turns culture into an 'aesthetic battlefield' between the organic plane and the machinic phylum of silicon chips 'which together deploy not a transparent apparatus of communication but instead a fractal architecture of events'.[80] In order to make sense of a system which 'lacks spatio-temporal solidity'[81]—or, more precisely, which belongs to a spatio-temporal realm of which humans are increasingly a by-product—it is not so much a matter of 'resistance' to this logic anymore, or a matter of looking for possible alternative scenarios, as it is perhaps a call to invent always anew potential space-times—new Worlds, new Universes, as Guattari would call them—that

---

77. Ibid., pp.311–312 .

78. Elie Ayache, *The Blank Swan: The End of Probability*, Wiley, Chichester, 2010. To Ayache, the market is the medium of contingency that algorithms cannot ever axiomatize. Here it is argued that contingency precisely departs from the open axiomatic immanent to the ontogenesis of algorithmic objects.

79. Gilles Deleuze and Félix Guattari, *A Thousand Plateaus: Capitalism and Schizophrenia*, Minneapolis: University of Minnesota Press, 2005.

80. Parisi, *Contagious Architecture: Computation, Aesthetics, and Space*, p.80.

81. Mirowski, *Never Let a Serious Crisis Go to Waste*, p.34.

would harness the surplus value of algorithmic objects, precisely by grasping its 'techno-aesthetic feeling', in order to orient individuation away from contemporary modes of power. 'A process of change of contexts ... not of possibilities' as Elie Ayache calls it.[82]

BEYOND POWER: TRANSGRESSION

In other words, one needs not stop at the infinity of algorithmic occasions of experience vis-à-vis the finitude of human life. Instead, it is precisely by crossing this threshold that one can counter the implosive acceleration of neoliberal power. The only way to do so—to make sense of it, as it were—is through a techno-aesthetic insertion that would break with the current postcybernetic mode of control and give a new directionality to individuation. At this point a distinction needs to be made between the crash and the break. The crash is a momentary collapse of the abstract infrastructure of power, an accident inbuilt in the operational logic of the machine that doesn't necessarily equate with a veritable change. Financial crashes are an instance of this as they constitute occasions for neoliberal contingents to respond to market crises with more financialization. Conversely, a break entails the opening up of a discontinuity for the insertion of novelty—a transgression. Discontinuous relation is what allows for a veritable invention.[83]

The relation between man and technical object that allows for such an invention doesn't follow the temporal regime of labour.[84] This is because the inventor is a 'pure individual'—that is, a mediator between the collective and the inaccessible technical object, whose role is to allow for the invention to become a 'germ of civilization' by breaking with social structures and instantiating new relations among the collective.[85] The privileged realm from which such a break can depart is the realm of the arts. As Simondon again puts it, the artist is an inventor, whose role is to exceed the finitude of the physical world and to imbue her works with virtual potential:

> Every inventor in the matter of art is futurist in a certain measure, which means that he exceeds the *hic et nunc* of needs and ends by enlisting in the created object sources of effects that live and multiply themselves in the work; the creator is sensitive to the virtual, to what demands, from the ground of time and in the tightly situated humbleness of a place, the progress of the future and amplitude of the world as a place of manifestation.[86]

The attunement of the artist-inventor to the new forms offered by technical invention is manifested today in many experimental fields that point toward the exigency to divorce aesthetics from the realm of representation and neoliberal value, to distance it from a phenomenological perspective and open it up to the

---

82. Ayache, *The Blank Swan*, p.6.

83. Gilbert Simondon, *L'invention dans les techniques: cours et conférences*, ed. Jean-Yves Chateau, Seuil, Paris, 2005, p.101.

84. Simondon, *L'individuation À La Lumiere Des Notions de Forme et D'information*, p.340.

85. Ibid., pp.340–343.

86. Gilbert Simondon, *Imagination et invention (1965-1966)*, Chatou: Éditions de la transparence, 2008, p.182.

operations of thought in conjunction with the affordances of digital networked technologies, in order to uncover the techno-aesthetics behind the imperceptible operations of algorithmic media. As Mohammad Salemy aptly observes:

> At the level of production, the artist not only utilizes a "technique" in the larger sense of the term, but also introduces sufficient fidelity to maintain certain assumptions. The artist does so in order to maintain the functionality of the work, while speculating on how cognition automatically generates assertions about art's metaphysical availability to the viewer. The artist begins with a certain set of ideas and access to a level of already produced knowledge, as well as an understanding of how proactive risk-taking opens up the outcome of the artwork to contingency. This type of work is a process and is not that different from, for example, the way high-speed algorithmic trading works.[87]

Artists, inventors, software engineers are able to cut through the sensual, representational layer of experience in order to come into contact with imperceptible algorithmic operations. However, techno-aesthetics does not only become manifest in accidents but, importantly, entails the insertion of a break, a turning point, into the system man-world for the formation of a new logic. This may be true for the economic too. Creation, attunement, invention always already pertain to the aesthetic domain, and don't need to be relegated to the visual arts. In the words of Milton Friedman, one of the original MPS members: 'The construction of hypotheses is a creative act of inspiration, intuition, invention; its essence is the vision of something new in familiar material'.[88] As neoliberalism 'invented' a new mode of power through its alliance with cybernetics, today we are witnessing bursts of inventions in the financial world too, stemmed from new modes of relations with algorithmic media. Examples such as blockchain technologies and the parasitic hedge funds of the Robin Hood Cooperative[89] counter market logic through a singularization and distribution of values away from the homogenizing effect of capital, thereby inventing new ways of navigating the real away from neoliberal logic.

According to Kolozova, the decisionism characteristic of the speculative mode of neoliberal reasoning, based on an 'amphibiology between thought and the real',[90] is erasing 'the real-of-the-human which is presubjective and prelingual'[91] and instead it constitutes an 'onto-theo-political'[92] view of Being as inexorably linked to economic dynamics. Far from being a retreat into folk-political humanism, this observation is a call to invent new modes of relation between man and machine—new operations of individuation—that would overcome the

87. Mohammad Salemy, "Art After Machines," *E-Flux Supercommunity*, June 2, 2015, http://supercommunity.e-flux.com/texts/art-after-the-machines/.

88. Milton Friedman, 'The Methodology of Positive Economics', in *Essays in Positive Economics*, University of Chicago Press, 1953, 43.

89. 'Robin Hood Minor Asset Management', accessed August 15, 2014, http://www.robinhoodcoop.org/.

90. Kolozova, 'Metaphysics of Finance Economy Of Its Radicalization as the Method of Revoking Real Economy', p.30.

91. Laruelle in ibid., p.25.

92. Laruelle, *Au-delà du Principe de Pouvoir*, p.15.

reterritorialization on capital and economic value, and instead, reverse the contemporary 'sense' of power and generate new, irreversible, Universes. As Simondon provocatively asks: isn't it that all creation is a transgression?[93]

---

93. Simondon, *Sur la technique*, p.449.

10

The Murmur of Nothing:
Mallarmé and Mathematics

Christian R. Gelder

'I lisped in numbers, for the numbers came' —Alexander Pope
'A poem can at most let the murmur of [the] nothing be heard.' —Jean-Claude Milner

Despite the fact that no direct analysis of Stéphane Mallarmé's relationship to mathematics has taken place[1], the literary historian Thierry Roger notes that after the publication of Mallarmé's final poem *Un Coup de Dés* in 1897, the first considerations of his poetry were "d'ordre philosophico-mathematique, et non pas poétique."[2] Drawing on a series of late 19th century French and Belgian literary reviews, Roger suggests that for these critics the secret of Mallarmé's mystery took the form of a question. Why, they asked, did the poet encode his final poem, a poem that was to pronounce upon "the destiny of a future poetry"[3], in a series of quasi-mathematical images: "un coup de dés", "l'unique Nombre qui ne peut pas être un autre", "si c'était le nombre... ce serait... le hasard"[4]? According to Paul Valéry—who was taught about set theory and the latest developments in 19th century mathematics by the engineer Pierre Féline, a man he met

---

1. One notable exception is Steven Cassedy, who has written broadly about literary theory, the history of mathematics, and Mallarmé's poetry. See, Steven Cassedy, 'Mathematics, Relationalism, and the Rise of Modern Literary Aesthetics', *Journal of the History of Ideas*, Vol. 49, No. 1, pp. 109-132 and 'Mallarmé and Andrej Belyj: Mathematics and the Phenomenality of the Literary Object', *MLN*, Vol. 96, No. 5, pp. 1066-1083. I must also take this opportunity to sincerely thank Sigi Jöttkandt, Baylee Brits, and Robert Boncardo for their comments on earlier versions of this essay: three better readers one could not hope for!

2. Thierry Roger, *L'Archive du Coup de Dés*, Paris, Éditions Classiques Garnier, 2010, p. 53-4. "The first considerations on the *Coup de Dés*, given its title, were of a philosophico-mathematical order, and not poetic." [my trans.]

3. Quentin Meillassoux, *The Number and the Siren: A Decipherment of Mallarmé's* Coup de Dés, trans. Robin Mackay, Falmouth & New York, Urbanomic/Sequence Press, 2012, p. 7.

4. Stéphane Mallarmé, *Œuvre Complètes I*, Paris, Gallimard, 1998, pp. 367, 372-3, 382-3.

and befriend in Montpellier some time in 1889—these critics recognized something of the mathematical in Mallarmé because of the "pure and distinct notions"[5] at play within his poetry. The exactitude of Mallarmé's composition, his resistance to the endless play of signification, and his insistence on creating a perennially unachievable "Œuvre pure" led Valéry to remark that his most beloved poet did not belong to any lineage of great French artists, but rather to the "family of great scientists"[6].

That the philosophers turned to the question of Mallarmé and mathematics should not surprise. For Jacques Derrida, Mallarmé's mathematical relevance could be located in his ability to inscribe Gödel's logical and meta-mathematical concept of undecidability at the level of writing itself. Derrida writes, "when [Mallarmé's] undecidability is marked and re-marked in *writing*, it has a greater power of formalization, even if it is 'literary' in appearance... than when it occurs as a proposition in logicomathematics form"[7]. And again, this time for Jean-Claude Milner, Mallarmé turned to mathematics because it could be used "en exception de la science"[8]. While modern science literalized nature to the point where it became unable to think the constellation—the group of stars that appear as the final image in *Un Coup de dés*—in its presence and fullness, Mallarmé saw mathematics as an "alliée"[9] that would exempt and exonerate his poetry from the limiting particularities of post-Galilean science. Although each of these commentaries responds in one way or another to the above question, they are emblematic of the kind of analysis of Mallarmé and mathematics that has taken place: one appears in a letter, another in the middle of a much larger essay on mimesis, and the last in an occasional essay, rather than in his larger, more sustained, readings of the poet.[10] It may be possible, then, to sum up the relationship between Mallarmé and mathematics by purposefully (mis)quoting a line that has become somewhat of a slogan in Mallarmé studies: nothing has taken place but the place. No sustained comparison or treatment of the two discourses has taken place; and yet the place itself has been constantly taking place, continually suturing Mallarmé's poetry to mathematics.

One philosopher who has championed a kind of productive non-relation between Mallarmé's poetry and mathematics is Alain Badiou, who has situated his own philosophy between the poem and the matheme. Badiou's first reference

---

5. Paul Valéry, 'Letter to Mallarmé,' Paul Valéry, *Leonardo, Poe, Mallarmé*, trans. Malcolm Cowley and James R. Lawler, London, Routledge, 1972, p. 243.

6. Valéry, 'Letter to Mallarmé', p.242

7. Jacques Derrida, 'The Double Session,' Jacques Derrida, *Dissemination*, trans. Barbara Johnson, Chicago, The University of Chicago Press, 1981, p. 222.

8. Jean-Claude Milner, 'Les Constellations Révélatrices', *Elucidation*, Vol. 8-9, 2003, p. 7.

9. Milner, 'Les Constellations Révélatrices', p. 7.

10. Jean-Claude Milner is an absolutely seminal - and quite remarkable - interpreter of Mallarmé's poetry. From his moving reading of *Un Coup de Dés* and Lacan's R.S.I knot in *Les Noms Indistincts* (1983) to his fascinating political diatribe against the 20th century's "mallarméens stricts" in *Mallarmé au Tombeau* (1999), Milner has consistently turned to Mallarmé as both a comrade and an enemy. I do hope that his work will appear in English someday soon, as it represents an important and often forgotten moment in the fascinating history of Mallarmé's reception. See Jean-Claude Milner, *Les Noms indistincts*, Paris, Éditions du Seuil, 1983, pp. 48-9 and Jean-Claude Milner, *Mallarmé au Tombeau*, Paris, Éditions Verdier, 1999, p. 88.

to Mallarmé appeared in "Mark and Lack", an essay that countered Jacques-Alain Miller's "heterodox"[11] reading of Frege in "Suture (Elements of the Logic of the Signifier)" by arguing for "the impossibility of a logic of the Signifier that would envelop the scientific order."[12] Because of the autonomy and self-sufficiency of mathematical writing—its status as an integrally ruled universe—Badiou writes that "Science is an Outside without a blind-spot"[13]. Accompanying this neat slogan-like proposition is a footnote that aligns the self-sufficient nature of formal language to the orientation of Mallarmé's poetic project: "If one wants to exhibit writing as such, and to excise its author; if one wants to follow Mallarmé in enjoining the written work to occur with neither subject nor Subject, there is a way of doing this that is radical, secular, and exclusive of every other: by entering into the writings of science, whose law consists precisely in this." While Badiou is by no means conflating science and mathematics here—he uses the terms interchangeably to refer to formal language as such—the general sense is that he, like Valéry, identifies a kind of family resemblance between Mallarmé's poetry and formal language. In this particular instance, however, his preference is given to mathematics: what Mallarmé wanted, mathematics completes.

This remark is the first part of a longer note that I shall attempt to make sense of at the end of this chapter, but the fact that Badiou links Mallarmé's project to mathematics may strike the reader as strange, not least because his later work is predicated on the separation of art and mathematics *tout court*. Perhaps it is surprising, then, to find that Badiou often reads Mallarmé's attempt to found a non-subjective poetics, a poetics that would perform the elocutionary disappearance of the poet, alongside mathematics. As he elsewhere remarks, "let us note in passing how inexact it is to say that such a poem is subjective. What Mallarmé wants is the very opposite: a radical anonymity of the subject of the poem."[14] While this chapter is not an analysis of Badiou's writings on Mallarmé - nor of his work on mathematics, even though I shall draw on it - the specificity of a potential syllogism between Mallarmé and mathematics is given fuller form in an essay on logic, mathematics, and the linguistic turn. Here Badiou writes the following: "Can the infinite be a number [*chiffre*]? This is what Mallarmé, *Cantor's unconscious contemporary*, contends in the poem. That the infinite is a number is what a set-theoretic ontology of the multiple finally made possible after centuries of denial and enclosure of the infinite within theology's vocation." [my italics and modified trans.][15] Against its theological and Romantic manifestations,

11. Tom Eyers, *Post-Rationalism: Psychoanalysis, Epistemology, and Marxism in Post-War France*, London & New York, Bloomsbury, 2013, p. 32.

12. Alain Badiou, 'Mark and Lack', in Peter Hallward and Knox Peden (eds.), *Concept and Form: Volume One Key Texts from the Cahiers pour l'Analyse*, London & New York, Verso, 2012, p. 160.

13. Badiou, 'Mark and Lack', p. 172.

14. Alain Badiou, 'A French Philosopher Responds to a Polish Poet', in Alain Badiou, *Handbook of Inaesthetics*, trans. Alberto Toscano, Stanford, Stanford University Press, 2004, p. 30.

15. I've chosen to translate "multiple" as "multiple", rather than "manifest". Norman Madarasz also chooses to translate Badiou's use of "chiffre" as "integer," whereas I have selected to opt for "number" because it is both more faithful to the developments of set theory and more in line with Mallarmé's own terminology. Alain Badiou, 'First Provisional Theses on Logic', in Alain Badiou, *Briefings on Existence: A Short Treatise on Transitory Ontology*, trans. Norman Madarasz, New York, SUNY, 2006, p. 124.

both Mallarmé and Cantor treat the infinite as a number.

Badiou's short analysis primarily focuses on the question of the infinite, which I shall not address here. However, it does formalize a relationship between Mallarmé's poetry and its mathematical counterpart: Cantor and post-Cantorian set theory. While the infinite operates within these two discourses in fascinating and unique ways, they also share another central concept: the nothing. In this essay I shall pose the question of Mallarmé's relationship to mathematics by way of the nothing: if post-Cantorian mathematics deals with the *mark* of the nothing unproblematically, how does Mallarmé, in the poem, achieve or formulate this nothing? In other words, is there any sense in which poetry and mathematics have similar conceptions of the nothing—and if so, how is this manifested in their respective particularities? To answer this, I shall provide a close reading of what is to my mind Mallarmé's greatest meditation on the concept of the nothing, his sonnet *Ses purs ongles*. I argue that Mallarmé attempted to imbue poetry with a type of nothing that shares a number of qualities with the set theoretic counterpart. As I hope to show, this can be thought of as the literal inscription of the presentation of what cannot be presented: not the mark of lack, but a mark that makes up for that which has a lack of a mark. However, by examining the linguistic, sonic and material facets of the poem, I conclude by suggesting that although the mathematical nothing is impossible for poetry to replicate, the concept of the nothing nonetheless serves to highlight a productive point of separation between the two discourses

*

The 19th century mathematician Georg Cantor did not inscribe his mathematical concept of the nothing with any particular philosophical importance. According to Joseph Warren Dauben, Cantor thought that his discovery of the transfinite—the proof that there are infinite infinities—had great philosophical, mathematical, and theological implications, whereas the nothing did not[16]. In the simplest terms, the basic gesture of Cantor's naïve set theory and its more complex 20th century axiomatization is to treat everything as a set. In Cantor's own words, the definition of a set is a follows: "*Definition*: By a 'set' we mean any collection M into a whole of definite, distinct objects m (which are called the 'elements' of M), of our perception or of our thought."[17] This philosophically-inflected statement clearly outlines what the basic orientation of set theory is: take a collection of anything—for example the numbers 1, 2, and 3—and set theory provides a way to schematize these parts into a whole, so that there is now a set m whose members are ($\emptyset$, 1, 2, 3). While this determines the basic thrust of what sets are, it leaves the question of where sets begin unanswered.

As one canonical textbook puts it, "all the basic principles of set theory… are designed to make new sets out of old ones"[18]. These "basic principles" re-

16. See in particular Joseph Warren Dauben, *Georg Cantor: His Mathematics and Philosophy of the Infinite*, Cambridge, Massachusetts, & London, Harvard University Press, 1979, pp. 120-148.

17. Quoted in Dauben, *Georg Cantor: His Mathematics and Philosophy of the Infinite*, p. 170.

18. P. R. Halmos, *Naive Set Theory*, New York, Springer, 1974, p. 4.

fer to a set of axioms developed by Ernst Zermelo in 1908, which were further refined and reformulated over the first half of the 20th century. In Badiou's ontological transliteration of set theory, the axiom that takes precedence is that, which states that "there exists a set which has no elements"[19]. As a formal proposition, this is written as follows:

$$\exists x \, \forall y \, \neg(y \in x)$$

For Badiou, because set theory is a theory of the multiple, which is to say a theory of *inconsistent* multiplicity that is retrospectively counted-as-one when presented in the world, what lies behind the multiples is precisely the empty set: a set that has no members. This set is marked by the following symbol, (Ø), and this symbol belongs to every subsequent set. The importance of the empty set for Badiou has to do with the metaontological consequences he draws from it. As he writes, "In its metaontological formulation the axiom says: the unpresentable is presented, as a subtractive term of the presentation of presentation… or: being lets itself be named, within the ontological situation, as that from which existence does not exist."[20] The empty set—or the "void" as Badiou comes to call it—formalizes the presentation of what cannot be presented. For this reason, Badiou *decides* to treat the empty set as the "proper name of being",[21] since it is what names being within each situation.

Following Lacan, it is the inscriptive, deductive, and axiomatic nature of set theory that allows Badiou to use it as a condition for his ontology. Since mathematics always irreducibly knows of what it speaks—what its limits and propositions are—it provides a counter-model to the poetic and linguistic ontology of Heideggerian and post-Heideggerian thought. The key point is that mathematics, insofar as its terms and the relations are univocal and integrally rule-governed, is subtracted from the problems of interpretation and iterability. There are not several voids or different orders of nothingness, instead the set-theoretic "the void is unique"[22] - and, as such, it operates as a proper name.

Set theory, then, begins with the nothing—and it is here that Mallarmé returns. Just as in set theory, Mallarmé positions the nothing as the ontological starting point for poetry. The poem that opens his canonical 1887 collection *Poésies* is entitled *Salut*, which, as Jacques Rancière has noted, is often wrongly considered to be nothing more than one of the "Occasional verses"[23]. Instead, it was written for an occasion. Composed for a banquet held by the French literary magazine *La Revue indépendante* on the 9th of February 1893, *Salut* begins by reciting and defining the tripartite movement of poetic composition: "Rien, cette écume, vierge vers"[24]. Poetry, then, begins with nothing—a proposition that led Michel Deguy to suggest that "Mallarmé introduces the zero into the poetic

19. Alain Badiou, *Being and Event*, trans. Oliver Feltham, London , Continuum, 2007, p. 67
20. Badiou, *Being and Event*, pp. 67-8.
21. Badiou, *Being and Event*, p. 86.
22. Badiou, *Being and Event*, p. 69.
23. Jacques Rancière, *Mallarmé: The Politics of the Siren*, trans. Steven Corcoran, New York & London, Continuum, 2011, p. 5.
24. Mallarmé, *Œuvre Complètes I*, p. 4.

calculus."[25] But if Mallarmé truly is Cantor's unconscious contemporary, and if, for set theory, the number zero is not the name of nothing but rather a member of a preexisting set, then what is this "rien" that poetry begins with? Is it possible to see exactly what Mallarmé means by this in terms of his own poetry's relationship to mathematics?

*

My reading of *Ses purs ongles* begins by distinguishing between two different orders of the nothing that are frequently invoked throughout Mallarmé's *oeuvre*. The first, signified by the existential term "le néant" or "nothingness", appeared during the Spring of 1866. This is the period during which Mallarmé underwent his infamous "spiritual crisis"[26]; a monumentally important moment in the poet's career that was triggered by, in the words of Marchal, the "découverte du néant"[27]. From this almost Nietzschean confrontation with the prospect - and perhaps even the challenge - of nothingness, Mallarmé entirely reformulated his aesthetic principles, writing in a letter to his friend and confidant Henri Cazalis on the 13th of July 1866 that "… after having found Nothingness, I have found beauty [modified trans.]."[28] But alongside this night of nothingness is what Blanchot calls Mallarmé's "other night"[29]. Signified this time by the more mysterious "rien", this order of the nothing designates "the 'presence' of nothing"[30] or, what Badiou might term, the presentation of the unpresentable. It is not for nothing, as Justin Clemens has remarked, that Badiou uses the term "rien" when discussing the void in set theory as a point of differentiation from Sartre's existential "néant"[31]: in the latter's reading, Mallarmé is precisely the poet of "néant". By contrast, I would like to suggest that Mallarmé is actually the poet of "rien" and that *Ses purs ongles* represents the purest and most forceful example of his attempt to instil and begin his poetry with the nothing by marking the point of unpresentation.

As Roger Pearson has argued, "the obvious way to begin reading 'Sonnet allègorique de lui-même'", the title of Mallarmé's first draft of *Ses purs ongles*, "is in terms of [Mallarmé's] own commentary."[32] If this is the case, then there are perhaps two key points that should orient any analysis of the poem. The first refers to the infamous "ptyx" that appears in the first line of the second quatrain.

25. Michel Deguy, 'The Energy of Despair', in Robert Greer Cohn and Gerald Gillespie (eds.) *Mallarmé in the Twentieth Century*, trans. Christopher Bryan Elson, New Jersey, Associated University Presses, 1998, p. 25.

26. For two excellent accounts of the spiritual crisis see, Pascal Durand, *Mallarmé: Du sens des formes au sens des formalités*, Paris, Editions du Seuil, 2008, pp. 35-53 and Bertrand Marchal, *La Religion de Mallarmé: Poésie, Mythologie et Religion*, Paris, José Corti, 1988, pp. 55-64.

27. Mallarmé, *Œuvre Complètes I*, p. 1373.

28. Stéphane Mallarmé, *Selected Letters of Stéphane Mallarmé*, trans and eds. Rosemary Lloyd, Chicago & London, The University of Chicago Press, 1988, p. 65.

29. Maurice Blanchot, *The Space of Literature*, trans. Ann Smock, Nebraska, University of Nebraska Press, 1982, p. 162.

30. Barnaby Norman, *Mallarmé's Sunsets: Poetry at the End of Time*, London, Legenda, 2014, p. 74.

31. Justin Clemens, 'Doubles of Nothing: The Problem of Binding Truth to Being in the Work of Alain Badiou', *Filozofski vestnik*, Vol. XXVI, No. 2, 2005, p. 104.

32. Roger Pearson, *Unfolding Mallarmé: The Development of a Poetic Act*, Oxford, Oxford University Press, 1996, p. 144.

The debate about this mark—thought by Marchal to be an "problème intellec-tual"[33]—centres around whether or not the word, or any word for that matter, can actually *mean* nothing. While there have been numerous attempts to pin-down an etymological root that would give the "ptyx" a decisive meaning, Mal-larmé himself was more than comfortable with its lack of meaning, writing the following to Eugène Lefébure in May 1868: "… I may write a sonnet and as I have only three rhymes in -ix, do your best to send me the true meaning of the word ptyx, for I'm told it doesn't exist in any language, something I'd much pre-fer, for that would give me the joy of creating it through the magic of rhyme… "[34]. This curious little phrase, "the magic of rhyme", is ambiguous: even on the face of things, the process of "magic" seems immediately juxtaposed to the care-ful and rigorous principles at work in mathematical reasoning and creation. However, it is precisely this guiding operation that allows Mallarmé to create a word that does not so much signify nothing, but rather inscribes unpresentation itself into his poem.

The second point responds to the use of the word "allègorique" in the po-em's original title: how can a poem refer only to itself? Much of Mallarmé's post-1866 career was dedicated, in various different ways, to creating an "Œu-vre pure"—and in some senses this manifests itself in *Ses purs ongles* through "an internal mirage created by the words themselves,"[35] a phrase drawn from his 1868 letter to Cazalis. To achieve the transition from nothing (rien), to the state of the poem (cette écume), to pure verse (vierge vers) in *Ses purs ongles*, Mallarmé looks to the internal operations of poetic composition—the way the words can reflect one another to create the effect of internal unity. One should observe, as Pearson does, the influence of Poe's *The Philosophy of Composition* (1846) on Mal-larmé's method. In this particular essay, which Mallarmé himself translated into French, Poe writes that works of poetry should proceed "with the precision and rigid consequence of a mathematical problem"[36]. This would seem to apply to *Ses purs ongles*, where the words are so tightly arranged and carefully placed that they almost take the form of a sequence of mathematical demonstrations, referring and reflecting only upon themselves.

Here is Badiou's prose summary of the poem's first two stanzas, which is useful in that it gives form to Mallarmé's otherwise impenetrable "hypothèse"[37]:

> In an empty room, at midnight, agony alone prevails, fuelled by the disap-pearance of the light. Such is the torch in the form of raised hands, which bear only an extinguished flame, that the anguish of the void cannot be cured by any trace of the setting sun, not even by the ashes that might have been gathered in a funerary urn.

33. Laure Dardonville, 'Entretien avec Bertrand Marchal', *Tracés. Revue de Sciences humaines* [On-line], 4 | 2003, online since 26 January 2009, connection on 01 June 2015. URL: http://traces.revues. org/3973; DOI: 10.4000/traces.3973.

34. Mallarmé, *Selected Letters of Stéphane Mallarmé*, p. 85.

35. Ibid, pp. 86-7.

36. Edgar Allan Poe, 'The Philosophy of Composition', in Leonardo Cassuto (eds) *Literary Theory and Criticism*, Toronto, Dover, 1999, p.102.

37. Mallarmé, *Œuvre Complètes I*, p. 391.

The poet, as master of places, has departed for the river of death, taking
with him a signifier (the ptyx) which does not refer to any existing object.[38]

The first stanza, then, works through a series of images that invoke nothingness: the initial scene is set in the "salon vide" of the second stanza, the poem
takes place at midnight (the time of Néant), there is the "angoisse" of nothingness present in the room, and there is also an empty "cinéraire amphore." In the
second stanza, the "Maître" or poet descends into the river Styx on a quest to
find nothingness in the realm of death. It should be noted that these particular
instances of nothingness in the poem are somewhat different from the "ptyx",
whose composition is spontaneous and forced into creation by "the magic of
rhyme".

While the above images represent possible states of nothingness, the "ptyx"
is not a signifier that signifies or represents the nothing. The poem's other
rhyme, the "or", means "gold" or "well" in English. But Mallarmé, who au-
thored a book on the English language in 1878, was prone to punning on English words in his poetry. Derrida, for example, reads the "or" rhyme as a term
that points to undecidability—it is either this *or* it isn't—and the same argument
can be extended to the "yx" rhyme. If the words are to reflect upon one another
and, following Poe, if the composition of the poem is to be as precise as a mathematical equation, then the question of whether the "ptyx" means nothing is inscribed within *Ses purs ongles*' opposing rhyme: is the "ptyx" something *or* nothing? In this sense, the "ptyx" does not follow the strict relation of signifier to the
signified; instead, its meaning or lack thereof is left to be determined.

What I have been calling the "orders" of nothingness in the poem are in fact
catalogued by Mallarmé through his use of the "yx" rhyme. Starting with the
"ptyx", the following rhyme is "styx", which is an allusion to the kind of nothingness found in death. As Badiou writes, the quest for nothingness through the
poet's perennial descent into the river styx, "renders poetry, even at the most
sovereign point of its clarity, even in its peremptory affirmation, complicit with
death"[39]. The next rhyme is "nixe", which is a mythical water creature that appears and disappears in the mirror described in the third tercet. The etymological roots of the word "nix" lie in the 18th century German word for nothing or
nul, "nitch" or "nix", which originated from the High Middle Germanic word
"nihtes". So this particular order of the nothing signifies absence, the mythical
nixe that is also "nitch". Lastly, Mallarmé uses the word "fixe" or "fixed" to fix
the three orders of nothingness to one another: "rien" to the "ptyx", death to
the river "styx", and absence to the "nixe." Moreover, the actual X sound produced by this rhyme orients the entirety of the poem. The poem's volta occurs
in the break between the nothingness that is described in the first two quatrains
and the emergence of the stars in the tercets, something I shall return to shortly. What characterises this turn is found on the poem's seventh line, where the
"avec ce" works to create the sonic presence of the X sound and links togeth-

---

38. Alain Badiou, 'Mallarmé's Method', in *Conditions*, trans. Steven Corcoran, London & New York,
Continuum, 2008, p. 54.

39. Badiou, *Being and Event*, p. 54.

er all of the orders of nothingness. It is in this sense, as Marchal writes, that the "'ptyx' est donc par excellence le mot qui ne désigne rien"[40]; its presence is everywhere in the poem, and yet it has no presence beyond its own material inscription.

There is in fact another reason to suspect that the creation of the "ptyx" is an attempt to convey the presentation of unpresentation in the poem. In a fragmented piece entitled "Notes sur la language", which documents the sole remains of a linguistic project pursued, but never completed, by the poet between the years 1869-1870, Mallarmé makes one of his few explicit references to a philosopher. Speaking of the "la grande et longue période de Descartes," an age that includes La Bruyère, Fénelon, "un parfum de Baudelaire" and also, curiously, "langage mathématique"[41], Mallarmé places himself at the closing point of the Cartesian age. This reference to Descartes is curious because it is not entirely clear whether the poet had actually ever read the philosopher. Nonetheless, Mallarmé concludes his discussion with the following, rather cryptic, remark:

> We have not understood Descartes; other countries have taken him over, but he did arouse French mathematicians.

> We have to take up his momentum, interrogate our mathematicians— and not use any foreign land, whether Germany or England, except as a counter-proof: helping us in that way with what they have taken from us

> Besides, the *hyperscientific* momentum only comes from Germany, not England, which cannot adopt a pure science, because of God, whom Bacon, its legislator, respects.[42]

Poets, for Mallarmé, must study and interrogate the mathematicians who are, as in the case of Cantor, too hesitant to "adopt a pure science" because of their respect for God: it is God who stifles or interrupts the "hyperscientific" momentum. However, what is odd about this particular passage, composed around the same time as the early version of *Ses purs ongles*, is that Mallarmé seems to suggest that French mathematicians have not understood Descartes precisely because of this fact. The usual interpretation of this passage assumes that Mallarmé's invocation of Descartes shows his own attempt to construct a concept of "fiction" that would be synonymous with the nothing that begins Cartesian method.[43] However, the radical doubt - the quest to begin, like poetry and mathematics, with nothing - that so often defines Descartes' cogito does not necessarily doubt the existence of God. In fact, the very opposite is true. Descartes may well be credited as the first rationalist philosopher but his rationalism is routinely subjected to the whims of the Divine. As he writes in *Principles of Philosophy*

40. Bertrand Marchal, *Lecture de Mallarmé*: Poésies, Igitur, Coup de dés, Paris, José Corti, 1985, p. 179. "'ptyx' is par excellence the word that designates nothing." [my trans.]

41. Mallarmé, *Œuvre Complètes I*, p. 872.

42. Mallarmé, *Œuvre Complètes I*, p. 872-3. This is Mary Ann Caws' translation. See, Stéphane Mallarmé, 'Descartes', in Mary Ann Caws (eds.) *Mallarmé in Prose*, trans. Mary Ann Caws, New York, New Directions, 2001, p. 76.

43. See Rancière's concept of 'fiction' in Rancière, *Mallarmé: The Politics of the Siren*, pp. 21-22, as well as Roger Dragonetti, 'Le Coup du Cogito de Descartes dans le Jeu Poétique de Mallarmé', in Jacques Berchtold (eds.) *Echiquiers d'Encre: le Jeu d'Échecs et des Lettres*, Genève, Droz, 1998, pp. 49-74.

(1644), "The reasons for doubting... mathematical demonstrations" are that the "omnipotent God who has created us" could change even that which is "hitherto considered to be self-evident."[44] This is why Ian Hacking once suggested that Descartes does not know what a mathematical proof is: for Descartes, *contra* Leibniz, as rational as they may appear mathematical proofs are nonetheless contingent properties of the world.[45] Moreover, while Mallarmé was clearly preoccupied with the nothing, no such concept is allowed for Descartes since God is perfect and "what is more perfect cannot be produced by... what is less perfect"[46]. In other words, God does not emerge from nothingness, since nothingness is less perfect than God. This doctrine, then, seems to be directly at odds with Mallarmé's thought—in which case it is worth thinking about what exactly the poet takes from the philosopher.

In *Ses purs ongles* one aspect of the relation between Mallarmé and Descartes lies in the materiality of the "yx" rhyme. Because of the rarity of the "yx" rhyme in the French language, Pearson again comments that "X marks the spot" and is therefore "a symbol of rhyme: like rhyme, it is a reflection, a mirrored V, the v... stands for 'vers'"[47]. For him, the letter X must be treated as a single signifier that stands in for the concept of rhyme. This is certainly an interesting reading of the function of the letter X, but due to the proximity of "Notes" to the composition of *Ses purs ongles* I am more inclined to read this in mathematical terms. While Descartes did not formalize the graph currently called the Cartesian plane—this was done by Pierre de Fermat in the 17th century—in the 19th century it was generally considered to be invented by the philosopher. Taken together, the "yx" rhyme points to the site of the nothing on the Cartesian plane: the y,x or x,y coordinates refer to the middle point of a graph, a point that is also marked by a double 0, a point of pre-Cantorian mathematical nothing. In line with the close relationship the poem has with the English language, the "pt" sound that opens the "ptyx" could then literally be read as "point", spelt the same in French, which inscribes "ptyx" with the following meaning: the "pt" of "yx", the point of the nothing on a Cartesian plane. The "ptyx" is thus an attempt to present the mathematical nothing in the poem. It is not a signifier that signifies nothing, for "rien" or "Néant" serve this purpose accordingly. Nor is it a word that simply represents nothing, for to suggest so would ignore its spontaneous creation. It is instead an attempt to present the unpresentable, to force a mark into the poem, through the random operation of "the magic of rhyme".

Mallarmé himself confirms the relation between the nothing, the "ptyx" and mathematics in the poem's final line: "De scintillations sitôt le septuor." There is a long tradition in Mallarmé studies of reading the seemingly arbitrary punctuation and titles of the letters in his poetry as signifiers themselves. For example, Quentin Meillassoux closes *The Number and the Siren* by pointing to

44. René Descartes, *The Philosophical Writings of Descartes Volume I*, trans. John Cottingham, Robert Stoothoff, and Dugald Murdoch, Cambridge, Cambridge University Press, 1985, p. 194.

45. See Ian Hacking, 'Leibniz and Descartes: Proof and Eternal Truth', *Proceedings of the British Academy*, Vol. 59, pp. 175-188.

46. Descartes, *The Philosophical Writings of Descartes Volume I*, p. 199.

47. Pearson, *Unfolding Mallarmé: The Development of a Poetic Act*, p. 145.

the significance of Mallarmé's use of the dash in *Crise des vers*: "what is this good for—for a game"[48]. Also, in terms of the poem's last line, the dots hanging over the word "scintillations" materialize the emergence of the stars; an emergence that, in the moving words of Milner, show how "la rencontre réelle est possible, où lalangue, un court instant, scintille"[49]. But not all the graphemes at play in this final line have been deciphered. The caret that rests upon the 'ô' of 'sitôt' points, as if like an arrow, back to a word from the previous line: "fermé", meaning "closed" or "shut off". What does it mean for the o, the zer-o, to be closed? Due to the internal mirage created by the two rhyme schemes—the undecidability (or) of the nothing (yx)—Mallarmé both closes and answers the question of whether the nothing exists in the poem through the hidden marks and graphemes placed above his letters. The question of the nothing is closed because the "ptyx" has been given a decisive non-meaning: it is the inscription of the nothing in the poem that presents the unpresentable. Further toward a mathematical mark in a poem, perhaps, one could not get.

While I have argued that Mallarmé aligns "rien" to the mathematical nothing, a close reading of the poem shows this to be immediately undone: mathematics and poetry unknot themselves at the very moment a knot is revealed. The narrative of the final two tercets suggests that it is possible for poetry to speak of something other than the nothing. As the unnamed narrator stands nude and defunct in front of the mirror, the stars begin to emerge: the seven shining lights in the sky that comprise the "septuor". Robert Greer Cohn notes that the "septuor" should be thought of as a "musical term" like Pythagoras's "*nombre*", which is used by Mallarmé to annex the concept of number to music and, finally, to letters[50]. More generally, though, the poem itself contains a series of puns on the French word for sound, "son". The opening line, for example, binds the "purs" to the "ongles" to create the effect of "pur-son", pure sound, which can be located in a number of other places in the poem. As if anticipating the question in advance, the Mallarmé of *Ses purs ongles* hides the clue to the relationship between his poetry and mathematics precisely in the term sound, the "sonore" of the second quatrain. If it is accepted that the "or" rhyme is to be read as "pur Anglais", pure English, then Mallarmé separates poetry from mathematics on the basis of the poem's inherent musicality: for mathematics is never said, only inscribed. The poet's use of the word "sonore" in the second quatrain can be read in terms of its immediate reflection, which would refer it back to the "ptyx" in order to highlight the sound of this mark—the sound of nothing. But if it is read it terms of its literality, the "sonore" presents the reader with the following choice[51]: "son-or" that is, "son-or" nothing, sound *or* the unpresentable.

---

48. Meillassoux, *The Number and the Siren: A Decipherment of Mallarmé's* Coup de Dés, p. 223.

49. Milner, *Les Noms Indistincts*, p. 49. "The real encounter is possible, where lalangue, in a brief instance, scintillates." [my trans.]

50. Robert Greer Cohn, *Towards the Poems of Mallarmé*, Berkeley/Los Angeles/London, University of California Press, 1965, p. 144.

51. Pearson also notices this. However, since his analysis does not focus with the concept of the nothing as such, his choice is "son or" X, the symbol of rhyme. Pearson, *Unfolding Mallarmé: The Development of a Poetic Act*, p. 146.

After writing about the magic of rhyme in his previous letter, Mallarmé tells Cazalis that the "ptyx" should be "murmured".[52] This is not a particularly uncharacteristic instruction on Mallarmé's behalf, as the poet often defined poetry through the mutual relation of music and letters. But the inherent sonic quality of poetry means that the "ptyx" cannot be wholly thought of as nothing. As soon as it is marked on the page in terms of its literality, it is immediately remarked in terms of its musicality. For Rancière, the relationship between music and poetry implies a notion of the spectator, one who is there to witness—and indeed hear—poetry. The immediate and necessary relation between poem and spectator means that the nothing in Mallarmé is always "almost-nothing"[53]; always in the symbolic and not—like mathematics—pressing up on the border of the real. Mallarmé himself confirms the impossibility of the nothing—of the "ptyx"—in his sonnet when he writes that there is "nul ptyx". Reading the double negation of the "nul" and the "ptyx" literally, there is *no nothingness* for the poet, who is forced to both murmur and hear any meaningless word that may arise out of the magic of rhyme. This musical quality of poetry is therefore always outside of the imminent relation to itself, which renders the internal mirage of *Ses purs ongles*, the attempt to present unpresentation in and on its own terms, an impossibility a priori.

Despite the fact that appears to be Mallarmé more of an "unconscious contemporary" of Pythagoras than Cantor, it is nonetheless worth ending by referring once more to Badiou's footnote in "Mark and Lack", this time in full:

> If one wants to exhibit writing as such, as to excise its author; if one wants to follow Mallarmé in enjoining the written work to occur with neither subject nor Subject, there is a way of doing this that is radical, secular, and exclusive of every other: by entering into the writings of science, whose law consists precisely in this.
>
> But when literary writing, delectable no doubt but obviously freighted with the marks of everything it denies, presents itself to us as something standing on its own in the scriptural Outside, we *know* in advance (this is a decidable problem...) that it merely sports the *ideology* of difference, rather than exhibiting its real process.
>
> Those writers who balk at the prospect of taking up mathematics should limit their agendas to the honourable principle of their own productions: to be *ideology exposed*, and thereby irreducibly sutured, even if autonomous.[54]

It seems to me that these particular observations exemplify the argument I have been advancing—albeit in a radically different manner. While Mallarmé, that poet intent on "interrogat[ing] our mathematicians," may have had the presentation of unpresentation in mind when writing *Ses purs ongles*, according to Badiou "we know in advance" that any literary work attempting to present an Outside, any rigorous removal of the subject from his or her work, will always

---

52. Mallarmé, *Selected Letters of Stéphane Mallarmé*, p. 87.
53. Rancière, *Mallarmé: The Politics of the Siren*, p. 19.
54. Badiou, 'Mark and Lack', p. 172.

be "freighted with the marks of everything it denies." There is no nothing—nul ptyx—for the poet, for whom the nothing is always already the son-thing.

II

Accelerationism, Prometheanism and Mythotechnesis

Simon O'Sullivan

In a previous meditation on accelerationism—in relation to a modality of art practice that I gave the name (following Sun Ra and Mike Kelly) myth-science—I attempted to get to grips with the concept of hyperstition, and, more particularly, with the mythos of Nick Land.[1] Myth-science, in that essay, was defined as the production of alternative fictions and the calling forth of a different kind of subjectivity attendant on this.[2] Here, in the second part of my enquiry, beginning with a commentary on two essays by two more recent accelerationist thinkers—Reza Negarestani and Ray Brassier (both of whom were inspired by Land)—I want to move from myth-science to a concept of 'mythotechnesis', when this is again defined as a 'fictioning' of reality, but also as a form of libidinal engineering involving the construction of what David Burrows and I call patheme-matheme assemblages.[3] Just as an attempt was made in my previous essay to differentiate myth-science from hyperstition per se, so, here, I attempt to differentiate mythotechnesis from an overly rational (and technological) Prometheanism, whilst also learning from the latter (mythotechnesis might be understood as a form of aesthetics after finitude in this last sense).[4]

---

1. See 'Accelerationism, Hyperstition and Myth-Science', in Tim Matts, Ben Noys and Dane Sutherland (eds.), *Accelerationism and the Occult*, New York, Punctum Books, 2015.

2. In terms of Sun Ra see Kodwo Eshun's discussion, 'Synthesizing the Ominiverse', in *More Brilliant than the Sun: Adventures in Sonic Fiction*, London, Quartet, 1998, pp. 154-163). Mike Kelley, in an essay on Öyvind Fahlström ('Myth Science', in *Öyvind Fahlström: The Installations*, Ostfildern, Hatje Cantz, 1995, pp. 19-27) links the term more particularly to an expanded contemporary art practice.

3. Both Negarestani and Brassier themselves point to their indebtedness to Land. The former in a footnote to the essay 'Drafting the Inhuman: Conjectures on Capitalism and Organic Necrocracy', in Levi Bryant, Nick Srnicek and Graham Harman (eds.), *The Speculative Turn: Continental Materialism and Realism*, Melbourne, re.press, 2011, pp. 182-201; the latter in the 'Inroduction', written with Robin Mackay, to Nick Land, *Fanged Noumena: Collected Writings 1987-2007*, Falmouth, Urbanomic, 2013, pp. 1-54.

4. What follows draws on and develops some of the arguments first sketched out in my review essay (of

ACCELERATIONISM (AND THE INHUMAN)

I began my previous essay by looking to the proposals for an accelerationist aesthetics made by Alex Williams (one of the co-authors of the 'Manifesto for an Accelerationist Politics') in his essay 'Escape Velocities', and to the idea that, as well as hyperstition, this aesthetics might take the form of 'processes of epistemic conceptual navigation'.[5] Williams names Negarestani as the key figure in the development of this philosophical but also—for Williams—aesthetic project. I want to return to this particular proposal as a way into Negarestani's own take on accelerationism:

> The spatialized conception of the navigation and ramification of conceptual spaces at the core of Negarestani's notion of epistemic acceleration has an immediately aesthetic dimension, a highly visualized approach, grounded in the mathematics of topos theory. This abstract mathematical aesthetic of gesture, navigation, limitropism, and pathway-finding re-routes the philosophy of mathematics away from a basis in set theory and logic, and instead seeks an ultimately geometric ground.[6]

In fact, Williams' fourth proposal also connects with Negarestani's outline for a renewed Prometheanism, naming, as it does, a more design-orientated programme to run alongside the strictly philosophical. Again, it is worth quoting:

> Finally, we have the aesthetic of action in complex systems. What must be coupled to complex systems analysis and modeling is a new form of action: improvisatory and capable of executing a design through a practice which works with the contingencies it discovers only in the course of its acting. This can be best described through the Ancient Greek concept of *metis*, a particular mode of cunning craft.[7]

The first question I want to ask is whether these two forms of aesthetics (very broadly construed)—conceptual navigation and a pragmatic *metis*—have a place in art practice, especially one conceived of as a libidinal engineering that might operate against what Gilles Deleuze, following William Burroughs, once called 'control' (and more specifically the production of a normative and standardized subjectivity that is attendant on this). I am also interested in what might be left out of this particular aesthetic (if, indeed, it can be called as such)—that is to say, the limits of philosophical accelerationism when it comes to art practice and the production of subjectivity.

Certainly Negarestani's key accelerationist essay—'The Labour of the Inhuman'—is orientated against a reified idea—or image—of the human that, for Negarestani, can restrict the possibilities of thought, and, indeed, of politics more generally (the 'human' as control we might say).[8] In fact, it is with-

---

#Accelerate: The Accelerationist Reader) 'The Missing Subject of Accelerationism', *Mute*, available at: www.metamute.org/editorial/articles/missing-subject-accelerationism (accessed 14 August 2015). In that essay the term 'myth-science' was used to describe the practices and productions that in the present article come under the heading 'mythotechnesis').

5. Alex Williams, 'Escape Velocities', *E-Flux*, no. 46, 2013, p. 9.

6. Williams, 'Escape Velocities', p. 9.

7. Williams, 'Escape Velocities', p. 9-10.

8. Reza Negarestani, 'The Labour of the Inhuman' in Robin Mackay and Armen Avanessian (eds.),

in a 'kitsch Marxism' that Negarestani sees this particular yoke (the 'consumption of norms') at play, and, in this, his essay harks back to Nick Land's notion of a broadly Left 'Cathedral' as that which places a break on the Promethean impulse.[9] Negarestani's essay is not, however, antihuman (the labour of the inhuman is defined against the antihumanist refusal to revise and construct), but, rather, involves a continuation or 'extended elaboration' (precisely, an acceleration) of the humanist project itself.[10]

This is to attend to an inhuman impulse that is, as it were, 'within' the human, when the former names the commitment to an on-going experimental but also rational process—of conceptual navigation—and the latter names the fetters on this (the 'folk' (everyday and common-sensical) sense of a human self—or 'myth of the given'—that can limit this other adventure insofar as it relies on pre-existing categories and definitions). The labour of the inhuman then involves the continuing interrogation of the category of the human, a program of endless revision and updating that is itself a commitment to always reassess previous commitments. This, we might say, is the human's self-overcoming through reason, albeit of a specifically experimental and speculative type.[11]

In fact, for Negarestani, the human (as a kind of processual project) is defined by reason, and more particularly, by the relation between seeing and doing (inferences and actions) and the task of giving and asking for reasons. This manifests itself most obviously in a shared language and common vocabulary (alongside other 'discursive practices') and it is this 'communal seeing and doing' that defines the labour of the inhuman as a collective, indeed, Universalist project (as well as marking the difference between sapience and sentience).

Although the case for a labour of the inhuman is compelling, we might note a first caveat in relation to the emphasis on language and discourse, insofar as the opposition Negarestani draws between 'stabilised communication through concepts' and 'chaotically unstable types of response and communication', that itself leads to a certain definition of the human and the privileging of the discursive, leaves out other forms of thought that might be said to operate between, or even outside of, these poles (LI, pp. 431-2). Indeed, it seems clear that art practice, for example, tacks between these two, if, indeed, its logics could be said to be staked out by them at all. Certainly questions of aesthetics—and, crucially, of affect—are left aside in this particular labour, but, more generally, there is also the question, following Félix Guattari, of a-signifying semiotics and other forms of expression that do not operate on a discursive register (or not exclusive-

---

#Accelerate: The Accelerationist Reader, Falmouth, Urbanomic, 2015, pp. 427-66 (referred to in text as LI).

9. See my discussion of Land and Neoreaction—or NRx—in the essay mentioned in footnote 1.

10. François Laruelle, in his focus on reclaiming and foregrounding a 'generic' humanity has something in common with Negarestani's labour of the inhuman in this sense, although, it has to be said, the non-philosophical project *per se* orientates itself against any philosophical Mastery—and with that a strictly philosophical definition of the human.

11. We might note the connections with Alain Badiou here and his proposal that a subject, as opposed to a human, is animated by a certain fidelity, or 'idea', that 'raises' them above the creaturely.

ly). These other, often complex semiotics (what Deleuze and Guattari call becomings) somewhat complicate the definition of the human as solely a rational animal.

For Negarestani, however, to dispense with—or even underplay—discursive practices in particular and the 'space of reason' more generally means
'everything lapses either toward the individual or toward a noumenal alterity where a contentless plurality without any demand or duty can be effortlessly
maintained' (LI, p. 434). Although this is to effectively dismiss practices outside
of the space of reason, it is also clear that these discursive practices—and indeed
reason itself—are, for Negarestani, not to be thought of in terms of the habitual and typical (to rely on already existing concepts and categories in this sense
would be to promote an antihumanism). As such, although Negarestani implic-
itly positions himself against a thinker like Henri Bergson (and, by extension,
any vitalist ontology) it might equally be claimed that a form of intuition—or
what we might call a thinking outside of ourselves—is at stake in these non-rea-
sonable operations of reason. [12]

For Negarestani the labour of 'seeing and doing' implies an interventionist
attitude to systems and the mobilisation of atypical forms of thought ('synthetic forms of inference'). This constant updating of one's commitments (which,
again, involves a re-vision of the category of the human itself) cannot but be
experimental—guided by 'complex heuristics' that in themselves produce new
frontiers of action and understanding. A system that does not intervene and interrogate its own norms of understanding and action—again, does not renew its
commitments—is irrelevant at best and obstructive at worse to this other fundamentally constructive and affirmative project.

In terms of aesthetics, and following my brief comment about intuition
above, a key question is what the more speculative types of reason, and 'abductive inference', might 'look' like (especially as the labour of the inhuman itself accelerates ever further beyond familiar categories and concepts). Could
it be, in fact, that it is within art practice that we see complex sets of heuristics
(some of which are not conceptual) at work? Certainly art is involved in 'ma-
nipulable, experimental, and synthetic forms of inference whose consequences
are not simply dictated by premises or initial conditions' (LI, p. 436). Indeed,
in many ways, this kind of experimental pragmatics—*metis*—seems a pretty
good definition of artistic practice. [13] Negarestani gives a footnote here on ab-

---

12. Bergson, no doubt, is who Negarestani, Brassier and others have in mind when they contrast the
private thinker-mystic—and idea of intuition—to a rule based and reasonable sapience that grounds
a collective 'us'. The question here is whether Bergsonian intuition, or indeed Deleuze-Guattarian becomings, are private and individualistic in this sense, or whether they are an instance of the world
thinking through us—or, more simply, a connection between 'us' and the world. I attend further to
this—in relation to Deleuze and Guattari's concept of becoming—in my 'Memories of a Deleuzian: To
Think is Always to Follow the Witches Flight', Henry Somers-Hall, Jeff Bell and James Williams (eds.),
A Thousand Plateaus and Philosophy, Edinburgh, Edinburgh University Press, 2016.

13. In relation to this Negarestani does turn to contemporary art in his essay on Jean-Luc Moulène,
Torture Concrete: Jean-Luc Moulène and the Protocol of Abstraction, New York, Sequence Press, 2014. Here the
labour of the inhuman becomes the labour of abstraction when this names a similar project of turning
away from reified images of thought (especially, here, those that rely on notions of interiority and exteriority) and, indeed, a continuous and experimental redefinition of the latter (involving 'bootstrap-

ductive inference that is worth quoting at length:

> Abductive inference, or abduction, was first expounded by Charles Sand-
> ers Peirce as a form of creative guessing or hypothetical inference which
> uses a multimodal and synthetic form of reasoning to dynamically expand
> its capacities. While abductive inference is divided into different types,
> all are non-monotonic, dynamic, and non-formal. They also involve con-
> struction and manipulation, the deployment of complex heuristic strate-
> gies, and non- explanatory forms of hypothesis generation. Abductive rea-
> soning is an essential part of the logic of discovery, epistemic encounters
> with anomalies and dynamic systems, creative experimentation, and ac-
> tion and understanding in situations where both material resources and
> epistemic cues are limited or should be kept to a minimum. (LI, p. 436,
> footnote 7)

Might we make a further claim that these abductive inferences, and especially 'non-explanatory forms of hypothesis generation' are similar to what I
have elsewhere called fictioning?[14] This involves an experimental (but also lived)
modelling of different realities that proceeds through imagining and imaging,
performing and making, alongside more speculative reasoning (and, in this last
sense, art practice itself often has a conceptual aspect to it). Certainly this kind
of art practice involves the suspension of dominant habits of thought, operates
outside of pre-existing frameworks and protocols, questions accepted 'realities'
and so forth—as well as, crucially, producing something that is of one but not
of one at the same time. There is a kind of politics implied here: in a situation
in which options are increasingly limited (a veritable hemming in of subjectivity
by neoliberalism), these forms of fictioning—again, the production of a different
reality—become crucial and in and of themselves politically charged.

In Part 2 of Negarestani's essay the experimental labour of the inhuman is
portrayed as more specifically navigational, and, indeed, one might say, more
restricted—or, at least, more rigorous and focussed in its unfolding:

> Interaction with the rational system of commitments follows a navigation-
> al paradigm in which the ramifications of an initial commitment must be
> compulsively elaborated and navigated in order for this commitment to
> make sense as an undertaking. It is the examination of the rational fallout
> of making a commitment, the unpacking of its far-reaching consequences,
> and the treating of these ramifications as paths to be explored that shapes
> commitment to humanity as a navigational project. Here navigation is
> not only a survey of a landscape whose full scope is not given; it is also an
> exercise in the non-monotonic procedures of steering, plotting out routes,

---

ping' from the local to the global). Art itself is positioned as one mode of thought amongst others in this
sense—a diversification which fosters novelty and exploration and, as such, serves to redefine the unity
of all modes of thought. In relation to art practice per se Negarestani also lays out a compelling case for
the reciprocal determination of thought on matter/matter on thought, itself 'led' by the positioning of
'generative points' that destabilize pre-existing images and habits. It is here that he also outlines an idea
of knots—between the mathematical and the libidinal for example—as a preeminent example of this
abstraction (and which, as such, have something in common with my own outline of patheme-matheme
assemblages) (see also footnote 27 below on Moulène's idea of the protocol).

14. See my essay 'Deleuze Against Control: from Fictioning to Myth-Science, *Theory Culture Society*, vol. 33, no. 7-8'.

suspending navigational preconceptions, rejecting or resolving incompat-
ible commitments, exploring the space of possibilities, and understanding
each path as a hypothesis leading to new paths or a lack thereof—transits
as well as obstructions. (LI, pp. 443-4)

As Williams remarks this is a highly visual (and, again, compelling) account
of the adventure of reason—abstracted from any specific content and understood as a specifically geometric project (in another essay Negarestani defines
geometry as 'the controlled organization of space as a precondition for the articulation of the unarticulated and the extraction of intelligibility').[15] The routes
and pathways are themselves the hypotheses, with the labour of the inhuman
becoming a form of experimental cartography. That said, despite the focus on
experimentation, there is still a certain normativity at play here insofar as this
navigation involves the positing and unpacking of consequences for humanity
per se. Thought might be untied from a specific telos, but it is, nevertheless, directed toward the immanent 'evolution' of the human. If art practice is also involved in these forms of navigation—again, an experimental cartography that
is both conceptual *and* affective—it seems to me that this is not always in the
service of any ethics in this sense. If art practice is a labour, it is one untethered
from the human (or, indeed, the inhuman).

For Negarestani this conceptual navigation involves a positive feedback loop
effectuated by the deracinating of any origin or fixed definition of the human
insofar as new definitions—inhumanism—feed back to inform the very idea of
the human. As Negarestani remarks: 'As soon as you commit to human, you effectively start erasing its canonical portrait backwards from the future' (LI, p.
446)). This revisioning and updating is the movement of reason itself, its autonomous self-actualisation through the superseding of any previous idea of what it
'is' (and, in this sense, as Negarestani says, his project must be seen in the tradition of Enlightenment thinking). We might note a further connection with Nick
Land here, insofar as the labour of the inhuman shares with teleoplexy (the time
loops of hyperstition) both a certain autonomous and self-evaluating character,
as well as a strange temporality: it retroactively operates back on the past/pres-
ent from a future it has helped construct (not least in the feeding back of the consequences of its understandings and actions into its own self-definition).

The self-actualisation of reason (which turns out to be the real labour of the
inhuman) involves the bootstrapping of more complex functions from simple
ones.[16] Reason's self-assemblage as it were which, in itself, ultimately involves
the augmentation of any given reality (hence the Prometheanism). But reality
(including the reality of a life) is not simply a construct of reason. Or, to put this
another way: reason might well outstrip the human (understood as a particular
psycho-biological platform), but the human (as complex psycho-biological entity) outstrips reason. In terms of any Prometheanism, this is not to instate a border between the given and the made exactly (more on this below), but it is to say

---

15. Reza Negarestani, *Torture Concrete*, p. 17.

16. Negarestani is clear, however, that this self-actualization needs must be accompanied by communal assessment and methodological collectivity; that is, by a politics.

that the made must involve other procedures and materials beyond the conceptual. We might make the case here that the augmentation of reality by the conceptual and technological, but also the affective and fictional is the raison d'être of art practice, at least post Duchamp.

It is at this point that we get one of the most compelling parts of Negarestani's essay which describes this process of construction and revision (and the heuristics mentioned above) as an 'engineering epistemology' in which attention is given to the different levels and hierarchies of any given system (with 'lower level entities' operating as guidance and enhancement of upper levels, and the latter reciprocally operating back down to correct and 'renormalize' so as to allow further construction and exploration) (LI, pp. 460-1). Negarestani suggests the compelling idea of an engineering loop between these different levels—and, as such, the labour of the inhuman is also to draw a map of syntheses that 'ensures a form of descriptive plasticity and prescriptive versatility' (LI, p. 463). Again, could it be that art practice is also involved in this kind of a 'patchwork structure', as Negarestani calls it—of belief and action—and, in particular, that it involves its own engineering loops between different levels albeit these must be seen as affective as well as conceptual (the mapping out of a Spinozist—molecular—unconscious in this sense, or a microphysics of force as Nietzsche might have it).[17]

In this revisionary programme the figure of the engineer becomes the key conceptual personae (in place of the 'advocate of transgression or militant

17. In an earlier essay—'Globe of Revolution: An Afterthought on Geophilosophical Realism', *Identities: Journal of Politics, Gender and Culture*, vol. 8, no. 2, 2011, pp. 25-54—Negarestani writes about these navigational loops in terms of different syntheses between the local and the global, or, more specifically, between a local horizon (man, the earth, and so forth) and the 'open universal continuum' out of which they have been cut. Here the trauma of excision defines us as individuated beings, but also points to the possibility of other pathways to the open besides those that position the latter as an 'unbindable exorbitance'. Indeed, man himself is made up of these nested 'traumata' (that go back to the inorganic) and the role of the revolutionary subject, for Negarestani, is to connect them together, to 'bring about all types of eccentric neighbourhoods between regional horizons of the universal continuum and establish topological transfer between seemingly discrete regional domains' (Reza Negarestani, 'Globe of Revolution', p. 38). It is in this sense that the revolutionary work of what Negarestani also calls the 'Modern Man' has something in common with the labour of the inhuman insofar as it involves a kind of construction that is attendant on an 'unrestricted synthetic vision' and the drawing of a geophilosophical navigational map (Negarestani's thesis on geotrauma has something in common with Deleuze and Guattari's own writings on geophilosophy in this last sense—but it also resonates with Badiou's theory of the subject insofar as the Modern Man is defined by his particular relation to the open (trauma operates in a similar fashion to the event)). Negarestani's essay is concerned with different types of syntheses, diagnosing an exogenic response to the outside (resulting in a terrestrial myopia), whilst also calling for '*alternative* modes of openness'. As he remarks: 'the responsibility of the revolutionary subject is to adopt and grow these germs [defined earlier as: 'asymptopic behaviours, neighbourhoods, overlaps and universal passages between regional fields'] as alternative modes of openness' (Reza Negarestani, 'Globe of Revolution', p. 52). Might we make the case that these alternative modes of openness, by definition, cannot be restricted to one domain of thought—and that, as such, they will include other work besides the conceptual (certainly Negarestsani's comments about how the counter-revolutionary is defined 'by their reactionary and restricted attitude against alternatives, their dismissal of tactical improvisation and unwritten plans, and their fear of asymmetrical fields of synthesis or relation to the open' would imply an openness to this idea (Reza Negarestani, 'Globe of Revolution', p. 35). It seems to me that the accessing of ever deeper nested trauma (understood as points of passage to the open) cannot but involve practices that are, as it were, atypical and non habitual—and that these needs must involve attention to the affective insofar this is the very register of trauma, at least on and in the human subject.

communitarian') and liberation becomes a work of construction—a labour—
that amounts to an *'unlearning* of slavery' (LI, pp. 464-5). *'Freedom is intelligence'*
as Negarestani puts it (LI, p. 465). In passing, we might note Michel Foucault's
late work on technologies of the self here, and, more specifically, Foucault's
remarks about the 'Care of the Self' in which the decision by the subject to
self-apply certain ethical codes brings about a kind of space of freedom.[18] For
Foucault, however, these practices are as much a-signifying and affective as
they are conceptual and discursive—although in both cases—Foucault and
Negarestani—it is a kind of autonomous decision making that, ultimately, defines freedom.

The artist has certainly often been positioned as a transgressor—as outside
(or against) 'the' system—just as more activist-artists have been positioned as
critics of the same. Negarestani suggests a third way: the working within a system that is itself dynamic and progressive. Could we understand the artist as engineer in this sense? On one level, to return to Foucault, this is an injunction to
treat life as experimental matter, as a 'work of art' to be produced. On another
it might mean the construction of artefacts that augment life, though not necessarily in a overly technologically determined manner. It might also be a combination of these two: the libidinal engineering of new and different forms of synthetic life. I will return to this—and develop some of my other comments on
Negarestani's important text (especially around the absence of the affective)—
in the final section of this essay.

PROMETHEANISM (CONTRA FINITUDE)

Like Negarestani, Ray Brassier's philosophical Prometheanism—as laid
out in his own accelerationist essay, 'Prometheanism and its Critics'—identifies a constructive and future-orientated impulse within the human, one that is,
again, rule-based and rational and that, ultimately, might be pitched against all-
too-human preoccupations such as finitude.[19] For Brassier the category of finitude also includes birth and suffering—which, along with death, are typically

---

18. See, for example, Foucault's *The Hermeneutics of the Subject: Lectures at the College de France 1981-82*, F.
Gros (ed.), trans. G. Burchell, London, Palgrave, 2005. Interestingly, Nick Srnicek and Alex William's
'Manifesto for an Accelerationist Politics', in Robin Mackay and Armen Avanessian (eds.), *#Accelerate:
The Accelerationist Reader*, Falmouth, Urbanomic, 2015, pp. 349-378—which lays out a Promethean politics in parallel with Negarestani's philosophy—makes some cryptic remarks regarding the need for
'self mastery' that might be said to resonate with Foucault's Care of the Self: 'We need to posit a collectively controlled legitimate vertical authority in addition to distributed forms of sociality' (Nick Srnicek and Alex Williams, 'Manifesto', p. 358). For a more detailed account of the Care of the Self—
in relation to the production of subjectivity and Lacan's Ethics of Psychoanalysis, see Chapter 2, 'The
Care of the Self versus the Ethics of Desire: Two Diagrams of the Production of Subjectivity (and of the
Subject's Relation to Truth) (Foucault versus Lacan)', of my *On the Production of Subjectivity: Five Diagrams
of the Finite-Infinite Relation*, Basingstoke, Palgrave Macmillan, 2012, pp. 59-88. It is worth pointing out
that the idea of freedom that Foucault outlines—the product of a certain work on the self by the self—
has resonances with Negarestani's own definition of freedom as a work of the human, albeit, again, for
the latter it is a specifically rule based—rational—work: 'Rather than liberation, the condition of freedom is a piecewise structural and functional accumulation and refinement that takes shape as a project of self-cultivation' (LI, p. 464).

19. Ray Brassier, 'Prometheanism and its Critics', in Robin Mackay and Armen Avanessian (eds.),
#Accelerate: The Accelerationist Reader, Falmouth, Urbanomic, 2015, pp. 469-87 (referred to in text as PC).

portrayed as essential and existential givens—limits as it were—that define us *as* human (Brassier has Heidegger and his followers in mind). Brassier's argument is that the positing of an existential authenticity of the given (as in the 'human', 'life', *Dasein* or what have you) *against* the made means that Prometheanism (simply, for Brassier, the idea that we can (re)make ourselves and our world without limits) is ruled out *tout court* or seen as a sin (involving, as it does the heresy of making, or attempting to make, the given).

In fact, in a recourse to Hegel, Brassier suggests that this Prometheanism, with its introduction of a disequilibrium into the world, is also the 'enabling condition of cognitive processes' in general insofar as the latter cannot but involve opposition (understanding) in tandem with conciliation (reason) (PC, p. 470). Prometheanism is not an attempt to heal any subject-object division, but is precisely enabled by it. Alienation begets freedom in this sense.

Brassier's particular take on finitude, and specifically his implicit idea of what suffering might be, could be fine-tuned somewhat insofar as from a certain perspective it is not suffering itself that is the given but, impermanence which, when encountered by a subject desiring permanence, causes suffering as a secondary effect (this is the fundamental insight of Buddhism). The possibility of a state of subjectivity that does not rail against impermanence (does not desire permanence), in particular one that does not identify itself as a separate self (and thus does not suffer in this sense), but instead 'identifies' with the world in general (and its impermanence)—or perhaps does not identify at all—might be said to be gestured towards by Brassier in what he tantalizingly calls a 'subjectivism without selfhood' (although, no doubt for Brassier such a state is to be rationally and scientifically produced rather than through any meditative practice) (PC, p. 471). Brassier's Prometheanism might be said to involve the promise of an existence beyond finitude (an infinite subject perhaps?) in this sense.

Indeed, for Brassier, finitude is less the determining factor of any given subjectivity per se than, again, a fetter on the Promethean impulse itself (this desire to go beyond finitude is a refrain of accelerationism in more or less all its articulations). As with Negarestani there is then both a critique of the human (again, as folk or 'manifest image' and thus as fetter), and an affirmation of it (as sapient rational being—as 'scientific image') and, as such, potentially unbounded.

We might note a specifically technological variant of this contemporary Prometheanism in Benedict Singleton's writings (including his own essay in *#Accelerate: The Accelerationist Reader*), in the impulse to escape planetary gravity and thus the ultimate 'prison': earth.[20] Hence, also, the accelerationist interest in the Russian cosmists (and the inclusion in the aforementioned Reader of 'The Common Task' by Nicolai Fedorov).[21] As Robin Mackay and Armen Ava-

---

20. Benedict Singleton, 'Maximum Jailbreak', in Robin Mackay and Armen Avanessian (eds.), *#Accelerate: The Accelerationist Reader*, Falmouth: Urbanomic, 2014, pp. 491-507.

21. Nicolai Fedorov, 'The Common Task' in Robin Mackay and Armen Avanessian (eds.), *#Accelerate: The Accelerationist Reader*, Falmouth, Urbanomic, 2014, pp. 85-90. We might note here a figure important to the accelerationist aspects of *Anti-Oedipus* and one similarly interested in leaving the planet: William Burroughs. For the latter such an escape, however, was to be achieved not through the latest technological prosthesis (at least as presented by NASA) but by various aesthetic practices involving time-space

nessian's 'Introduction' to the same Reader suggests, Singleton's interest in the technological 'platforms' that capitalism produces, and the concomitant navigational spaces opened up by them, parallels Negarestani and Brassier's own projects of conceptual navigation (Singleton was also the first to deploy the concept of *metis* in relation to the latter).[22]

In passing we might also briefly quote a contemporary anti-Promethean thinker so as to sharpen the differences. Here is Simon Critchley from the very beginning of his relatively recent *The Faith of the Faithless*:

> Our culture is endlessly beset with Promethean myths of the overcoming of the human condition, whether through the fantasy of artificial intelligence, contemporary delusions about robotics, cloning and genetic manipulation or simply though cryogenics and cosmetic surgery. We seem to have enormous difficulty in accepting our limitedness, our finiteness, and this failure is a cause of much tragedy.[23]

For Critchley the human tragedy is not finitude, but precisely the wilful denial of it. Indeed, finitude, in Critchley's account, defines authentic human existence and experience. Such a position, according to Brassier, maintains a structure of transcendence in relation to the human, implying (when not simply asserting) that there is a difference in kind between the latter and other forms of life (it also, crucially, implies that finitude—and suffering—is meaningful). Following Heidegger (and Kant) this is an ontological difference that implies that we can never wholly know ourselves (or 'jump on our own shadow' as Brassier puts it) (PC, p. 476). Or, at least, if we do objectivate ourselves—make ourselves into an object of knowledge (a particularly complex machine)—then we risk losing something essential about our humanness (and, indeed, risk losing any position from which to maintain an 'ought' or other normative principles).[24]

This anti-Promethean philiosophical attitude might be summed up with the idea that man cannot be understood as merely a 'catalogue of empirical properties', and that there is also a fragile equilibrium between the made and the given that ought to be respected (or, more simply, the idea that the world was made at all) (PC, p. 477). Brassier's audacity (which gives his essay its striking quality) is simply to question this ought, this idea of a given equilibrium (or, again, the idea that the world was made at all), and thus to 'free' the Promethean impulse itself and with it the potential of the human (who, in this sense, does not have a defining limit; Brassier's Prometheanism, as he remarks, refuses the ontologiza-

---

disruptions: the cut-up, dream-machine and so forth (thanks to David Burrows for this point)).

22. Robin Mackay and Armen Avanessian, 'Inroduction', in Robin Mackay and Armen Avanessian (eds.), *#Accelerate: The Accelerationist Reader*, Falmouth, Urbanomic, 2014, pp. 32-3.

23. Simon Critchley, *The Faith of the Faithless: Experiments in Political Theology*, London, Verso, 2012, p. 1. I want to thank Nicole Denham for alerting me to this explicitly *non*-accelerationist character of Critchley's writings.

24. We might note here that Negarestani's labour of the inhuman, insofar as it involves a commitment, proceeds from an ought, one that arises from an idea that there is a difference of the human *qua* reason. On the one hand then Negarestani provides an ethics, in Spinoza's sense, to Brassier's colder empirical work—but, on the other, Negarestani might be accused, from Brassier's perspective, of smuggling in a difference in kind—an ontologization of the human?—under the cover of reason itself.

tion of finitude) (PC, p. 478).

It seems to me that art practice, at least of a kind, is also Promethean in this sense insofar as it refuses a certain kind of finitude (one thinks, again, of Duchamp and his 'explorations' beyond typical space-time) but also other limits more generally (one thinks of the very movement of the avant-garde that specifically refuses any predetermined parameters or logics of what art is). Indeed, art practice also interferes in the equilibrium of the world—its fictions disrupt the normal run of things, or, philosophically speaking, its representations and simulations undo truth claims. On the other hand it must also be remarked that art is often the name for practices concerned with finitude (with mortality and so forth), and, more generally, cannot but concern itself with finite materials (it is a concrete rather than abstract practice in this sense). Art, as Félix Guattari once suggested, is necessarily a practice of the finite, but one that opens towards the infinite.

That said, clearly, art is not simply or narrowly technological—it does not produce anything 'useful' in this sense, but operates in a different paradigm (to reference Guattari once more, we might say an ethico-aesthetic paradigm as opposed to a techno-scientific one). If art practice has its own Promethean impulse this is not necessarily to further human evolution (even when this moves beyond the human per se)—or, indeed, to further the progress of reason. It is less teleologically driven it seems to me (at least, since the end of a certain kind of Modernism), involved in its own experimental constructions that draw as much on past resources as contemporary and future-orientated ones. Indeed, it is often this mobilization of what Raymond Williams once called the residual (alongside more emergent culture) that gives certain art practices their peculiar traction and political efficacy in the world (after all, the past (as well as the future) can be mobilized as a powerful resource against the impasses of the present).[25] In fact, the present is never simply homogenous, temporally speaking, but involves a heterogeneity of times (Raymond Williams' writings provide a useful mapping of this complexity). This complex make up of the contemporary can sometimes be occluded in the accelerationist pre-occupation with the future.

As with Negarestani, the Promethean project is expounded in Brassier's essay as ultimately the desire to 're-engineer' the human itself (and, in this, as Brassier remarks, the project is again the direct successor to Enlightenment thought and practice, as most obvious in the pre-eminent Promethean thinker of modern times: Marx). In part this involves a refusal of transcendence and, instead, a kind of tracking of immanence via rule governed activity. To quote Brassier:

> ...rather than trying to preserve the theological equilibrium between the
> made and the given, which is to say, between immanence and transcend-
> ence, the challenge for rationality consists in grasping the stratification of
> immanence, together with the involution of structures within the natural

---

25. I will be attending to this in a further essay on 'Myth-Science as Residual Culture and Magical Thinking'—which, in part, will involve an encounter between Williams' temporal mapping and Gilbert Simondon's work on phase-shifts (the emergence of technicity from an originary magical mode of existence—and the latter's contemporary analogue in aesthetics).

order through which rules can arise out of physical patterns. According to this conception of rationality, rules are means of coordinating and sub-suming heterogeneous phenomena, but means that are themselves histor-ically mutable. (PC, p. 486)

We might ask here where this leaves a pursuit like art practice? Is it a rule-governed activity in this sense? More broadly we might ask (once again) whether art can be understood as producing any rational knowledge, even in the minimal sense of rule-governed behaviour? When it comes to art it seems to me that it might be better to replace this particular concept of rules (concerned with 'coordinating and subsuming heterogeneous phenomena') with a concept of rules that are more like protocols for experimentation.[26] Rules as a means of 'going on' in practice.[27] Indeed, art practice here is like a move in a game for which the precise rules, in fact, are unknown—or are made up as the 'game' progresses. This might, for example, involve the production of fictions within fictions (and so on). Ultimately this is to produce a kind of density, even an opac-ity, built up by this nesting of one set of fictions in another. Art, when it is a prac-tice, can constitute its own world in this sense.

Brassier suggests that it might be Alain Badiou who opens the way for a con-tinuing of this Promethean project in relation to the subject (albeit Badiou's ac-count of the subject and event would need to be linked, for Brassier, to 'an anal-ysis of the biological, economic, and historical processes that condition rational subjectivation' (PC, p. 487)). In a sense Badiou is indeed the template insofar as philosophy, for Badiou, is not itself involved in the production of the subject (as opposed to art, politics and science), but, rather, is a reflection on these process-es. Likewise, Brassier's philosophy is really a meditation on science as Promet-hean—rather than itself a form of Promethean practice—although, certainly, a different kind of scientific image of the subject is at stake in Brassier's work.

In 'The View from Nowhere', Brassier turns his attention more explicitly to

---

26. Negarestani has something similar in mind when he writes about Moulène's practice in relation to 'protocols of cruelty':

What Moulène calls 'protocol' when describing his *modus operandi* in making art is a performative system or germ of procedurality. It is a thought-manual furnished with materially influenced be-haviours and evolving logics of operation. It is called protocol insofar as it governs the artist's con-duct according to entanglements between (normative) laws of thought, (representational) laws of im-agination and (dynamic-natural) material laws. To follow protocol is to be prepared to change one's approach in accordance with how interactions of matter and thought develop and how the space of abstraction is reorganized and diversified. In other words, the protocol offers new choices of disequi-librium for the entanglement between thought, imagination and material (Reza Negarestani, 'Tor-ture Concrete', p. 9).

In Brassier's terms Negarestani's definition of protocol is Promethean insofar as it involves the inro-duction of a productive disequilibrium into the world.

27. Brassier is certainly not oblivious to this idea that an experimental practice requires protocols—rules—even if these are to do with what to avoid or negate. See for example his earlier essay 'Genre is Obsolete', *Multitudes*, no. 28, 2007, available at: http://www.multitudes.net/Genre-is-Obsolete/ (ac-cessed 13th August 2015) that considers 'Noise' performances and practitioners in this respect. That said, for Brassier, 'Noise', when it is 'successful', is less about aesthetics or affect (or, indeed, 'experience') than about producing a certain cognitive dissonance and negation of genre (a 'generic anomaly' as Brassier puts it). Brassier links this in his essay to some developments in neuroscience—and thus, we might say, the essay gestures to more recent work (such as the essay in the footnote immediately below).

this other mode or form of life—the nemocentric subject (a subjectivism without self)—that might be produced through the advanced operations of reason as it is manifested in neuroscience (this being a subject (if that is still a useful term) that shuttles between the folk and scientific image of the human).[28] The account of this future non-self agent—'a physical entity gripped by concepts: a bridge between two reasons, a function implemented by causal processes but distinct from them'—is compelling (as is the critique of phenomenology), but is it not also the case that the rational (and communist) Promethean project—especially as manifest in science—needs must be married with a more affective—libidinal—type of engineering (that deals with desire), and would it not be this kind of encounter and experimental conjunction that really produces a radically different kind of subject?

And what about the theme of fictioning in all this? Would these new forms of life need new kinds of fiction (different kinds of narrative and/or image as cohering devices)—or, perhaps, it is in fiction itself (rather than philosophy) that we might actually find blueprints and prototypes of these new forms. Science Fiction is clearly an important resource in this respect. Indeed, towards the end of 'Prometheanism and its Critics' Brassier himself turns to J. G. Ballard for future-evidence of this new kind of human who, as it were, both engenders and is engendered by the Promethean project. Ballard's protagonists live a Prometheanism that is far from comfortable, or, indeed predictable ('the psychic and cognitive transformations undergone by Ballard's protagonists are nothing if not savage and violent' (PC, p. 486)). In fact, these characters—could we call them Brassier's conceptual personae?—are also libidinal figures (Ballard's novels track this other alien, often inorganic sexuality). They are inventions, experimental configurations of reason and affect given proper names—forms of synthetic life that might be gestured towards in philosophy, but are given life in art.[29]

MYTHOTECHNESIS (AS PATHEME-MATHEME)

In a short commentary on the 'Manifesto for Accelerationist Politics' Antonio Negri lends his support to a renewed accelerationism, but also gestures to certain caveats such as the overly technologically determined nature of the thesis, and to certain key omissions such as a consideration of the commons and questions to do with the production of subjectivity, including 'the agonistic use of passions'.[30] For myself, following on from my commentaries above, this last

---

28. Ray Brassier, 'The View from Nowhere', *Identities: Journal of Politics, Gender and Culture*, vol. 8, no. 2, 2011, pp. 7-23.

29. Ballard's books are, precisely, of the imagination in this sense. In fact, ultimately, for Brassier, the imagination has a part to play in Prometheanism, which cannot but have a phantasmagoric aspect (albeit one that might be diagnosed, analysed and, presumably, 'cured'): 'Prometheanism promises an overcoming of the opposition between reason and imagination: reason is fuelled by imagination, but it can also remake the limits of imagination' (PC, p. 487).

30. Antonio Negri, 'Some Reflections on the Manifesto', in Robin Mackay and Armen Avanessian (eds.), *#Accelerate: The Accelerationist Reader*, Falmouth, Urbanomic, 2014, pp. 365-78. There is also Patricia Reed's critical commentary, 'Seven Prescriptions for Accelerationism', in Robin Mackay and Armen Avanessian (eds.), *#Accelerate: The Accelerationist Reader*, Falmouth, Urbanomic, 2014, pp. 523-36, which points to a number of possible variations and further accelerations of the Manifesto, perhaps most interestingly (at least in the context of my own essay) the call to 'fictionalize'. For Reed this is tied

theme is perhaps the most crucial missing aspect of accelerationism (and, indeed, of any aesthetics that leads from this) at least as the latter is presented in the essays by Negarestani and Brassier or, indeed, in the Manifesto which might be said to be a political instantiation of the philosophical work. Indeed, more often than not the focus of recent accelerationism is specifically not the affective make up of subjectivity—with claims, rather, about the latter's obsolescence, especially in the wake of the 'rise of the machines', the foregrounding of only the rational subject, or, as in the Manifesto, the offering of no detail on this crucial area beyond a passing swipe at 'affective self-valorization'.[31]

In relation to an explicit politics, this non-engagement with the affective complexities of life means accelerationism offers only a partial picture of the issues and problems at hand—and, indeed, of their possible solutions. For capitalism is not just an abstract inhuman agency 'out there', instantiated in forms of technology, and so forth (that is, as a supra-molar entity). It is also 'in here'— producing our very subjectivity on what we might call a molecular level. Capitalism goes all the way down, determining our affective states, as well as our very desires, dreams and the contours of our innermost worlds. Subjectivity, then, is not solely a rational business in this sense or, at least, those aspects not involved in the project of reason are also crucial to our sense of who and what we are—or, indeed, what we might become.

Any subjectivity 'beyond' capitalism (even one produced from within the latter) will have to deal with this, and, indeed, get involved in the whole complex mess of being alive, not least addressing the various affective tonalities that capitalism engenders (from an omnipresent ambient anxiety, to resentment and depression, to all out paralysing fear). It will not be enough to take on—or commit to—a new set of ideas, or put our faith solely in technological progress; subjectivity has to be produced differently at this level. This is not to say that giving attention to this area is the most important aspect of any ethico-political project today, but it is to say that without an account of (and experimentation with) the affective production of subjectivity (very broadly construed), any diagnosis of the problems produced in and by capitalism, or strategy to deal with them (including a renewed Prometheanism), remains too abstract (or, remains abstract in only a partial way).[32]

---

to the production of a new *demos*, or new collective will and, more generally to the role of belief within any radical politics. In relation to my own take on accelerationism, Reed also points to the need both to attend to the 'distribution of affect' in any accelerationist agenda ('in equal partnership with calls for operational, technological and epistemic restructuration') and to the more Guattarian idea of a 'commitment to an eccentric future' (although it is not entirely clear what Reed has in mind here) (Patricia Reed, 'Seven Prescriptions', p. 528 and 527).

31. Nick Srnicek and Alex William, 'Manifesto', p. 351.

32. To a certain extent all this is also the business of schizoanalysis especially as Guattari understood it—as a form of expanded analysis and accompanying experimental technology of the subject (involving non-human encounters as well as other models of and for a non-typical (and non-standard) subjectivity). I go into more detail on this in the section on 'Mapping the Diagonal: on the Production of Subjectivity' of my review mentioned in footnote 4 where I suggest that Guattari's writings might offer the missing framework for thinking a post-capitalist subjectivity (in this regard see especially Guattari's 'The New Aesthetic Paradigm', in *Chaosmosis: An Ethico-Aesthetic Paradigm*, trans. Paul Bains and Julian Pefanis, Sydney, Power Publications, 1995, pp. 98-118).

It is important to note that this does not imply the reinstatement of a phenomenological self that experiences the world (an individual that *has* the affects) nor, a straightforward vitalism that is pitched against a colder abstraction. Affects—or becomings—are themselves abstract. They take the subject out of themselves—or they involve the irruption of something different—non-human—within the subject (when 'human' names a very particular historical configuration and self model). Indeed, molecular encounters—that might well involve the biological and chemical in conjunction with the technological and digital—produce unforeseen compounds that themselves are generative of other forms of thought and, indeed, themselves determine what thinking itself might become.[33]

It is here where the conceptual meets these other kinds of thought (defined in its broadest possible sense) that we might then find a role for art practice understood as also a technology of the inhuman (the production of something that does not—as Jean-François Lyotard once put it—offer a reassuring image to and of a subjectivity already in place). But also as a practice that attends to, and experiments with, the different registers of subjectivity, including, crucially (but *not* exclusively), the affective. Here art's ability to produce that which was previously unseen and unheard, untimely images and other forms that 'speak' back to us—as if they came from an elsewhere—is especially important and, again, takes on a political character (the imaging/imagining of alternatives). These other, perhaps stranger, image-worlds and fictions are an address not to us, but to something within us (or, to the collectivity that we are 'behind' any standardized molar identity).[34]

Besides the essay by Alex Williams with which I began this article (itself part of a special *e-flux* issue on 'Accelerationist Aesthetics')—and the inclusion of an extract from Shulamith Firestone's *The Dialectics of Sex* in *#Accelerate: the Accelerationist Reader*—there is little to be found in core accelerationist texts that significantly addresses the issue of aesthetic production itself, and even with Firestone the latter is seen as something to be overcome as technology renders the utopian imaging of art redundant.[35] In fact, it seems to me, accelerationism does not really have a place for art practice, tending to position it as secondary—at

---

33. Deleuze writes well on these new kinds of compound, or folds, in the appendix of his book on *Foucault*, trans. Sean Hand, Minneapolis, University of Minnesota Press, 1988, pp. 124-32.

34. In relation to this idea of art's inhospitableness to the already constituted subject (but that nevertheless offers something) see my 'Art Practice as Fictioning (or, myth-science)', *diakron*, no. 1, 2014, available at: http://www.diakron.dk (accessed 13 August 2015).

35. There is, however, an increasing amount of essays and publications on aesthetics and Speculative Realism—some of which, such as the anthology on *Speculative Aesthetics* (Robin Mackay, Luke Pendrell and James Trafford (eds.), Falmouth, Urbanomic, 2014), contain writing directly related to an accelerationist agenda (indeed, the latter volume contains a contribution by Brassier amongst others, that ends with this intriguing reflection:

... perhaps it's not so much a question of pitting the conceptual against the aesthetic, or concepts against affects, but of developing a conception of aesthetics which is not exclusively governed by either: one dedicated to reconstructing sensation on the basis of new modes of conceptualization. A Promethean constructivism will engineer new domains of experience, and it is these new domains that will need to be mapped by a reconfigured aesthetics (Ray Brassier, 'Prometheanism and Real Abstraction', p. 77.).

best a forerunner to the real business of technological development, a poor cousin to philosophy.

But art practice—especially today, and more generally since the expanded field of the 1960s (if not post Duchamp)—is more than just this folk image. Indeed, as I suggested above, it involves its own experiments and navigational strategies that parallel the rational and technological and even, in some respects (in terms of the production of images and fictions) outrun it. It is also with art, or with aesthetic productions more generally, that we see real attempts at libidinal engineering—again, forms of synthetic life. These more expanded and performative practices can involve the kind of conjunctions I also gestured to above: non-human becomings (animal, plant … molecular) alongside, for example, other experiments in and with digitally produced sound and image and, indeed, with what has become known as a 'post-media aesthetics' in general. This is to say nothing of practices that might involve even stranger conjunctions between man and machine, especially around biology, coding and algorithms—or, to return to some of my comments above, practices that might utilize the residual alongside the emergent (or even pre-emergent). In these kinds of 'performative fictions' desire is invested and mobilised in a manner rarely encountered within more narrowly focused conceptual work. Might we reiterate the claim I made earlier in this essay that art practice in this sense is itself Promethean (precisely, artifice)?

In this respect I am very much in agreement with Patricia Reed's critical commentary that ends the *#Accelerate: The Accelerationist Reader*, and which takes the 'Manifesto for an Accelerationist Politics' to task for, amongst other things, not attending to the constructive project of imagining alternatives (to 'eccentricate' as Reed puts it), and also, in fact, to the editors' own call (towards the end of their 'Introduction') for 'new science-fictional practices, if not necessarily in literary form'.[36] Although, in the 'Introduction' the claim is made that the more recent accelerationist treatises are a response to a situation in which the polemics and experiments of a 1990s cyberculture have been blunted, then assimilated, in web 2.0 and the general algorithmic character of social media (and, indeed, that these essays are intended as a mapping out of something more conceptual as a corrective to that other more aesthetic scene), nevertheless it remains the case that something has been lost in the sole focus on the rational (even when, as with Brassier and Negarestani, this might involve more speculative kinds of reason and also imply a kind of human/inhuman subject). In fact, once again, my suspicion is that this omission is also apparent to the editors of the Reader themselves. Why else end the 'Introduction'—after an account of how a machine-produced 'transformative anthropology' requires a newly thought rational subject—with the claim, entirely correct in my opinion, that this latter subject will also need to be a vitalist one?[37]

Elsewhere David Burrows and I have attempted to map out some of this terrain analytically, in terms of patheme-matheme assemblages, where the former

---

36. Patricia Reed, 'Seven Prescriptions', p. 524; Mackay and Avanessian, 'Introduction', p. 37.

37. Mackay and Avanessian, 'Introduction', p. 46.

names the formal (or we might say vertical) character of subjectivity, and the latter names an equally abstract—though in a different sense—more vitalist, 'creaturely' and affective character (something more horizontal).[38] The reader will recognize both Lacan and Guattari here, and, indeed, our intention was to produce a transversality between the two—to metamodelize (to use Guattari's phrase) these two analysts. This experimental diagramming—when it is drawn out, but also performed—is also, it seems to me, a kind of schizoanalysis. Or, in fact—and following François Laruelle—a non-schizoanalysis (it uses the tools and models of schizoanalysis but not necessarily for therapeutic aims).

In terms of the Lacanian matheme we might suggest a resonance with certain aspects of accelerationism, especially that of Negarestani and Brassier, insofar as, in Lacan's terms, the matheme is a kind of inhuman—again, formal—parasite on its animal host. Indeed, the matheme, especially as it is later developed and deployed by Badiou, is that which renders the human animal subject. In terms of the patheme, once again, it seems to me that this is the missing subject of more recent accelerationist texts. But it is also worth noting that certain pre-cursors to accelerationism had a pathic aspect—or, again, an affective charge, as I suggested in this essay's companion piece—on hyperstition and Nick Land.[39]

I mentioned Badiou above and, in fact, it seems to me that he—rather than Deleuze-Guattari—is a key progenitor of the inhumanism of recent accelerationism insofar as Badiou is also explicitly not interested in the affective make up of subjectivity (and, indeed, follows a war of attrition against the human animal).[40] Badiou might be said to be on the side of accelerationism (if it makes sense to take sides) in so far as he affirms a subjective process that is alien to the human animal itself. That said, Badiou does, of course, offer a theory of the subject (this is at the core of his philosophical œuvre), and, as such, it might be argued that Badiou himself offers us the missing subject of accelerationism. Certainly Negarestani's labour of the inhuman has something in common with both Badiou's fidelity to an event (in *Being and Event*) and his 'Living for an Idea' (in *Logics of Worlds*) and Brassier, as we saw in the previous section of this essay, refers to Badiou when thinking about the relation between a renewed Promet-

---

38. See 'S/Z or Art as Non-Schizoanalysis', in Ian Buchanan and Lorna Simpson (eds.), *Schizoanalysis and Art*, London, Bloomsbury, pp. 253-78. In this essay we also attempt a metamodelization of Guattari (specifically his four ontological functions) with the late Lacan's RSI knot (Lacan's sinthome is also allied with what we call a 'mytheme' that might function as kind of cohering device for an art practice). Many of the ideas that follow—on mythotechnesis specifically—were developed with Burrows and in the context of our collaborative art practice—or 'performative fiction'—*Plastique Fantastique* (see www.plastiquefantastique.org).

39. See footnote 1.

40. Things are, of course, more complex and overdetermined than this, with a whole cast of philosophical precursors to accelerationism. Alongside Badiou, and in the distancing of Deleuze-Guattari, we might note, for example, for Negarestani, Wilfred Sellars and Robert Brandom; and for Brassier (as well as the previous) Thomas Metzinger and Paul and Patricia Chruchland (indeed, we might suggest that accelerationism is at least partly characterized, philosophically speaking, as a synthesis between continental and analytic traditions (and departs from Speculative Realism, in this respect—as well as from those Object-Orientated trajectories that constitute the other main philosophical offshoot from the latter).

heanism and a subject adequate and appropriate to this.

Could it be argued that what characterizes some aspects of more recent accelerationism—as opposed to something more Landian—is the replacement of Deleuze-Guattari (and especially the thesis of *Anti-Oedipus*) with Badiou, and, with this, a foregrounding of the formal (and of mathematizeable thought in general)? It has often been argued that Deleuze is the key interlocutor for Badiou, but, in relation to the matheme, I think it is really Guattari who is Badiou's opposite insofar as Guattari attends specifically to the affective (as well as being precisely a non-philosopher).[41] The basic philosophical-analytic schema looks something like this:

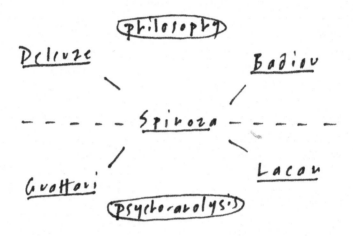

There is more to be said here, about two different trajectories of French thought, the animal (on the left) and the formal (on the right)—and both Brassier and Badiou have written on this. An especially interesting line of thought is Deleuze's difference to Lacan particularly around the idea of the unconscious.[42] Of particular note in the diagram is the figure of Spinoza as common root to both the philosophical and psychoanalytical categories, but also as purveyor of both the creaturely (affect) and the rational (reason), depending on what one reads of *The Ethics* and indeed *how* one reads it. We might map some of the accelerationist texts, in particular Negarestani and Brassier, between Badiou and Lacan (insofar as both are philosophical, but also attend to a kind of subject (albeit, a rational one) which means they have an psychoanalytic aspect (though, crucially, no account of an unconscious)). This very partial and reductive schema (which leaves out any analytic philosophical precursors) also allows a more

41. For more on these distinctions see Chapter 3, 'The Aesthetic Paradigm: From the Folding of the Finite-Infinite Relation to Schizoanalytic Metamodelization (to Biopolitics) (Guattari)', and Chapter 4, 'The Strange Temporality of the Subject: Life In-between the Infinite and Finite (Deleuze contra Badiou)' of my *On the Production of Subjectivity: Five Diagrams of the Finite-Infinite Relation*, Basingstoke: Palgrave Macmillan, 2012, pp. 89-124 and 125-168.

42. For a fine study of this area see Christian Kerslake's *Deleuze and the Unconscious*, London: Continuum, 2007.

pointed reflection on the differences between an accelerationism positioned on the right of the diagram (again, between Badiou and Lacan) with that on the left, between Deleuze and Guattari (where we might place Land and Ccru more generally). It also gestures, pace Spinoza, to a composite subject—between the right and left sides—and, more crucially, to what *different* composite subjects might look like.[43]

Art practice, it seems to me, can be involved in this kind of experimental and synthetic modeling. Again, this is not exactly a therapeutics (art practice does not have any kind of clinical responsibility in this sense). In fact, it is also, ultimately, not simply the production of subjectivity (at least when this is only narrowly construed), not least as it tends to produce something to be encountered by others. The essay I mentioned above—written with David Burrows—develops the idea of art practice as a holding pattern for points of collapse in this sense —maintaining only a minimum consistency, whilst also operating as a scene of rupture. Indeed, such practices are not *for* a human subject that is already in place, or, at least, they threaten to undo this subject. But certainly these practices offer up something—different models, diagrams, performances—different fictionings—for more experimental modes of being (or becoming) in and with the world (for a subjectivity to come perhaps?).

If reason and science are of the matheme, broadly construed, which is to say the Promethean impulse in its rational and technological form, then mythotechnesis might be a name for these practices that attend to a kind of vitalism alongside the more artificial constructs of the human, practices that involve an abstraction that is both formal and affective (or, to put this another way, mythotechnesis is a diagonal between the rational and the animal). Any accelerationism, it seems to me, will need to explore, and experiment with, this terrain—participate in the construction of its own kinds of mythotechnesis, its own kinds of images and fictions, assemblages and figures, so that it might have a transformative traction on the world, and especially on those who dwell within it.

If this mythotechnesis is part of what a 'radical political response to capitalism' might look like then these different synthetic forms of life will also need to express and capture our collective desires. They require, precisely, libidinal engineering—as well as our participation in this. This project of reclaiming and then deploying a new collective—optical, aural *and* libidinal—unconscious is the necessary accompaniment, it seems to me, to any focus on reason and rationality and operates as a corrective to any faith in technological development as itself the sole progenitor of new and different ways of being in the world.

---

43. It seems to me that Mark Fisher's writings are pertinent here—see in particular those on his blog at http://k-punk.org (accessed 15 August 2015)—especially in their prescient call for new libidinal figures adequate and appropriate to a reanimated Left (could we position Fisher on a transversal between Deleuze and Lacan?).

12

Pink Data: Tiamaterialism and the Female Gnosis of Desire

Tessa Laird

Reza Negarestani's *Cyclonopedia* has been described variously as apocalypse the-ology, aberrant demonology, a living cauldron and a philosophic grimoire.[1] Yet in falling under the spell of Negarestani's crypto-archaeological tract, it's easy to forget its preface: a semi-autobiographical narrative penned by the American artist Kristen Alvanson. She calls it 'Incognitum hactenus', which Negarestani later translates as 'Anonymous-until-Now', or, a 'mode of time connecting abys-sal time scales to our chronological time', in which 'anything can happen for some weird reason; yet also, without any reason, nothing at all can happen'.[2]

Nothing really does happen in Alvanson's preface, except that she further mongrelizes *Cyclonopedia*'s already deeply questionable pedigree by creating a quasi-fictional status for herself and Negarestani, as characters alongside other fictional inventions, including the living manuscript of *Cyclonopedia* itself.

Reading 'Incognitum hactenus' against Alvanson's art practice shines a beam of pink light on a desire I will code *female*, one which begs penetration, not by the fallible phallus, but by an influx of *data*. Parallels can be traced in the very differ-ent, but equally data-hungry art practices of two other women, Camille Henrot (France) and Jess Johnson (Australia). The most profound example of pink pene-tration, however, comes in the form of science fiction: Philip K. Dick's 1981 cult classic *VALIS*. Dick's novelistic worm holes perform a sci-fi invagination which unwillingly enacts the Tiamaterialism propounded in *Cyclonopedia*, a return of the repressed 'nested-vaginas' of the archaic-chaotic mother goddess, Tiamat.

Alvanson begins her narrative with the story of a woman flying into Istan-bul, and taking up residence in a hotel where she awaits a rendezvous with an

---

1. I've been thinking of it as a kind of ()hole Earth Catalog (with an 'evaporative W'), a dystopian psychedelia, the bad trip to end all bad trips...

2. Reza Negarestani, *Cyclonopedia*, Melbourne, re.press, 2010, p. 49.

entity indicated in the text by a Persian initial unpronounceable in English. Whether he is an avatar of Negarestani, and she of Alvanson, remains unclear. The rendezvous never occurs. Instead, 'Alvanson' finds a box of notes written in black pen and pink highlighter under her bed. Ostensibly by Dr. Hamid Parsani (another Negarestani avatar), these end up forming the basis of the *Cyclonopedia* text.

The pestilent palimpsest of the Parsani-Negarestani notes aren't all that Alvanson finds inside the dusty box—there is also a pink mother of pearl bracelet which fits her perfectly, and a card for a computer repair shop, with directions to retrieve a laptop there. Hot on the trail of intrigue, Alvanson visits the shop but declines to pay for the dodgy laptop, instead surreptitiously stealing the CD from its drive. We never get to hear what, if anything, is on this CD, because Alvanson's narrative jumps from the computer shop to a liquor store, and then states, rather obliquely, 'If I can't pass through these plot holes, then it is the best to leave my own holes'.[3]

Alvanson's *holes*, it turns out, are pink. She perforates Negarestani's petroleum-black scrawls with vivid pink highlights, (and, incidentally, a highlighter is a textual tool which is also known as a *magic marker*). The colour pink, for Alvanson, operates as a marker of magic, or of (willfully embodied) desire, or is that the same thing anyway? As if virally infected by the dodgy CD, Alvanson vomits this hallucinogenic pink paragraph:

> Pink magnolias, NYPL, NYBG, cherry blossoms in DC more pink... a fleshed out nipple, a bleeding heart, little girls' pink velvet ribbons, pink spaces, pink sweater set, Christos' [sic] pink, pink blush, or the lack of need for blush cotton candy Pink poodles or pink cats pink cover of Laches the most perfect shade of pink lipstick pink cd holders pink pearl necklace pink pearl earrings pink camisole pink highlighter pink Christmas lights and pink flowers—peonies, tulips, Christmas Cactus in bloom in my room, pinkish lilac, pink hydrangea, pink rose of sharons, rare pink poppies, carpet roses, spinning in pink flowers... begonia, spider flowers, cosmos, sweet peas, toadflax, moonwort, petunias, phlox!, butterfly flower, sun moss, wax pink lilies, caprifoliaceae, pink wisteria, malvaceae, oyster plant in pink, floxglove [sic], caryophyllaceae, heather, theaceae, magnolias, chinese crab apple flash by my eyes, Pink torrent.[4]

A BitTorrent is a file-sharing protocol enabling the exchange of large amounts of data over the Internet. Alvanson's interlude in the seedy computer shop seems to have opened a channel for the inflow of information via the colour pink. This is strangely reminiscent of Dick's *VALIS*, which tells the pseudo-autobiographical story of the author's own theophany, or 'in-breaking of God'[5] via a *beam of pink data*. In *VALIS*, it's Dick's alter-ego, the improbably named Horselover Fat, who has 'beam after beam of information-rich coloured light" fired at his brain, 'blinding him and fucking him up and dazing and dazzling him, but

---

3. Kristen Alvanson, 'Incongnitum hactenus', ibid, p. xviii.

4. Ibid.

5. Philip K. Dick, *VALIS*, Vintage Books, Random House, New York, 1991, p. 39. '...a theophany is an in-breaking of God, an in-breaking which amounts to an invasion of our world...'

imparting to him knowledge beyond the telling'.[6]

As with Alvanson's preface, *VALIS* turns the autobiographical into a series of nested fictions. Dick personally experienced theophany (or a schizoid turn, depending on your perspective) after painful dental surgery. Apparently, Dick was listening to that pinkest of songs, *Strawberry Fields Forever* when he was blinded by the pink light, and the words in the song were rearranged to tell him that his son had a birth defect which would kill him if it wasn't operated upon immediately. Dick commented that the pink colour operated like binary code, and talked with a female AI voice.[7]

So, while we're thinking about binaries and codes, such as female versus male, and pink versus blue, let's not forget that this particular assignation of colour to gender is a relatively recent cultural phenomenon (post World War I) and indeed, during the great war, pink was recommended for boys as the baby version of warlike, masculine red.

By contrast, pink has become, in recent years, a crypto-capitalist cult for female children, in a way which is terrifying, sickening, and deeply fascinating. Alvanson's pink torrent of language betrays a desire for the more *grown up* aspects of pink culture, with her 'pink sweater set', 'Pink poodles', 'Pink lipstick', and a litany of pink flowers.

That Alvanson's brush with the infected CD leads to a supra-digital influx of pink-tinted *information* is made obvious at the start of her rosy rant, which namechecks NYPL, the New York Public Library: second largest library in the world, exceeded only by the Library of Congress in Washington DC. Alvanson notes 'cherry blossoms in DC more pink', as though 'more pink' equates to *more data*. Indeed, Dick claims of *his* pink beam, that 'it fired whole libraries at him in nanoseconds'.[8] Another of Alvanson's acronyms is NYBG, the New York Botanical Garden, where a different kind of data is stored. Michael Pollan writes that '…the flowering garden is a place you immediately sense is thick with information, thick as a metropolis, in fact'.[9]

Alvanson's floral list includes Caryophyllaceae, more commonly known as the pink or carnation family, but Dianthus is the genus within that family that contains the 300 or so species we recognise as 'pinks'. *Dianthus* is from the Greek words *dios* (god) and *anthos* (flower)—so the common pink is the flower of God, and Alvanson's enthusiasm for the colour is like the original Greek 'Enthousiasmos'—the God's 'inbreaking' into you as Dick puts it. This piercing is pertinent, since pinks are not named for their colour, but for their serrated edges, which look like they have been 'pinked', that is, in the Old English, 'pierced' or 'stabbed', as with dressmakers' pinking shears, which cut cloth in a zigzag, or

---

6. Ibid, p. 71.

7. Robert Crumb, 'The Religious Experience of Philip K. Dick', *Weirdo #17*, 1986.

8. Dick, *VALIS*, p. 71. Note also that Camille Henrot held an exhibition which asked, 'Est-il possible d'être révolutionnaire et d'aimer les fleurs?' (Is It Possible to Be a Revolutionary and Like Flowers?) (2012). This exhibition consisted of floral arrangements that interpreted books from Henrot's personal library. As Claire Moulene asks in her review of the exhibition, 'aren't all libraries revolutionary?' *Artforum*, 2013, Vol. 51, Issue 5, p. 219.

9. Michael Pollan, *The Botany of Desire: A Plant's Eye View of the World*, Random House, New York, 2001, p. 73.

meander (a motif I will return to later). Across Europe most languages name the colour pink with a variation of the word rose, but English stands out for naming this seemingly gentle colour 'to pierce', a prick that Dick was no doubt aware of when he made it the colour of theophanic penetration.[10]

When Horselover Fat tries to recall the exact colour of the blinding beam, he studies a chart of the visible spectrum. But the colour is absent, because it lies 'off the end' of the Fraunhofer Lines, 'past B in the direction of A'. In 2011, popular science had a field day with the idea that 'pink light can't exist' because it is made of a combination of red and violet, which are at opposite ends of the spectrum, and that if you rolled up the spectrum there would be a gap in which radio waves, microwaves, infrared, ultraviolet, x-rays, gamma rays exist. 'Since we can't see any of those wavelengths, we replace all of that hidden grandeur with pink'.[11] Perhaps this is why David Andrew Sitek of the indie rock band TV on the Radio opined that 'All music since the beginning of time has been an attempt to aurally convey the colour pink'.[12]

Indeed, the synaesthetic properties of pink seem boundless. Thomas, an ancient Roman Christian inhabiting Fat's brain, achieves life-in-death because he 'engrams' himself—stores his memory traces—on the *ichthys*, or Christian fish symbol, and eats 'some strange pink food'.[13] Perhaps Dick is referring to the Eucharist, the body of Christ, since flesh, regardless of skin colour, is searing pink, and a pink beam of data represents Logos, or the 'word made flesh'?[14]

At the nexus of sign and sensation, or data and desire, Alvanson's real life art practice involves a project called *dESIRE for Sale*, in which she sells her intangible desires in units, and 1 unit equals 100 consecutive desires, as well as 100 photographic representations of said desires.[15] Each unit is sold on a CD, and for

10. 'Penetration' is a term I use deliberately, since Dick refers to living information as a 'plasmate' which 'uses the human brain as a *female* host in which to replicate itself into its active form'. (Dick, p. 61, my emphasis). This has a strange resonance with the 'facehugger' alien which Barbara Creed refers to as 'orally raping' Kane in Ridley Scott's film *Alien*, (1979), in order to 'impregnate' the male crew member who essentially 'births' a baby alien in what is one of cinema's most climactic and memorable moments. Creed, *The Monstrous Feminine: Film, Feminism, Psychoanalysis*, New York, Routledge, 2012, p. 28. Jess Johnson's Gnostic sci-fi drawings are populated by tentacle- and vulva-faced aliens which inspire a kind of genital panic in the viewer.

11. Youtube's MinutePhysics, 'There is no pink light,' October 16, 2011. *Scientific American* takes this illogic to task (Michael Moyer, 'Stop this Absurd War on the Colour Pink', March 5, 2012). But while the colour may be a 'pigment of the imagination' (another waggish phrase doing the pop science rounds) its irreality makes perfect sense in terms of Dick's theophany. See Robert McRuer, 'Pink' *Prismatic Ecology: Ecotheory Beyond Green*, ed. Jeffrey Jerome Cohen, University of Minnesota Press, Minneapolis, 2013. McRuer fleshes out a queer pink, something this essay tacitly acknowledges but does not attempt to speak for.

12. Thanks to Kristen Alvanson in personal communication for this quote.

13. Dick, p. 111.

14. 'Because everyone knows, regardless of meaningless exterior coloration, it's all pink inside'. Mike Kelley on his use of pink crystals in the exhibition *Deodorized Central Mass with Satellites*, 1999. He goes on to connect human flesh to the earth's glowing underbelly: 'Crack any dull geode, and inside is its fiery heart: the crystalline core of beauty and wonder'. Quoted by Karl Schawelka, 'Showing Pink—Biological Aspects of the Colour Pink' in *Pink, The Exposed Colour in Contemporary Art and Culture*, Hatje Cantz Verlag, Ostfildern, 2006, p. 70.

15. This project embodies the 'practice of photography as the technic-erotic perpetuation of love-at-first-sight'. Kristen Alvanson, Nicola Masciandaro and Scott Wilson, 'Desire Gloss: A Specimen', *Glossator: Practice and Theory of the Commentary* 3, 2010, p117. For Alvanson, the camera is literally a desir-

US$525, the unit price at the time of writing, the viewer can be infected with Alvanson's desires in the same way she herself was infected by the CD from the Turkish computer store. A preview of some very pink desires includes Persian pastries with pomegranate seeds, a blurry Sophia Loren in a pink towel-turban caught on an old colour TV, marble tiles depicting a rose paradise garden, a dresser with pink candles and a pink highlighter pen…

In *Pink—The Exposed Colour in Contemporary Art and Culture*, Barbara Nemitz suggests that pink addresses our *senses* more than other colours, because it can be closely related to certain skin tones, eliciting the sense of touch, as well as a sense of taste associated with sweetness and fruitiness, and the sense of smell, as in the fragrance of blossoms,[16] all of which are evoked in Alvanson's photographic desires. In the same book, Karl Schawelka's essay "Showing Pink" points out that shocking colour's appearance in primates' lips, genitals, and nipples, and that the blood-engorged posteriors of baboons, chimpanzees, and bonobos signal willingness to mate.[17] He links pink language with human sexual mores, such as the expression 'showing pink' which refers to nude female models exposing their genitals. In Japan, the sex industry is known as the 'Pink Industry' while across Europe, the rose has long been a euphemism for the vagina, with rather charming terms such as 'Rose Lane' and 'Rose Corner' denoting places of prostitution.[18]

The relation of gentalia or euphemistically *private* parts with the colour pink is nothing new; to the ancient Romans, the term *sub rosa*, meant 'under the seal of confidentiality'.[19] In *VALIS*, Ancient Rome is superimposed over Southern California in the early 1970s, and Horselover Fat shares his already paranoid psychic space with Thomas, the persecuted Christian who secretly ate pink food to time-travel posthumously via a beam of pink data.

Dick problematises my attempt to claim pink as an especially feminine gnosis, although the female archetype looms heavily over his text. Fat is engaged in writing a cosmological exegesis, known as the *Tractates: Cryptica Scriptura*, which explains that there are two realms, the upper 'hyperuniverse I or Yang' which is 'sentient and volitional', while the lower yin realm is 'mechanical, driven by

---

ing-machine, while Roland Barthes' 'punctum' or 'little prick', the detail of a photograph which 'pierces the viewer' which he discusses in *Camera Lucida*,1980, might have some relevance here especially considering the etymology of pink.

16. Barbara Nemitz, *Pink—The Exposed* Colour, p. 27.

17. Karl Schawelka, "Showing Pink—Biological Aspects of the Colour Pink," ibid, p. 44.

18. Ibid. Zona Rosa, on the other hand, is one of Mexico City's *zonas de tolerancia*, home to the city's gay population, and a major gay tourist destination, see McRuer, 'Pink'.

19. Schawelka, p. 45. Pink heralds a liminal space, a *marker* of transition, as with the *magic* hours of dawn and dusk. Pink represents the threshold of a new order, the change from yang to yin and vice versa, and thresholds the world over are visioned as vulvas—portals to new dimensions, from the Maori *pare* (door lintels) in which female ancestors display their vaginas, to the infamous, grinning Sheela na gig of Celtic lore. This idea of being 'under the vagina' brings to mind the moment in Nicholas Roeg's film *Insignificance* (1985), when 'Marylin Monroe' performs her famous subway-grating skirt-lift, and one of the men below the grating looking up says, 'I Saw the Face of God'. Compare this to the story of the Devil taking flight when a woman showed him her vulva. (Freud in his essay 'Medusa's Head', quoted by Creed, p. 2.) This leaves no doubt that *VALIS* a.k.a. the living beam of pink light, emmanates from the Goddesshead.

blind, efficient cause, deterministic and without intelligence since it emanates from a dead source'. Fat believes that we are unknowingly trapped in the lower realm, concluding that 'The Empire never ended',[20] which is the gloomy signature phrase of *VALIS*.

Predictably, the sick and evil cosmogonic twin ruling the yin realm is female, and must be killed by the healthy twin, whose gender is never stated, but is presumably male.[21] Within the *VALIS* narrative, two of Dick's female friends die, and his coping mechanism involves creating his alter-ego, Fat, who pens the exegesis in an attempt to explain cosmic disunity. The *Tractates* states that within measured time, the yin twin remains alive, but in eternity, she has been killed—of necessity—by the healthy twin 'who is our champion'. As with *Cyclonopedia*, chronological time and abyssal time are engaged in coitus, the result being that in *VALIS*, the universe is grieving over the tragic death of a woman… without knowing why.[22]

Primordial femicide is a pan-cultural motif dramatically epitomised by the story of Tiamat, who in Mesopotamian religion was both chaos monster and primordial goddess of the Ocean. In the *Enuma Elish*, the Babylonian epic of creation, she gives birth to the first generation of deities, one of whom is Marduk, god of storms. In a matricide symbolic of the overturning of archaic goddess worship and matriarchal societies, Marduk dismembers the archaic mother and institutes order in the Cosmos, creating man to be 'servant and labourer of the gods'.[23]

Hakim Bey's cult classic TAZ *(Temporary Autonomous Zone)*, brings the Babylonian myth into the present, in which 'Chaos has been overthrown by younger gods, moralists, phallocrats, banker-priests, fit lords for serfs'.[24] Bey calls for nothing less than a 'clandestine spiritual jihad' to be waged under the banner of Tiamat, who he calls 'the anarchist black dragon'. Opposing Dick's doleful chant 'The Empire Never Ended', Bey proclaims that 'Chaos never died'.[25]

In her study of the monstrous feminine in horror cinema, Barbara Creed uses Kristeva's theory of abjection to connect the archaic mother with chaos. Kristeva terms the abject as that which does not 'respect borders, posi-

---

20. Dick, *VALIS*, pp. 47-48.

21. Fat invokes Dogontology to explain the Nommos or divine twins, one of whom rebelled and had to be slain. But for the Dogon of West Africa, the Nommos are fish-like and hermaphroditic, while Dick feels the need to ascribe a specifically female gender to the 'defective' twin. Incidentally, Camille Henrot dabbles in Dogontology, which is attested to in the title of her exhibition *The Pale Fox* (2014), taken from Marcel Griaule and Germaine Dieterlen's 1945 study of the same name, which charts the cosmology of the Dogon.

22. Dick, *VALIS*, p. 238.

23. Thorkild Jacobsen. 'The Battle between Marduk and Tiamat', *Journal of the American Oriental Society*, Vol. 88, No. 1 (Jan. - Mar., 1968), p. 105. Within the *VALIS* narrative, other creation stories featuring sick female twins are alluded to, including that of the Dogon, as well as the Japanese myth of Izanagi and Izanami, in which the 'female twin dies giving birth to fire; then she descends under the ground. The male twin goes after her to restore her but finds her decomposing and giving birth to monsters'. Dick, *VALIS*, pp. 61-62.

24. Hakim Bey, *TAZ*, Autonomedia, New York, 1991, p. 18.

25. Ibid.

tions, rules', that which 'disturbs identity, system, order',[26] and Creed uses abjection theory to understand movies like *Alien*, in which 'The archaic mother is
the parthenogenetic mother, the mother as primordial abyss, the point of origin and of end'.[27]

Bey embraces the anarchist black dragon, while in *Cyclonopedia*, the fictional archaeologist Dr. Hamid Parsani posits a Tiamaterialism, in which it
is archaeology's goal to turn the Earth itself into an artefact, and to vision the
Earth as 'the coiling body of Tiamat, the Sumero-Babylonian Mother-Drag-
on'.[28] This *Tellurian insurgency* is Earth's 'uprising against its own passive plan-
etdom. Once freed from its solar slavery, the earth can rise against the onanis-
tic self-indulgence of the Sun and its solar capitalism',[29] for the *Empire of the Sun*
has given rise to 'terrestrial orders, politics and modes of living based on its
hegemonic stardom'.[30]

Are Dick's Empire, Bey's Chaos and Negarestani's Tellurian Insurgency
all the same dark force, seen via different spectacles, rose-tinted or otherwise?
Dick the crypto-Christian exults Apollo and fears Dionysus, and sees the female principle as sowing disorder in the universe. And yet, her death fills the
universe with remorse, so that 'All the information processed by the Brain—experienced by us as the arranging and rearranging of physical objects—is an attempt at this preservation of her; stones and rocks and sticks and amoebae are
traces of her'.[31] The propensity to find meaning in stones and rocks and physical objects, mimics the archaeological impetus, which has literally dug up thousands of prehistoric goddess figurines, but also, in the process of ex-humation,
what Negarestani would call *ungrounding* has created a fissured earth, in which
narratives of stability and solidity are increasingly less convincing.

Camille Henrot's *Grosse Fatigue*, 2013, is a thirteen minute video which attempts to be a history of everything, yet is anything but a stable narrative. Accompanied by a spoken-word hiphop track fusing a range of global creation
myths, images of museum collections and anthropological texts jostle with the
data storm that is the Internet—pictures of cats proliferate amongst softcore
porn scenarios. Of relevance to Alvanson's pink torrent of public libraries, the
bulk of Henrot's imagery comes from her residency at the Smithsonian Institution, Washington DC, the world's largest museum and research complex. Henrot's fable of endless beginnings is Tiamaterialist: an ungrounding in which the
earth becomes an artefact made of artefacts, in endless fractal recursion.[32]

---

26. Julia Kristeva, in Creed, p. 8.

27. Creed, p. 17.

28. Negarestani, Cyclonopedia, p. 50.

29. Ibid, p. 44.

30. Ibid, p. 42. Perhaps, then, it is not so much that "The Sun is a whore," as Daniel Paul Schreber
once put it (quoted in Ben Woodard, On an Ungrounded Earth: Towards a New Geophilosophy, p.
88), but that the sun makes a whore of earth. Indeed, it is worth noting the similarities (and differences) between Dick's beam of pink data and Schreber's sexual assault via sunbeams. I think also of the relationship between the sun and the earth in terms of Barbara Kruger's classic feminist work, *Untitled:
Your Gaze Hits the Side of My Face*, 1981.

31. Negarestani, *Cyclonopedia*, p. 37.

32. Both artists appear to suffer from Walter Benjamin's 'cataloguing psychosis', or Jacques Derrida's

Henrot's manipulation of images has been called 'Dionysian dismember-ing',[33] but what ties together the imagery of *Grosse Fatigue* are what another crit-ic referred to as its 'black hole of browsers', which are 'progressively nested with-in one another in an infinite regress'.[34] I can't help but be reminded of 'the nested-vaginas of Tiamat's swirling body, engorging their curls, opening their curves and experiencing the contorting movement of each concave and convex wall'.[35] Indeed, '…everything related to the Middle East emerges, moves, diffus-es, escalates and engenders itself through and out of the holey *Hezar'to* (A Thou-sand Insides; the Persian word for labyrinth)'.[36]

The recurring motif of a pair of highly manicured female hands codes the encyclopaedic *Grosse Fatigue* as feminine. Obsessively lacquered nails gently ca-ress pieces of fruit, eggs, stuffed birds and books, creating an intimate snapshot of female lust for information via a highly eroticised interface of the gaze and touch.

In *Grosse Fatigue*, manicured nails are micro-chips of vast databases encoded in the resins and adhesive polymers that fix colour (that most data-rich of sub-stances) to the tips of the fingers. Fingernails, when painted, take on inhuman associations—they become the talons of birds, the scales of serpents, or even, in Henrot's case, hint at an alien culture encountering our own. Long or coloured fingernails are the stuff of goddesses and female chaos monsters. 'Red in tooth and claw,', while referring to the violence of the natural world, can also be ap-plied to the red nails of seductresses, prefiguring vagina dentata.[37]

Like Alvanson's photographed desires, Henrot's subjective catalogue makes no attempt to be exhaustive, rather, as the title suggests, it is the ex-haust*ing* auto-erotic summary of the universe from the perspective of a procre-atrix: she whose desires are generative. In one key sequence, the female hands are thrust into a pair of panties, provoking a torrent of browser windows to open, one upon the other, in an orgasmic infinity of *mille plateaux*. Nested va-ginas, indeed!

'Archive Fever'. I'm thinking of positing the term 'Data Slut' for this kind of work, as long as it is read as a prideful reappropriation of shaming language. In fact, Henrot's latest project includes drawings of rap star Nicki Minaj, as a repudiation of the slut-shaming responses to Minaj's videos. Minaj is a par-agon of pink love; all three of her studio albums to date have "pink" in their title. Eerily, in relation to *VALIS*, the second album is called *Pink Friday: Roman Reloaded* (2012).

33. Federico Nicolao, *Domus*, 4 June 2013, http://www.domusweb.it/en/art/2013/06/4/camille_hen-rot_grossefatigue.html

34. Pamela M. Lee, 'The Whole Earth is Heavy', *Artforum*, September 2013, Vol. 52, Issue 1, p. 306.

35. Negarestani, *Cyclonopedia*, p. 51.

36. Ibid, p. 43. A Thousand Insides can surely be related to A Thousand Plateaus, especially since 'Everywhere a hole moves, a surface is invented', ibid, p. 50. It was Deleuze's *The Fold: Leibniz and the Baroque*, Minneapolis, University of Minnesota Press, 1993, which first alerted me to the shared etymol-ogy of labia and labyrinth, as well as the term 'invagination'.

37. Maori legend has two vivid examples of these female archetypes: Mahukia, the goddess of fire, who Maui tricked into giving humankind the knowledge of fire by asking for her fingernails, one by one, and Hine-nui-te-po, goddess of death, who Maui tried to vanquish by entering her vagina in the form of a lizard as she slept. She was awoken, however, and her vagina snapped shut, 'beheading' Maui in his phallic, lizard form. Lisa Reihana has made a series of photographic images of Maori forebears including *Mahuika* 2001 who is modelled by the artist's aunt, and is a superb example of the primordi-al goddess figure.

In *VALIS*, lacquered nails are mentioned in relation to Fat's suicidal friend Gloria. At the beach, Fat notices that Gloria 'had pink-painted toenails and that they were perfectly pedicured. To himself he thought, she died as she lived'.[38] This sentiment presages the idea that measured time and eternity coexist, the former in which Gloria is alive, and the latter where she is always already dead. The pink-painted toenails allow Fat to see this because they engram the all-knowing beam of pink data.

Eventually, the living intelligence that is *VALIS* finds human form in a little girl—Saint Sophia, the divine feminine avatar of wisdom.[39] Fat's exegesis states that 'St. Sophia is going to be born again; she was not acceptable before'.[40] However, the little girl, who represents Godhead and the Logos, is accidentally killed by a laser beam, becoming the third female death in the narrative, (or fourth, if you count the evil cosmogonic twin).[41]

Exposure to the ichthys awakens Thomas within Dick's body and allows for the *inbreaking* of God to occur. But there are many symbols far older than ichthys, symbols associated with goddess cults which archaeologist Marjia Gimbutas catalogues in her encyclopaedic text *The Language of the Goddess*. The meander or zigzag was more than merely decorative, in paleolithic art it symbolised fertility and was closely associated with water goddesses and snake goddesses, who were eventually killed by their cosmic offspring but recycled as female chaos monsters such as the Greek whirlpools Kharybdis and Scylla, or, indeed, Tiamat, whose name was the Akkadian word for sea.[42]

Fat writes that the beam of pink light is 'exactly what you get as a phosphene after-image when a flashbulb has gone off in your face'.[43] Indeed, multiple studies have shown that paleolithic art bears the telltale signs of phosphene activity—flashes of light seen under the influence of drugs or sensory deprivation. These meanders indicate entry into a sacred psychic space in which pattern operates, not as vapid wallpaper, but as living data.

In *VALIS*, Fat calls living information 'Zebra' because 'Normally it remained camouflaged'.[44] Fat meets an archetypal mad scientist, who tells him that he (Fat) has been given 'a set-ground discriminating unscramble'. Most hu-

---

38. Dick, *VALIS*, p. 13.

39. Indeed, in Alvanson's *Incognitum hactenus* she is given instructions by 'he with a Persian initial' to visit the Hagia Sophia, completed in 537 AD and for a thousand years the largest Christian Church in the world, named for the manifestation of wisdom in female form.

40. Dick, *VALIS*, p. 229. It isn't made clear why she wasn't *acceptable*, but the inference is that it was because she was female, and therefore *imperfect* or rather, *unwhole* and therefore *unwholesome* (in Freudian/ Lacanian/ Kristevan terms) lacking a phallus.

41. Dick just doesn't seem to have any luck with the ladies, indeed, underpinning all of this is the real-life fact that his wife Tess leaves him after one too many discussions about Thomas the Ancient Roman who is inhabiting his body.

42. Jacobsen, 'The Battle between Marduk and Tiamat'. Creed quotes Roger Dadoun in *The Monstrous Feminine*, whose writing on horror film denotes 'a mother-thing situated beyond good and evil, beyond all organised forms and all events. This is a totalising and *oceanic* mother, a 'shadowy and deep unity,' evoking in the subject the anxiety of fusion and of dissolution.' Creed, p. 20, (emphasis mine). Alvanson's pink mother-of-pearl bracelet might be read, then, as the oceanic vagina of Tiamat, that mother-of-all plot holes.

43. Dick, *VALIS*, p. 20.

44. Ibid, p. 69.

mans can't distinguish set from ground. But once *VALIS* has fired the unscrambler at you, you see set as colour and ground as black and white, in order to understand 'The false work that's blended with the real world'.[45]

The sacred meander, phosphenes, games of camouflage with set and ground, are integral to the holographic, hierophantic imagery of New Zealand born, Melbourne-based artist Jess Johnson. Her earlier works (c2010) played on the transmoggification of ancient Egyptian cat worship into Internet kitty porn, and delighted in drawing beleaguered, bearded, Dick-like men. Johnson's more recent work has become increasingly arcane, a mesh of grids, brickwork, towers, pillars, and textual proclamations, patrolled by aliens with demonic, bat-like faces with super-sensory noses and ears. As with Zebra, in Johnsons' highly patterned, data-rich work, it is difficult to discern set from ground.[46] In her parallel worlds information is 'engrammed' on symbols which, if viewed under the right conditions (perhaps, as with Dick's ichthys, a mixture of pain medication and psychosis), are capable of unleashing a data storm.

Fat's *Tractates* quotes Hermes Trismegistos' fundamental: 'That which is above is that which is below'. Fat interprets this as meaning that the universe is a hologram, and that the great Hermetic sage simply lacked the term.[47] Put another way, inverted by Parsani/ Negarestani, 'the ()hole complex carves ultra-active surfaces from solidus when it digs holes… Everywhere a hole moves, a surface is invented'.[48] The practices of Alvanson, Henrot and Johnson are just such ultra-active surfaces.

In conclusion, Alvanson's preface is Tiamaterialism in action, an acknowledgement of the archaic feminine as first principle, before the arcane convolutions of petropolitics can begin: she essentially births the monster of *Cyclonopedia* from a 'box' under the bed. But while Alvanson vomits pink data with delight, Dick's penetration via pink data embodies in him that which he fears most—a feminine consciousness allied with the inexplicable urges of the yin realm and the inevitable return of the repressed, murdered ur-mother.[49] Hakim Bey on the other hand, has learned to lie back and think of chaos, like a good anarchist, while Negarestani complicates Bey's spiritual jihad, visioning the coiling tail of the black dragon Tiamat as ever more black and baroque. Artists Alvanson, Henrot and Johnson variously demonstrate that data itself is the locus of desire, that pattern and surface encode meaning, and that we are all, all-ways and all-ready, data sluts and encylonopediaphiles.

---

45. Ibid, pp. 183-184.

46. Tessa Laird, 'The Devil is in the Detail: Pattern and Power in Jess Johnson's Gnostic Architectures', commissioned for *Matters* (NZ), Issue 6, 2015, and reprinted in *Bloodfin and Whipwurm*, NGV, 2015, provides an even more convoluted appraisal of the relationships between Johnson's practice and *VALIS*.

47. Dick, *VALIS*, p. 230.

48. Negarestani, *Cyclonopedia*, p. 50.

49. That Henrot's *Grosse Fatigue* emanates from the yin realm is implied by this reviewer's caution, that 'Henrot's video is no paean to a transcendent collective unconscious. On the contrary, *Grosse Fatigue* shatters any image of a fully integrated system of knowledge or totality'. Pamela M. Lee, 'The Whole Earth is Heavy', *Artforum* September 2013, Vol. 52, Issue 1, p. 306. The (W)hole Earth, though, is infinitely perforated, and weighs less than the feather of Maat.

13

The Emergence of Hyperstition

Chris Shambaugh (and Maudlin Cortex)[1]

According to the tenets of Hyperstition, there is no difference
in principle between a universe, a religion, and a hoax. All involve an engineering of manifestation, or practical fiction,
that is ultimately unworthy of belief. [...] Because the future
is a fiction it has a more intense reality than either the present
or the past.
— Cybernetic Culture Research Unit

No one knows exactly when or how the Cybernetic Culture
Research Unit, or Ccru, came about. Even less is understood
of who (or what) speaks through it. Its existence has been denied more than once, and despite repeated attempts to excise
all record of its strange intellectual and aesthetic experiments
from institutional histories, it always seems to return, each
strain more virulent than the last.
— Prue Nort

---

1. Note from the editors: We asked Mr. Shambaugh if he could elaborate on the concept of hyperstition following his presentation in a similar vein at the Aesthetics After Finitude conference in February,
2015. After ignoring our emails for months, we finally received a single reply from him containing the
following line: 'My original endeavour, finding the solution to the problem of "explaining" hyperstition
is being annexed, if not virulently rerouted, by anonymous forces.' The email carried an attachment
containing an article titled 'The Krakatoan Chimera', which was supposedly written by one Chaim
Horowitz. We wrote to Mr. Shambaugh asking for clarification regarding the contents of the attachment but to no avail. After much deliberation, we have decided to publish the Horowitz document in this
volume, along with a transcription of the annotations that accompanied it, without alteration.—Eds.

'The Krakatoan Chimera'

Chaim Horowitz

THE LEMURIAN TURN

Echidna Stillwell spent much of her young life haunted by recurring nightmares of gargantuan explosions, chthonic tsunamis, and atolls swallowed whole. By the age of 18 she came to understand these nightly terrors as direct transmissions from the 1883 eruption of Krakatoa in the South Indies—an event she would later describe as the biggest bang heard on this earth within living memory. At the time of this realization, in 1911, Stillwell was one year into a Bachelor's Degree at the Pembroke Women's College in Providence, Rhode Island. Due in part to annoyance with her peers, as well as her anomalous nightlife, Stillwell became enraptured by the writings of Sigmund Freud.

While in Providence, she found herself compelled by the mechanics of various Semitic languages, developing a suspicion that many ancient dialects were not just elegantly stripped down communication devices, but perhaps simply more effective instruments for contact.[*] This idea led her to seek out one George Gammel Angell—the Professor Emeritus of Semitic Languages at Brown—with whom she spent long hours contemplating linguistic redundancies in the English language, intently considering topics such as the anthropomorphic listlessness of vowels and primitive logograms. These exchanges with Professor Angell would turn out to be far more constitutive than she could have known at the time. Meanwhile, the torments of Krakatoa returned more ferociously with every night, eventually resulting in a premonition that the surviving cultures of the Krakatoan explosion were somehow affiliated with the long lost continent of Lemuria, an enduring topic of fascination with Stillwell.[**]

---

[*] Not unlike those 'deviation-amplifying' runaway processes described by Magoroh Maruyama in his 1963 paper *The Second Cybernetics*, hyperstition surfaces as all runaway systems do, effectuating both qualitative and quantitative alterations in the perceptible. For this reason, formalizing hyperstition as a concept is quite an ironic venture, as the temptation to systematize its 'deviation-amplifying' operations, will inevitably bring on 'deviation-counteracting' gestures. The bottom line is that no one wanted to draw attention to autopoiesis in a time of war and uncertainty, preferring to see in Maruyama's diagnosis a stabilizing potential. (I'm reminded of Ian Hacking's 'looping effects', wherein expertly constituted descriptive or diagnostic categories regarding human behavior are assimilated, taken on by the subjects under scrutiny, thereby hyperstitionally ratifying and inflating the original fiction, resulting in ratcheting pathologies and the "making up of people". You get the picture. It's an escalational self-fulfilling paradigm.) Anyway, the heated up runaway is the kind of positive feedback Wiener was deathly afraid of and what hyperstition requires.

[+] 'There is a basic difference between communication and contact; communication is designed to avoid contact, to establish a distance across which communication can take place. Contact involves identification with the creature you contact, and this can be very painful.' - WSB

[**] Bateson called it schismogenesis, either escalatory or de-escalatory, but most definitely runaway. It could be brought on via a *cargo cult* scenario, typified by the sudden arrival of an alien artifact (or hyperstitional carrier) that contagiously revalences the field of relations constituting the invaded culture, desperately seeking to stabilize (rationalize) the anomaly's origin and function. Homeostasis, the perpetu-

It is worth remembering that the turn of the century generated much confusion surrounding the existence of Lemuria, although Stillwell had fortunately discovered the necessary reading materials. A most significant misapprehension arrived in the leap year of 1896, when the British photographer August le Plongeon equated Mu with Atlantis—the treasured island of the West. By the early 1920s Stillwell's diary indicates that she was engaged in readings of the Russian occultist Helena Petrovna Blavatsky's *The Secret Doctrine*—a highly inscrutable tome, but one which fully convinced Stillwell that Lemuria not only preceded Atlantis, but that this Western island was likely to have been nothing more than a peninsula of the far more substantial Lemurian megacontinent. It was then through documentation of Captain Mission's explorations in Madagascar that she discovered that the aboriginal word for 'lemur' translated directly to 'ghost'. Despite more credible accounts of Lemuria coming from both the German naturalist Ernst Haeckel and the English Zoologist Phillip Sclater, it was not until 1931, with the publication of James Churchward's *The Lost Continent of Mu*, that the forgotten landmass was solidified as a Pacific continent far older than Plato's precious Atlantis.

By the late 1920s Stillwell was living amongst the tribes which survived the Krakatoan calamity; having sailed through the Sunda Strait in 1925 in search of an explanation, if not a cure, for her own incessant torment by the caldera. Her early fieldwork there not only confirmed suspicions that the Land of Mu, or Lemuria, had indeed existed, but more remarkably that the tribal communities there held significant residual strains of the ancient Muvian polyculture. (◌) Over the next few years of concentrated island hopping, Stillwell came into contact with a multilateral set of tribal peoples, all of which shared an orienta-

---

al regulation of a system through adaptation and incorporation of noise, was more convivial to Wiener, who invented cybernetics (hijacking Ampère's hijack of the Greek *kubernesis*) to prosecute it, smack dab in the middle of WWII: communication and control between human and machine, very much prophetic of the inhuman modulatory capacities of digital technologies which capture and refigure in order to better predict and contain. Not to mention the cyborg feedback loops promoted by self-tracking devices...

(◌) Templexing—time folding—is central to hyperstition, as it exposes the control structures dependent on linear accumulation (language being a particularly insidious perpetrator). Brion Gysin and William S. Burroughs invented the cut-up in order to warp the binding lines of time, which constrain thought by forcing it into language-encoded linearity (WSB later picked up on Alfred Korzybski's *general semantics*, which included elucidations of mankind as a 'time-binding' class of life). Cut-ups are excellent germinal sources for potential hyperstitions, missives from the future—'when you cut into the present the future leaks out'—detonated preemptively. WSB also worked with tape recorders, playing back edited concoctions in public situations to trigger concomitant effects—to induce a *real* event out of a reproduction. Furthermore, he understood the following basic fact: If the arrow of chronological time is defined as entropic and irreversible by the second law of thermodynamics, and all complex beings are self-organizing, then they embody temporal reversal. In observing the manifold tractability of this temporal flip, coincidences detach from serendipity, and intensify.

The China Syndrome, a film released March 16 1979 documenting the partial meltdown of a fictional nuclear reactor hyperstitionally brought about the very real partial meltdown of a reactor on Three Mile Island (near Harrisburg, PA) March 28 1979, some 12 days later. Details regarding both cases were too proximate to be the product of coincidence, the most extraordinary being the malfunctioning of coolant-level indicators which led to nearly fatal human overcompensation in filmic space and in "reality" (understanding the fluid nature of the latter term). Indeed, WSB had correctly identified the volatile nature of speculative incursions into chronoportational modalities.

tion towards number so confounding, she deemed it utterly indigestible for the western mind.[∴]

With her only reference being the weathered journals of an explorer by the name of Cecil Curtis (who had himself died in the great Krakatoa eruption), Stillwell was able to identify two of three tribes by utilizing and adopting Curtis' overarching classification of the 'N'Ma'. While the actual etymology of this truncated designation remains unclear, some academics have since come to believe that it refers to a 'people of Nomo'.

The following description from *The Vault of Murmurs*, Stillwell's retrospective account of her experiences living amongst these proto-aboriginal peoples, offers an invaluable description of the state of the N'Ma at this moment:

> By the time I arrived in Indonesia, the tripartite N'Ma system was in shreds. In totally annihilating one tribe—Curtis's Tak N'Ma—and all but destroying another—the Dib N'Ma—the 1883 explosion of Krakatoa had wrecked the complex web of social exchange on which the Mu had traditionally depended.

In Stillwell's eyes, the Mu were the overarching cultural wellspring of the N'Ma and furthermore, as noted in her diary, 'that Transitional Pacific interculture providing a mainline conduit for Lemurian influences into human history.' Captivated by what she described as 'a fixation on the intrinsic materialism of number', Stillwell set out to study the atypical spatio-temporal practices[∵] of the Muvian people, with hopes of reconstructing their cultural sensibilities.

Complicating coincidences further, Stillwell noticed that Cecil Curtis' journal entries had also identified peculiar customs of dream sorcery amongst the

---

[∴] Apophenia—conventionally flagged as a pathological misrecognition of meaningful agglomerations of information within noise—may be positively valenced in terms of its capacity to find new patterns and therefore invent the future. It's a thin line between creativity and paranoia. (The obligatory Lovecraftian premonition: 'The most merciful thing in the world, I think, is the inability of the human mind to correlate all its contents…some day the piecing together of dissociated knowledge will open up such terrifying vistas of reality, and of our frightful position therein, that we shall either go mad from the revelation or flee from the deadly light into the peace and safety of a new dark age.') Didn't the godfather of cybernetic anthropology Gregory Bateson state that 'all that is not information, not redundancy, not form and not restraints is *noise*, the only possible source of *new* patterns'?

[∵] Where time folding is concerned, the numerous cases of *plagiarism by anticipation* unearthed by literary anachronism hunter, Pierre Bayard, loudly beckon. Due to normative habits in thinking the arrow of time in one direction only—forwards—Bayard contends that an entire realm of speculation has been unnecessarily occluded, setting into motion a chronoportational framework in which the idea of past authors literally plagiarizing from the as-yet-unborn becomes plausible. Read that pilfered passage in Maupassant that Bayard alleges was ripped off from (the chronologically subsequent) Proust, an anamnetic sequence redolent of madeleine rememoration. Resonating weirdly within its context, like a case of standard linear time plagiarism, it begs to be found out; the attempt to disguise the theft by coating this most Proustian of precognitions with Maupassant's usual dysphoric mien only further compounds this intuition, which ends up over-ratifying a certain form of paranoid reading which escapes the boundaries of the specific case to metastasize across *all* future literary engagement.

As oft underlined, future authors (pseudonymously) regularly chronoportate their work into the past in order to induce qualitative bifurcations, either through the amplification of existing weak signals or the implantation of radically alien constructs which have no basis on which to be evaluated. Bayardian Operators would then be those particular carriers instituting avant-la-lettre insinuations whose particular stickiness helps them circulate and gain traction, priming for realities which thereby become increasingly inevitable. The alien order of time is concealed within the folds of literature (WSB would concur) and only discoverable through both exo- and eso-teric readings.

Muvians. While her letters indicate that the nocturnal ruptures in her unconscious had dissipated dramatically since she had arrived there, Curtis' observations on dream witchery triggered an awfully disturbing thought for her, which she portrayed as 'the vicious possibility, not that I had never been awake, but that I have already died'. This rumination was purportedly short lived, however.[*]

Carrying on as the excellent scholar she was, Stillwell began to perceive the exactitude of Curtis' reflections. In a letter dating June 21, 1933, Stillwell proclaimed: 'It is utterly evident that Mu culture is indeed based on a system of dream magic, in which the Nago—or dream witch... holds a central, oracular role.'[**] Stillwell's notes suggest that the vast majority of the Mu sought out the dream witch's wisdom by visiting her temple, and that on the night following the ceremonial trial, would receive a 'nagwi', or dream visit.

It was around this time that Stillwell began to consider the intense possibility that one of these dream witches had interfered with her own destiny on Earth. With serendipity out of the question, she asked the Mu elders for permission to approach the Nago's temple ('[t]hey greeted [her] entreaty with the same sense of fated inevitability with which they seemed to accept all matters'). According to Stillwell, what transpired after her encounter with the Nago simply could not be reconciled by any account of the unconscious ever encountered in language.

THE NUMOGRAM

Although her retroactive descriptions of the Nagwi visit were fantastical to say the least (even at times illegible, to be honest), what was unveiled to Stillwell amongst the Mu N'ma was no neurochemical hiccup:

> As I looked down at my hands, they became translucent, and I saw, inscribed into impossible geometries on the dream cave's wall beyond, an arrangement of ten circles, a number of smaller circles, and a series of interconnecting lines. This was my first encounter with what came to be called the Numogram.

Dr. Echidna Stillwell liked to remind me that even though she'd begun sketching the twinning orbs and their circuitous flows before the phantasm faded, there was absolutely no need, as it had been branded in her mind. She began describing the occurrence as a 'a labyrinth in which my fate, that of the N'Ma, Cecil Curtis, and more cosmic presences had always been tangled together', insisting that the figure had not been constructed or preconceived by any mind

---

[*] Power operates most effectively not by persuading the conscious mind, but by delimiting in advance what can be experienced. Recall the Escher-like staircase in *Inception* (a thoroughly instructive film for the oneirically minded hyperstitionist) which harbors a gap inaccessible to the dreamer. As long as the model is transparent—it remains unavailable for *objective* processing (as during waking consciousness)—it can simulate expansiveness while maintaining tightly scripted, policed boundaries.

[**] Hyperstitional entities are indifferent to explanation or signification, only concerned with access, operating at the right nexus. (Schopenhauer got it too, in *The Art of Being Right*, a rhetorical arsenal keyed to winning an argument, not arguing for immutable truths.) Any reality frame is thereby provisionalized in the name of pragmatic engagement rather than epistemological hesitation. Friedrich Hayek, influential doyen of the Mont Pèlerin economic cabal, would agree that in a world indeterminably knowable analysis has its limits. You have to act; make a cut.

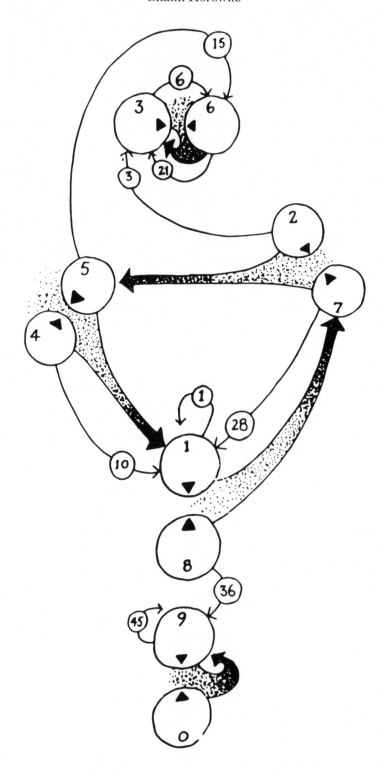

or body, but was rather a key embedded in the numeric undercurrents of matter itself. [(:):]

Stillwell's faith in the unremitting diagrammatic exactness of the Numogram led her to think that it had the capacity to arise from any alphanumeric culture in history. She would excitedly tell me things like, 'number is crucial for discovering the real boundaries under which we operate'. Throughout the 1930s and 40s, she navigated the South-East Asian cultural matrix seeking to unveil how the Numogram was invoked in Lemurian times—while also exploring how it might be of use to the present. Eventually she determined specific passages through the Numogram's contours, allowing her to begin a reconstruction of the decimal-based language of the Mu-N'ma, which lead to her famous assertion, 'N'ma culture cannot be decoded without the key provided by the Lemurian Time-Maze'. Frankly Stillwell's ethnographic analysis of Muvian numeracy during this period was nothing short of path breaking. [((:))]

In an unpublished paper from the summer of 1935, she announced that 'each numeral had a true name (although based on sounds intractable to modern human physiology)', asserting that these 'source words [were] derived from [an] 'Ur-Nma' culture, [which] provided the names of the decimal numerals and [their] basic morphological components [for] the entire Mu-Nma language (Munumuese)'. After identifying forty-five distinct pathways between the Numogram's ten zones, [(:):] she began unraveling the numeric phoneticism of each

---

[(:):] One always acts within an assemblage, a collective, in which machines, objects, and signs are at the same time *agents*. The anonymous agent (for instance, in Valéry's conception of a history without authors) produces ruptures by differentially surfing combinatorial processes. This collective investment can lead to the creation of an egregor (cf. Vodun ritual), an independent thought-form which may or may not be intentionally actualized, and which communicates with its adherents, who in turn modulate it via feedback. The entity often outlives its initial collaborators (think of corporate concoctions, political parties, media celebrities, any long-term myth sustenance) and will continue thriving as long as its components are periodically reenergized. The way in which the intensive gradient of a war belongs to the latter rather than to any of the constitutive parties is a profoundly egregoric phenomenon. 'John Frum' was an egregor hovering over Tanna (New Hebrides) that ended up becoming naturalized, institutionalized (reterritorialized!) in a political party in the 1950s. Dubbed an 'urumun' (spirit medium), 'John Frum' was/is a middleman, a servitor, a hermetic messenger travelling between the living and the dead mirroring the escapades of the *original* Frum, a temporarily human vector connecting America and Tanna.

[((:))] The number 9 holds absolutely no value in the digital reduction of the Assyro-Babylonian occult practice of Gematria (meaning that 9 can be eliminated from any complex kabbalistic reduction). Due to the fact that the division of zero by any number results in infinity, Zone-0 of the Numogram is necessarily paired with Zone-9—due to an elementary nine-sum coupling decimal procedure called zygonovism. This twinning process both divides and binds the ten decimal numerals (0-9) into five syzygys, or numeric twins. Basically each number designates a zone, and each numeric zone is coupled with its pair, and the smaller lines (considered channels), result from the simple addition of a numeral's component naturals. By subtracting a smaller number from a bigger number within a syzygy, a current is formed. Although Echidna was not always the most lucid with words, the neolemurian scholar Lendl Barcelos remains especially clear: 'The Numogram's profundity arises from basic arithmetic, in that its entire structure results from adding or subtracting the ten decimals running from 0 through 9. Imposing no rules that aren't already in the numeric operations themselves, it also decouples the arbitrary attributions of numerology.'

[(:):] Designed to avoid capture by pre-established codes, hyperstition not only reveals the exceptional arbitrariness of many belief systems in place, but the unavoidable departure from thought that occurs when any belief is accepted or dismissed. Hyperstition as strange attractor of *unbelief* induces engagement with concepts that defer judgment. ("I don't believe in it but it works.") It is through the praxis of

channel in the Lemurian decimal labyrinth, arriving at the conclusion that each of the forty-five corridors circulating the Numogram's transits were actually hosted by distinct (albeit dormant) demonic denizens.[(:)]

By drawing out the Numogram, and following its channels, Stillwell became convinced she could unlock its gates—summoning a legion of unimaginably ancient, time-travelling insurgents. Although I had come to trust her notion that the central region of the Numogram was in fact a hydraulic arena of chronological time, and was even willing to conceive of the Numogram (as a whole) as a map of time—I remained flabbergasted by the notion that there were forty five primeval demons occupying the transits (running from any one isolated decimal zone to all other possible zones available to it).

So in January 1949, in the former Burmese capital of Yangon (a city bearing the curious translation 'End of Strife'), I journeyed to test this most audacious hypothesis with one of my own. Across a table covered with spironomic diagrams and rhizomatic manuscripts, I handed Echidna my first rendition of what I was calling the Old Book—an ancient Munumese text that I had recently lifted from the Mu Archive in Tibet (and then feverishly translated). I had travelled there to entrust my first version to Stillwell, because I was certain she was the only person who could safely deliver the document to a new acquaintance of ours. This was the retired naval captain and occultist, Peter Vysparov. Although Vysparov had been intently following Stillwell's ethnographic work on the N'Ma for decades, Stillwell had not heard of him, or his Lemurian proclivities, until this transaction. Directly following Vysparov's reception of the package containing my B manuscript (now known as *The Book of Paths*), he initiated a most fortuitous correspondence with Dr. Echidna Stillwell, which lasted from mid March to late May 1949. After many years of searching, I finally acquired this exchange, containing many of the missing pieces in what I would like to call the Krakatoan Chimera.

PANDEMONIUM

In the first letter, Peter began by conveying his exceptional interest in Stillwell's research, before relaying a very recent and highly destabilizing encounter of his own, which took place amongst the Dib-Nma of Eastern Sumatra. Apparently he had been deployed to the region to catalyze a local insurgency against the Japanese occupation. Vysparov promptly admitted to having relied upon Stillwell's research there, with the goal of harnessing the sorcerous practices of the local witchcraft in order to incapacitate the enemy garrison. What followed was no routine insurrection, but rather a sorcerous war resulting in atrocious

---

unbelief that the hyperstitious are said to hold their premonitions at bay.

[(:)] The 'time-circuit' is occupied by three of the Numogram's five primary, syzygetic demons—Katak (4::5), Oddub (7::2), and Murmur (1::8). Both the lower and higher realms exist outside of sequential time, considered by the two respectively as 'the Plex' and 'the Warp' (these are the provinces of the other two principal Lemurian demons—occupied by Djinxx (3::6) and Uttunul (0::9)). She referred to the demons (or eventually, lemurs) within the Time-Circuit as Chronodemons; those that only circulate in the outer gulfs are Xenodemons, and finally those crossing all three expanses of the Numogram were Amphidemons.

mental breakdowns: 'from leadership dysfunction… to berserk derangement[::]; and paranoid ravings, culminating in suicide'. The successful episode, however horrific, left Vysparov irrevocably fascinated by the fact that the Dib-Nma sorcerers were 'able to telepathically communicate extreme conditions of psychotic dissociation'. After imparting his sincere admiration for Stillwell, and also thanking her for relaying my text, Vysparov closed the letter by describing the dates surrounding the Sumatran ordeal as strikingly Lovecraftian.

While Stillwell had never met the reclusive H.P. Lovecraft during her time in New England, she knew his writings through and through, and had in fact even engaged in a fleeting correspondence with the man. However, she had sensed an excessive and irrational terror[(:)(:)] in Lovecraft's tone (which she described to me as 'unusually hygienic racial paranoia') and thus cut off their communications.

I remember how distressing Vysparov's letter was for Stillwell, as it was clear evidence that the Indonesian conflicts were further devastating the long afflicted peoples of the N'Ma. Nevertheless, in her first response, Stillwell agreed that the dates in question possessed not only strong Lovecraftian resonances, but overtly Lemurian ones as well. While mid to late March (the period of the Spring Equinox) is of course explicitly emphasized in 'The Call of Cthulhu'—it was also what she called 'the intense-zone of Nma time ritual'. Vysparov's next letter opened with some lingering thoughts on his encounter with Dibbomese Sorcery. He wrote of an 'occult ammunition manufacture', 'complete personality disintegration', and then hurdled a much heavier thought: 'Dibbomese sorcery does not seem to be at all interested in judgments as to truth or falsity, it appears rather to estimate in each case the potential to make real.'[::::] Although Stillwell responded respectfully, her letter was undeniably critical.

In short, she was concerned Vysparov was potentially reducing Nma sor-

---

[:::] Think about the way in which (artificially-generated) anticipation bleeds into, infects, shapes the present while functioning as a probehead for potential future events. It's the essence of hype. The amygdala, emotional nexus of the brain, is adjacent to the hippocampus, lodging both hard drive and information retrieval mechanisms. Anamnestic experiences fuse the two in mutual excitation. Add significant portions of the frontal lobe involved in planning and impulse control and you have a machine for hyperstitional entrainment.

[(:)(:)] The integrity of a hyperstitional carrier is never relevant, only its capacity to conjure the desired effects, which assemble in the absence of discernable causes, much like within certain Vodun practices (as documented by Walter Cannon) that induce fatal biological consequences. The route is through the amygdala, the 'audition-to-fear' pathway, lubricated by cultural underpinnings. (The manner in which deprogramming effectively retroproduces the offending program is another classic effect-before-cause scenario. Recall that regressive hypnotherapy historically preceded the appearance of false memory syndrome!)

[::::] Peirce's idea of abduction—'leading away' (ab + ducere)—is at the core of his hyperstitional pragmatics. Thought becomes stifled when negative feedback reigns. Abductive reasoning does not need to follow logically from self-evident observables or premises at hand (as with deduction), or from excluded but necessarily implicated information (as with induction), being untethered to initial conditions, and although not analogous to discovery or justification, it is deeply intertwined with both. CSP sought to jumpstart alien vectors of investigation by changing headings abductively, without the benefit of provable theorems to lead the way. The British cyberneticists (bless their idiosyncratic minds) rejected the statistical, quantifying methods made possible by data correlation. Grey Walter (among them) knew the complexities of the world could only be accosted through materially contingent, temporally pressured interventions.

cery, 'to mere magic, or the imposition of change in accordance with the will'. While this seems like an easy misinterpretation to arrive at, Stillwell considered it catastrophically Western, and moreover a crude divergence from her life's work. Nevertheless, the exchange continued, perhaps climaxing with Vysparov's communiqué of May 7, 1949:

> Here in Massachusetts we have been convening a small Lovecraft reading-group, dedicated to exploring the intersection between the Nma cultural constellation, Cthulhoid contagion, and twisted time-systems. We are interested in fiction only insofar as it is simultaneously hyperstition—a term we have coined for semiotic productions that make themselves real—cryptic communications from the Old Ones, signaling return: *shleth hud dopesh.*[(::)]

Although Echidna Stillwell had always been wary of reading groups, Vysparov's enterprise caught her attention. As someone who had committed her life to the most urgent invariances, Dr. Echidna Stillwell was well aware that superstition only ever scratched the surface of reality. This notion of *hyperstition*, however, had strong Lemurian current, and got its grip on her.

While Stillwell had assumed Vysparov had read bits and pieces of her ethnographic work on Lemurian sorcery, she was startled that he had encountered as much as he had.[(:):] Although oddly flattered by Vysparov's bold claim that her 'recovery of the Lemurodigital Pandemonium Matrix', was none other than the implicit wellspring for Abdul Alhazred's fabled *Kitab al-Azif* (known as *The Necronomicon* by most Western occult-dealers), she still found it, 'absurd to imagine that Lemurian Pandemonium has One purpose or function'. While her final response to Vysparov did not at all imply commitment to this newly inaugurated reading group, she nonetheless congratulated him for the daring venture.

Stillwell had always presumed Lovecraft's writings were more factional than fictional, not only because the narratives oscillate between real and imaginary events, but simply since she had met several of his 'characters' in person. In fact, she once told me that the most excessively hyperbolized fictional quantities in Lovecraft's writing were simply outcomes of missing information, if not explorations cut short. Aware that much work had to be done in decoding Lovecraft's mythos, not to mention the many zones and channels of the Numogram, she thus closed her letter to Vysparov of May 28, 1949 conveying her profound interest in how these events all converged around hyperstition. There she wrote,

---

[(:):] Reality potency is a function of consistency, but a flair for staging helps. One should strive towards the construction of a consistent world that performs the reterritorializing necessary for hyperstition to take effect, inevitably requiring the mimicry of epistemological and formalist hierarchies and patterns by which something can be ratified into conceptual solidity. Any kind of nonsense or synthetic fiction as long as it's pressured through sense-making formalisms, protocols, narrative, institutional logics, parasites on them, can be successfully transitioned into effectiveness. You remember the "Welfare Queen" hyperstition that Reagan amped (dredged) up in order to justify the decimation of a social program? Or cyberspace, fictionalized by Gibson in 1984, then conjured into being via extensive investment in the concept. Then there was that Bush administration official: 'We're an empire now, and *when we act, we create our own reality*. And while you're studying that reality—judiciously, as you will—we'll act again, creating other new realities, which you can study too, and that's how things will sort out. *We're history's actors . . . and you, all of you, will be left to just study what we do.*'

'Hyperstition strikes me as a most intriguing coinage. We thought we were making it up, but all the time the Nma were telling us what to write—and through them'. As with the Numogram, it would seem that hyperstition was not something that could be attributed to Vysparov, or anybody else for that matter. [:::]

Stillwell presumed the prefix of this word was derived from 'hypodermic' (beneath the skin), but also approached this assumption cautiously— wondering whether this concept's potency wasn't also connected to hype (recent American slang for trick or swindle). Either way, she was amazed by the sheer grammatical rarity of a neologism that sought to outstrip its suffixation without any recourse to allusion or metaphor. Mindful that any entry into language entailed overcoding, she felt hyperstition was a concept that required delicate usage,[(:):] and decided that if it were to be employed at all, it would require covert engagement, as well as diversions. Cognizant that the word *fact* evolved from the Latin for *fabrication*, and the word *person* from *mask*, she understood that hyperstition could only be entrusted to the most depersonalized 'individuals'.

THE RIFT

It has now been over forty years since this exchange took place. I am writing this to tell the real Stillwell story. Having finally defeated the Vysparov estate in court, we are now in the process of publishing their correspondence in full. Roughly nine years ago, Stillwell vanished from the face of the earth.

What really happened between Stillwell and Vysparov? In the early 1970s— largely due to Vysparov's support—Echidna had been appointed Chair of the Hydro-History department at MVU (MIT's short-lived interdisciplinary appendage in Cambridge, Massachusetts). Vysparov's enduring enthusiasm, however, had the gradual effect of discrediting Stillwell's work via contamination with his own questionable interests. As rumours began to spread that her data had been falsified she recorded the receipt of several ominous 'cease and desist' letters in her diary, mentioning—fleetingly, as if paranoia had made her doubt

---

[:::] All epistemic activity composing a particular hyperstition needs cryptographic dispersement if it is to prove its contaminatory mettle. Hyperstitional carriers simulate personalities in order to consolidate a node of anegoic cognitive consistency: to think what no natural ego can. (Caillois' psychasthenic, de-pathologized: 'I know where I am, but I do not feel as though I'm on the spot where I find myself.') Carriers can be coincidence magnets, attractors, ferreting out previously veiled, subliminal linkages. They can attach themselves to other entities, holding them together in a correlative bind, resulting in a permanent fusional parasitic-syzegetic contamination. (Remember the lead up to GWII and the terms Atta, Prague, Saddam, 9/11 hanging out across vast swaths of media. It's only a matter time before you ascribe causal solidity to these relations, möbius-like, without anyone knowing the difference.) They can also be programmed to hijack existing (read: consistently deployed) symbols that already compress a preexisting set of relations and trajectories, normative temporalities and continuities, keeping in mind the thresholds above and beneath which such symbols shed their identity. Carriers are props articulating the ambiguous zones between the perceptual experience of actual reality and what can be imagined.

[(:):] Hyperstition benefits as much from smoke and mirrors as it does from collective excitation. Hyperstitional transmissions are always autocatalytic. The hyperstitional investment of Jerusalem as Holy City with a specific historical destiny entails certain geopolitical consequences. Likewise in finance: The Black-Scholes-Merton Model (in option pricing theory) becomes an engine (prescriptive) rather than a camera (descriptive). Derivatives are themselves hyperstitional. They are fictional quantities— no longer pegged to anything materially substantial like the *gold standard* (Nixon unmoored the US dollar in 1971)—transmuted into an effective world-historical force.

her own intuitions—the fact that each of the letters had been sealed with a strange insignia 'comprising five spheres arranged in the form of a cross'. Tragically, the university began to distance itself from Stillwell's career, and volumes of unpublished writings on Muvian folklore never saw the light of day.

Just weeks before her disappearance, I received what is considered to be her final letter. Dr. Edward Blake—the author of a forthcoming Stillwell biography—is convinced that the letter is authentic and contains many of 'Stillwell's characteristic stylistic traits', perhaps most notably her typically serpentine handwriting ... but to this day I remain suspicious. The letter of March 6, 1980 reads:

Chaim,

Despite considerable efforts, Vysparov and his Atlantean brothers will not rest without capitalizing on the Lemurian device. I had always thought he seemed too academic, but somehow convinced myself that his didactic compulsions were a militaristic tactic, if not just a remarkable sense of humor. Unfortunately, it is now dreadfully clear that he has had ulterior allegiances all along.

In order to protect hyperstition from encroaching tedium, we are in need of a sufficient detour, a sort of smokescreen. Do you recall the Phonocleric? "Liars retain respect for the truth"? Displace illation for the sake of transmission. A rigorous unfolding of the labyrinth (in all its folds) remains key, but for the sake of the last Lemurians, all processes intrinsic to hyperstitional praxis must forever be cloaked.

Parallels with particularly resonant dynamic systems could be drawn, but if the occultural traditions are amended, style must be encoded accordingly. While a fragmented hyperstitional mythos might help corrode your credibility, only with the most exacting conceit. I must go now.

- Echidna

PS—Hyperstition will find a way around this mess ... focus on buying the carriers some time.[::)(:]

[::)(:] Entrusting a concept to any real author always backfires. Territorializing manoeuvres emphasizing the pathology of original genius inevitably short circuit the hyperstition's potential virulence as it takes a cascading network of carriers for a hyperstitional multiplicity to gather its distinctively self-regenerative traction. In order to smuggle concepts into culture, avatars are indispensable, decoys are useful, and depersonalization is mandatory. (On encountering anomalous obstacles, carriers would be well advised to relay the hyperstitional eddy to a less encumbered vector.)

Designed to pursue a line of thought further than is prudent, decent, or reasonable, a carrier thinks only for the sake of the thought itself, rather than for what its thinking will mean for its own interests (of which it has none). It probes, or pings territories that no natural mind could navigate. Heraclitus advocated seeking out the invisible and inarticulate in the order of things, the invisible connection being the stronger one, the inconspicuous correspondence the most important. Pinging is a way of smoking out a *distribution of the insensible*—a motley array of weak signals, aberrant behaviors which rational models fail to apprehend—exposing the operative paradoxes and inconsistencies of a constellation which, when surfaced, often spiral out of control. Hyperstitional probeheads favor misconstruals of a system, foregrounding the latter's workings as it surfs the impersonal differentiating filters of language, media and communication.

Semiotic/material constitution is already thought as being implexed within an affective, semiotic, interpretative network which assigns these particular concoctions a certain productive virtuality or potential (The Phonocleric). A parasite, the carrier plays the position instead of the contents. Playing and preying on the relations and the points that constitute those relations as operators = a royal road to hyperstitional effectiveness.

14

Noise: An Ontology of the Avant-garde

Amy Ireland

When he first sights the vast unknown mountain range from the window of an aircraft with his scientific team in tow, geologist and academic William Dyer, the protagonist of H.P. Lovecraft's *At the Mountains of Madness,* is intensely troubled by the vision that confronts him. Like his colleague Professor Lake, Dyer struggles to determine the image's verity.[1] Lake attributes the queer effects to the pre-Cambrian slate, upheaved strata and volcanic quality of the highest peaks, but Dyer is not so sure. For this particular image (in which he discerns a 'seething labyrinth' housed in the range's uppermost slopes) 'has a menacingly novel and obscure quality' about it, giving the effect, Dyer recounts, of 'a Cyclopean city of no architecture known to man or human imagination...'.[2] Of course, the Professor is relieved when the image finally breaks up, dissolved by the shifting mists that screen the mountains—confirmation of its illusory status.

But this relief does not last for long. As is the case for many an unfortunate Lovecraftian protagonist, Dyer's scientific zeal compels him to return, only this time he traverses the peaks and discovers that the distorted image he originally perceived has an origin that is irrevocably real and disturbingly inhuman:

> The effect of the monstrous sight was indescribable, for some fiendish violation of known natural law seemed certain at the outset. Here, on a hellishly ancient tableland fully 20,000 feet high, and in a climate deadly to habitation since a pre-human age ... there stretched nearly to the vision's limit a tangle of orderly stone which only the desperation of mental self-defence could possibly attribute to any but a conscious and artificial cause. We had previously dismissed, so far as serious thought was concerned, any theory that the cubes and ramparts of the mountainsides were other than natural in origin. How could they be otherwise? Yet now the sway of reason

---

1. H.P. Lovecraft, 'At the Mountains of Madness', *Tales,* ed. Peter Straub, New York, Library of America, 2005, p. 492.

2. Lovecraft, 'At the Mountains of Madness', *Tales,* p. 508.

seemed irrefutably shaken, for this Cyclopean maze of squared, curved, and angled blocks had features which cut off all comfortable refuge. It was, very clearly, the blasphemous city of the mirage in stark, objective, and ineluctable reality. That damnable portent had had a material basis after all—there had been some horizontal stratum of ice-dust in the upper air, and this shocking stone survival had projected its image across the mountains according to the simple laws of *reflection*. Of course the phantom had been twisted and exaggerated, and had contained things which the real source did not contain; yet now, as we saw that real source, we thought it even more hideous and menacing than its distant image.[3]

As Dyer approaches and finally crosses the mountains of madness, straying over the threshold that encircles 'that mysterious farther realm upon which … no *human* eye had ever gazed' his relationship to the image of the alien city and the verity he accords to it shift dramatically.[4] What he first instinctively took to be real is demoted to the status of an illusion, a revelation that is followed by his discovery of its real source, a discovery that in turn restates the illusion as a problem of reflection and an epiphenomenal imprint of a very real thing—but a noisy, distorted one. If one were to diagram this in a cybernetic key—following the models of classic communications theory—the following configuration would emerge:

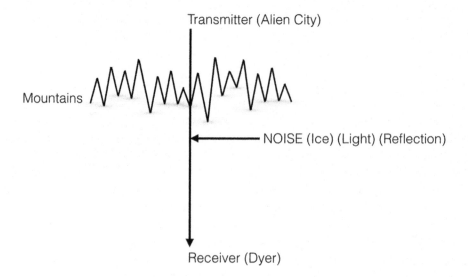

Transmitter (Alien City)

Mountains

NOISE (Ice) (Light) (Reflection)

Receiver (Dyer)

3. Lovecraft, 'At the Mountains of Madness', *Tales*, p. 522; p. 523 [emphasis added]. Among Lovecraft's notes is a diagram—drawn along the upper flap of an unfolded envelope—for the formation of the mirage on a 'layer of cloud' in front of the mountain range, with the alien city sketched in behind. Particularly significant is the suggestion that Lovecraft's mental image of the city's projection onto the dust and mist on the other side of the mountain range seems to have had its own material basis, informed by the shape of the envelope. H.P. Lovecraft, notes on 'At the Mountains of Madness', 1931. *Howard P. Lovecraft Collection, 1894-1971*, The John Hay Library, Brown University.

4. Lovecraft, 'At the Mountains of Madness', *Tales*, p. 522.

Here, the real city acts as a transmitter, the ice-dust, mist and most importantly, the Antarctic light, constitute interference to the transmitted signal, and Professor Dyer occupies the position of the receiver. The clear signal is scrambled as it passes over the mountains, but Dyer is, at least at first, content to call the distorted image he receives, real. As well as being an illustration of cybernetic noise, this image schematizes the basic cognitive operation of Enlightenment subjectivity, an operation of 'inhibited synthesis' to put it in the words of Nick Land, who clarifies this notion in one of his early essays on Kant:

> [Modernity] lives in a profound and uneasy relation to an outside that both attracts and repels it, a relation that it precariously resolves within itself from a position of unilateral mastery. [...] The paradox of enlightenment, then, is an attempt to fix a stable relation with what is radically other, since insofar as the other is rigidly positioned within a relation it is no longer fully other. If before encountering otherness we already know what its relation to us will be, we have obliterated it in advance. This aggressive logical absurdity (the absurdity of logic itself) reaches its zenith in the philosophy of Kant, whose basic problem was to find an account for the possibility of what he termed 'synthetic a priori knowledge', which is knowledge that is both given in advance by ourselves, and yet adds to what we know.[5]

Modern subjectivity, forged in the cool climes of Kantian critique and Enlightenment rationality, represents the object by passing it through the subject. It is in this way that Kant first sets in place the epistemological limit that would outlaw metaphysics—that is—by installing a representational one. Put another way, for the modern subject, freshly stripped of all metaphysical guarantees, the world cannot appear without the presupposition of a self.

Human subjectivities, of course, may vary wildly, but the objectivity of their experience, as pointed up by Land, is assured by virtue of a universally attributed a priori purification of all that is inputted into cognition. For Kant specifically, this 'signal from the outside' is cleaned up by the pure forms of intuition and the twelve categories, which obtain in all human creatures—Kant explicitly notes that his deduction does not hold for the non-human—thus underwriting the homogeneity and the intelligibility of the world as it *for us*. This constitutes the nub of what Kant would call transcendental conditioning. We no longer discover the order of phenomenal nature; we make it.

Modernity's unprecedented capacity to breed the individual arises from and feeds back into the constitution of objective reality and the truth of being by means of intersubjectivity. The proper functioning of our significative regimes is unimaginable without this intersubjectively-constituted objectivity. Regardless of whether we subscribe to a properly Kantian theory of cognition or not, it is important to recognize that Kant's badly named Copernican revolution continues to determine the configuration of our subject-object relationships, and thus our understanding of representation, right up until the end

---

5. Nick Land, 'Kant, Capital and the Prohibition of Incest', *Fanged Noumena*, eds. Robin Mackay and Ray Brassier, Falmouth, Urbanomic, 2012, p. 64.

of the twentieth century, surreptitiously informing, in turn, standardized notions of aesthetic representation. For it is there, in the early decades of the nineteen-hundreds that one sees the real maturation of this state of affairs which places its denizens in a queer situation of utter dependency on representation. The cumulative effect of two hundred years of human reflection confirms that the real will always-already be represented and that the material is always-already conditioned by the ideal. There is no such thing as matter *in-itself*. Originary moments of presentation and production are impossible for the moderns. Everything is mediated. Their world, our world, is one of representation and reproduction, right down to the ground—which here, is irrevocably anthropomorphic—the human mind.

As Land will tell us, almost fifteen years before a single theorist uttered the word 'correlationism', the ontological condition of the moderns comes down to the following fundamental premise: 'the outside must pass by way of the inside'.[6] To this I will append that claim that the inside is a condition known in cybernetic theory as 'noise'. What Kant sees as a clarifying process, Land sees as a process of interference, the difference is a simple matter of positioning.

In French the word '*parasite*' has several meanings. It refers, as it does in English, to an organism that subsists by feeding off a host in a non-reciprocal relation; it means *static*, *interference*, or *noise*; and it denotes a point that is beside another, more integral one: *para*-site—beside the site. Michel Serres, in his book of the same name, *The Parasite*, uses these various meanings to frame a logic that is anything but 'absurd' in the sense intended by Land above. Rather, in a flagrant, wholesale rejection of a priori thought-structures, Serres' elaboration of his logic takes the form of a series of interrupted meals.[7] Each meal is a message transmitted to a receiver—an act of consumption, digestion and signification. However, more often than not, the receiver is deprived of the message by means of an uninvited guest—a parasite, who para-sites or eats-next-to the host, effectively interrupting the transmission, only to be interrupted in their interruption (which is a message being transmitted in its own right) by another message or guest. It suits Serres' purposes that the words for guest and host are identical in French: '*hôte*'. The message here—although Serres makes sure it does not come through clearly—is that there is always an alternative position from which a guest may suddenly appear as a host; a message as a parasite; signification as noise.[8]

Borrowing Serres's method of using cybernetics as a means of articulating complex relationships between elements that are both internal and external to a system, we can diagram Kantian cognition from both the position of the human subject and the position of the non-human object:

---

6. Nick Land, 'Machinic Desire', *Fanged Noumena*, eds. Robin Mackay and Ray Brassier, Falmouth, Urbanomic, 2012, p. 320.

7. Michel Serres, *The Parasite*, trans. Lawrence R. Schehr, Minneapolis, University of Minnesota Press, 2007.

8. 'The host, the guest, breathes twice, speaks twice, speaks with forked tongue as it were ... we don't know what belongs to the system, what makes it up, and what is against the system, interrupting and endangering it. Whether the diagram [...] is generative or corrupting.' Serres, *The Parasite*, p. 16.

I. Inside Out

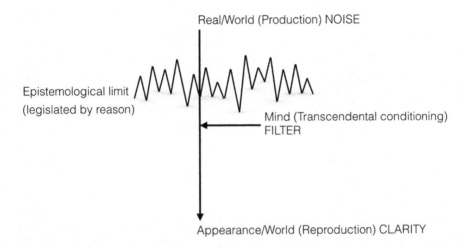

Real/World (Production) NOISE

Epistemological limit
(legislated by reason)

Mind (Transcendental conditioning)
FILTER

Appearance/World (Reproduction) CLARITY

II. Outside In

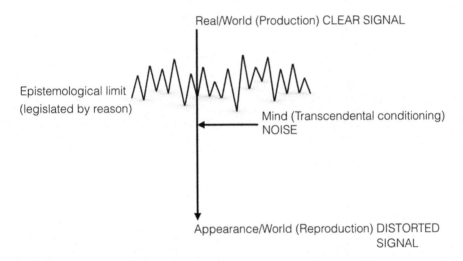

Real/World (Production) CLEAR SIGNAL

Epistemological limit
(legislated by reason)

Mind (Transcendental conditioning)
NOISE

Appearance/World (Reproduction) DISTORTED
SIGNAL

The advantage of transcribing a philosophical description of consciousness into a cybernetic register is that it allows us to move from a transcendent structure to an immanent one, and once within the latter, to move from one observer position to another. Hence, cybernetics affords us a vantage point from which to examine our own experience from the position of both the human and the nonhuman, effectively returning to the decentred Copernican viewpoint so slyly co-opted by Kantian philosophy. Looking from the inside out, the transcendental conditioning of experience establishes clarity by admitting certain contents of an unknowable site of primary production; yet from the outside in, the transcendental conditioning of experience is itself a degenerative noise that degrades the clarity of its external input, rendering it unintelligible and ultimately inaccessible to internal modes of apprehension. What, for the observer-as-subject is clarity, for the observer-as-object is noise. As Niklas Luhmann once remarked: 'Reality is what one does not perceive when one perceives it'.[9] Or (to collapse the first *Critique* into a single aphorism), '[t]he world is observable *because* it is unobservable.'[10] As the signal passes through the human—by virtue of this processing which ultimately renders it intelligible *to* the human—it becomes distorted. Signification, then, rests on a fundamental interruption and deformation. Here, the 'objectivity' of intersubjective experience is re-conceivable as interference in a primary signal that originates beyond the human in the unexperienceable (and unknowable) world of things-in-themselves. If Enlightenment subjectivity is constituted in this jamming of a signal from the outside, can we, by negating human noise (i.e. the a priori, the rational), reconstruct a vision of the source?

In *At the Mountains of Madness* as it is elsewhere, the perpetual Lovecraftian lesson is—of course—that the conditions upon which our Enlightenment subjectivity (figured in the hapless man of science) is founded and by which it is maintained, constitute a fundamental repression of something else, which, as is always the case in Lovecraft's prose, inevitably returns to invade the human from a point outside of it. I want to suggest that we take the Lovecraftian lesson here just as seriously as we take our Enlightenment genealogy and interrogate human representations of self and world from the *far side* of the mountains of madness in order to cultivate a properly inhuman notion of representation with which to reconsider certain moments of twentieth century aesthetic 'production'.

This widening of perspective to a point beyond the human afforded by thinking cybernetically brings with it new tools for the critique of critique, and, thereby, the critique of representation in art and poetics insofar as aesthetic representation is the representation of a representation that we can now grasp as a noisy one. Such a positioning is, of course, a form of philosophical speculation or better, a xenotheoretical act—one commensurate with the inversion Serres performs in his story of the rats' meal:

> At the door of the room, [the rats] heard a noise. What happened? The master is there; he disrupts the rats' feast. Why? He was sleeping soundly, after a good meal of ortolans, a heavy dish. Suddenly he awakens. He has heard a noise. Uneasy and anxious, he gets up and bit by bit opens the door. No one. The rats have left. A dream; he goes back to bed. Who, then, made the noise? The rats, of course... with their little paws and the gnashing of their teeth. All that wakes him up. The noise, then, was called for by noise. At the door of the room, *he* heard a noise.[11]

In the beginning, it is the noise of the master that interrupts the meal of the rats, but Serres then inverts the configuration by moving to the position of the human and now it becomes evident that the source of the noise is in fact the

---

9. Niklas Luhmann, 'The Cognitive Program of Constructivism and a Reality That Remains Unknown' in *Self-Organization: Portrait of a Scientific Revolution*, ed. Wolfgang Krohn et al., Dordrecht, Kluwer, 1990, p. 76.

10. Niklaus Luhmann, 'The Paradox of Observing Systems,' *Cultural Critique*, no. 31, 1995, p. 46.

11. Serres, *The Parasite*, p. 66.

rats' meal—although the master is left with nothing to confirm his speculation, and concludes, like Dyer, that it was only a dream. Perhaps if he had cultivated his insomnia a little longer, and sat up in the dark without a light—for it is light that turns the real into an illusion—he might have discovered the source … because the rats always come back. In fact, they've never left. Just as Serres conceives of the post-human as something that does not simply succeed the human, but precedes and subtends it too, the rats wait in the ground, perpetually ready to 'climb onto the rug when the guests are not looking, when the lights are out, when the party's over'.[12] The transmission itself begins in noise, but this noise is different from the noise of the human subject.[13] It is a rat noise. A noise from underground. A noise that is *post-*, *pre-* and *sub-* all at once.[14] Land would write in 'Spirit and Teeth' that '[the rat has] a hideous talent for decomposing interiorities,' that it is a 'sheer intensity, a potential for disaster' whose 'destructiveness is almost unlimited', and that, much in keeping with the thinking of Serres, there is no such thing as a single rat-unit, for as far as differentiation can occur within the rat-swarm, it is only 'differentiation within an illimitable series, [an] alogical dissimilarity, [an] indiscriminate proliferation of nonidentity'. 'This,' concludes Land, 'is the "logic" of the rat.'[15]

Serres differentiates the parasite-producer of the message, the one who is 'always attentive to the game of the things-themselves' from the parasite-reproducer 'who plays the position' or 'the location', which is to say, the one who positions themselves at the relation rather than at the object.[16] These latter lack the complexity and generative potential that Serres illustrates with the trope of fire; those at the relation are 'the cold ones', while those at the object, the producers, are hot. Their operation is one of deliquescence, dissolution, meltdown—the pursuit of a heat death in which the verticality of transcendence slips forwards or backwards into the ooze of immanence:

> Those of fire without location burn madly, so strongly that around them, objects change as if in a furnace or near a forge… They are not the masters [the one who plays the position plays the relations between subjects; thus, he masters men], they can be slaves, but they are the beginnings. They are the noise of the world, the sounds of birth and of transformations.[17]

---

12. Serres, *The Parasite*, p. 12.

13. 'In the beginning was noise…' Serres, *The Parasite*, p. 13.

14. 'Are not the rats… a positive antihistoricism?' Nick Land, 'Spirit and Teeth', *Fanged Noumena*, eds. Robin Mackay and Ray Brassier, Falmouth, Urbanomic, 2012, p. 192.

15. Land, 'Spirit and Teeth', *Fanged Noumena*, p. 193; p. 196; p. 199; and Serres: 'We are fascinated by the unit; only a unity seems rational to us… Disaggregation and aggregation as such, and without contradiction are repugnant to us … We want a principle, a system, an integration, and we want elements, atoms, numbers. We want them and we make them. A single god and identifiable individuals.' Serres, *The Parasite*, p. xii.

16. 'To play the position or to play the location is to dominate the relation. It is to have a relation only with the relation itself, never with the stations from which it comes, to which it goes, and by which it passes. Never to the things as such, undoubtably, never to subjects as such. Or rather, to those points as operators, as sources of relations. And that is the meaning of the prefix *para-* in the word *parasite:* it is on the side, next to, shifted, it is not on the thing, but on its relation. It has relations, as they say, and it makes a system out of them. It is always mediate and never immediate.' Serres, *The Parasite*, p. 38.

17. Serres, *The Parasite*, p. 38.

Here is the primary noise, the noise that produces, the site of genesis or primary production. An uninhibited 'primary synthesis', to put it in more Kantian terms, from which the a priori synthesis that Kant attributes to the human mind is itself drawn.

Land and Serres both theorize the productive element of Being as a pre-individuated, generative excess that precedes the mental processing which, under the direction of Enlightenment rationality, filters from it all that is inefficacious or problematic for the consolidation of the category known as 'the human', serving up experience as a single, anthropocentrically calibrated, signifying channel. Thus, we have two parasites/two noises: one that is an endlessly proliferating, generative, disorganized and unstable multiplicity and one that interrupts and interferes with this multiplicity by constraining it, and in doing so, maintains coherence in the reproduction of the conditions of its own possibility. One noise that is hot, that races, disperses and transforms; and one that is cold, a noise composed of structured rigidity and immobile formalism. For each, the other constitutes an interruption.

On the other side of the mountains of madness, the tunnel to the centre of the earth has its entrance. Professor Dyer and his assistant plumb the subterranean rat-holes looking for evidence of the architects of the alien city. What they find is Futurism.

> ... there was something vaguely but deeply unhuman in all the contours, dimensions, proportions, decorations, and constructional nuances of the blasphemously archaic stonework. [The reliefs] involved a peculiar treatment of perspective; but had an artistic force that moved us profoundly notwithstanding the intervening gulf of vast geologic periods. [...] It is useless to try to compare this art with any represented in our museums. Those who see our photographs will probably find its closest analogue in certain grotesque conceptions of the most daring futurists.[18]

As one approaches the heat at the centre of the earth, *pre-* collapses into *post-* and *sub-* intensifies. At the nadir of their descent, the scientific language with which Dyer controls his narration gives way entirely and it is only through the negative that his retelling is able to continue. Meanwhile his assistant can only chant the names of stations of the Boston-Cambridge subway line, portentous in their accelerating rhythm—'*South Station Under—Washington Under—Park Street Under—Kendall—Central—Harvard* ...' an analogy that is not lost on Dyer.[19] The legislative power of the a priori is waning, and this 'something else'—the Lovecraftian alternative to the professorial regime of sense—swerves abruptly into human experience:

> It was the utter, objective embodiment of the fantasy novelist's "thing that should not be"; and its nearest comprehensible analogue is a vast, onrushing subway train as one sees it from a station platform—the great black front looming colossally out of infinite subterranean distance, constellated with strangely coloured lights and filling the prodigious

---

18. Lovecraft, 'At the Mountains of Madness', *Tales*, pp. 535-536.
19. Ibid, pp. 580-581.

burrow as a piston fills a cylinder.[20]

'*It*' is an acephalous, alien thing, a 'nightmare plastic column of foetid black iridescence', a 'fifteen foot sinus', 'formless protoplasm'—utter noise—the pre-condition of life, and—'gathering unholy speed', it is also modernity.[21] But more profoundly, it is a certain element of modernity that—despite its ostensible development from it—comes back to Enlightenment rationality, to the human, from a position outside of it with the tremendous force of an interruption. This noisy drive to rupture and to race, to deform and disrupt, to collapse all boundaries between art and life, between life and machine—between the *reproduction-of-reproduction* and the *reproduction-of-production* (as a gesture towards the ultimate collapse between reproduction and production itself) belongs to the 'inhuman will' (to quote D.H. Lawrence) of the modernist avant-garde—an envoy from the future, definitionally 'out of time'.[22]

A figuration of the non-relation between human and world can only be posited within the aesthetic as an irruption of this primary noise into the secondary noise of human representation.

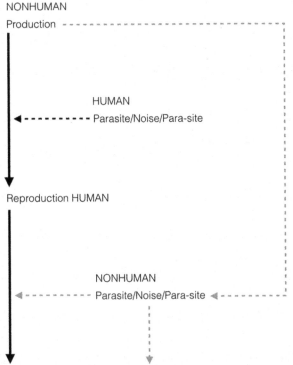

NONHUMAN
Production

HUMAN
◄ - - - - - - - - - Parasite/Noise/Para-site

Reproduction HUMAN

NONHUMAN
◄ - - - - - - - - Parasite/Noise/Para-site ◄ - - - - - - - -

Aesthetic Production (reproduction of the interruption of reproduction)

---

20. Ibid, p. 581.

21. Lovecraft, 'At the Mountains of Madness', *Tales*, p. 575; p. 581. See also, Luigi Russolo, 'Dynamism of a Car', (1912-1912), oil on canvas, Paris, Musée National d'Art Moderne, Centre Georges Pompidou.

22. D.H. Lawrence, 'Letter to Edward Garnett, 5 June 1914', *The Cambridge Edition of the Letters of D.H. Lawrence*, Vol. 2: *1913-16*, ed. George J. Zytaruk and James T. Boulton, Cambridge, Cambridge University Press, 1981, pp. 182-183.

Thus, F.T. Marinetti, Kurt Schwitters, and Sibyl and Lazlo Moholy-Nagy, for the most part reluctant guests at a banquet held in the name of the German Press Association—the epitome of legislative, a priori conditioning—demonstrate the doctrine of uninhibited synthesis: that entropy is generative.[23] Schwitters is on the point of getting himself arrested after insulting the official from the Folk Culture Organisation who is seated beside him at the table and, following the account of Sibyl Moholy-Nagy, shoots a desperate glance at his fellow artists for aid. But before he can incite anyone to action, Marinetti has risen from his chair, swaying considerably, his face purple. Moholy-Nagy continues the account:

> "My friends", Marinetti said in French. "After the many excellent speeches tonight"—the silent officials winced—"I feel the urge to recite my poem 'The Raid on Adrianople'." There was polite applause. Some nice poetry would break the embarrassing dullness of dinner.

> *Adrianople est cerné de toutes parts*

> *SSSSrrrr zitzitzitzitzi PAAAAAAAAAAAAgh*

> *Rerrrrrrrrrrrrrrrr,* roared Marinetti.

> *Ouah ouah ouah, départ des trains suicides, ouah ouah ouah -*

> The audience gasped; a few hushed giggles were audible.

> *Tchip tchip tchip —*

> *féééééééééééééééééééléz !*

> He grabbed a wine glass and smashed it to the floor.

> *Tchip tchip tchip————des messages télégraphiques,*

> *couturières Americaines*

> *Piiiiiiiiiii—————————————iiiiiiiiiiiing, sssssssssrrrrrrrr, zitzitzit*

> *toum toum Patrouille tapie———*

> Marinetti threw himself over the table.

> *"Vanitéeeeee, viande congeléeeeeeeee ———*

> *veilleuse de La Madone —*

> — expiring almost as a whisper from his lips. Slowly he slid to the floor, his clenched fingers pulling the tablecloth downward, wine, food, plates, and silverware pouring into the laps of the notables.[24]

The poet descends along the vertical to reassume a formless horizontali-

---

23. Put another way, negentropy increases local entropy (which occurs as a necessary ballast). See, for example, Alexandre Favre, Henri Guitton, Jean Guitton, André Lichnerowicz and Etienne Wolff, *Chaos and Determinism*, trans. Bertram, Balitmore, Johns Hopkins Univesity Press, 1995, p. 8.

24. Sibil Maholy-Nagy, quoted in *The Dada Painters and Poets: An Anthology*, ed. Robert Motherwell, Cambridge, Belknap Press, 1981, pp. xxix-xxx.

ty under the table, commensurate with the noise from which the avant-garde emerges, taking order with him (exchanging it for art) and reinstating, amidst the clamour of errant cutlery, the profound unreasonableness of an entropic regime—one that dissolves the borders between table-top and pleated pants, sauce béarnaise and boutonnière, Riesling, ramekin and wrist-watch. That which would legislate artistic production will be shown a thing or two: 'Départ de trains suicides'—the suicide train is leaving the station.

After After Finitude: An Afterword

Justin Clemens

It is very common for people to think that they live in times of dissolution and decay. In Christian Europe, for example, the book of *Revelations* was canonical: 'The Apocalypse was widely commended as utterly indispensable.'[1] Prophets of one kind or another would accordingly emerge to declare that the end of the world was nigh. It is still grimly amusing to see the phenomenon of firm dates for the End being given, then broken—and then further dates given, to be broken in turn. Year-after-year, the End has come and the End has passed, without the attitudes and forms of thinking for which the End is clearly necessary failing to remain popular. One might then propose with the poet Wallace Stevens that 'the mind is always at the end of an age': that is, that a certain apocalypticism is perhaps a condition for any possible or actual thinking as such.

Certainly, there have always been critics of the sense of an ending. Maurice Blanchot has wittily declared that 'the apocalypse will be disappointing,' given that we now know how miniscule our entire solar system is in the scheme of the universe.[2] What previous ages enthusiastically imaged as the total obliteration of created things turns out to have been an almost-risible irrelevance. For his part, Jacques Derrida has shown that the thought of the 'end of man' is itself inscribed within philosophical anthropology itself, such that all putative calls for a transcending of Man in fact repeat the fundamental operations of humanism.[3] Compatible contemporaneous critiques can be cited from across the post-World War II humanities.

Only apparently paradoxically, this recognition of the insufficiency of the concept of an end derives from analytics that draw their inspiration and methods from finitude itself. The discovery of finitude is one of the most profound developments in modern philosophy, and one of its greatest thinkers is Martin Hei-

---

1. C.A. Patrides, '"Something like Prophetick strain": apocalyptic configurations in Milton' in C.A. Patrides and Joseph Wittreich (eds.), *The Apocalypse in English Renaissance thought and literature: patterns, antecedents and repercussions*, Manchester, Manchester University Press, 1984, p. 207.

2. See 'The Apocalypse is Disappointing' in M. Blanchot, *Friendship*, trans. E. Rottenberg, Stanford, Stanford University Press, 1997.

3. See 'The Ends of Man' in J. Derrida, *Margins of Philosophy*, trans. A. Bass, Brighton, Harvester Press, 1982.

degger. Why finitude? The ancient Greeks were finite thinkers of the finite: they submitted all thought and being to the limiting order of the One, and found the formlessness of the *apeiron* repulsive. But this isn't finitude; quite the contrary, it is merely the finite (of which more below). In contrast, Christian theology found a way to render God infinite—in fact, found a way to give its deity a number of staggering predicates or anti-predicates, such as immortal, immutable, infinite, and so on. This is clearly not finitude, either. Yet this very 'infinity' was inscribed in transcendence, that is, of an attitude to time that renders the time of this world finite, integrally marked by the End. Although scientific thought, in particular modern physics and mathematical set theory, renovated the thought of an infinite universe and the status of infinity itself, it allegedly failed to comprehend being-as-time.

Among other accomplishments, Heidegger returned simultaneously to the necessity to rethink being, the traditions of thinking itself, and above all to the problematics of disclosure, eclosion, and unveiling. As Christopher Fynsk puts it: 'By virtue of its inescapable temporal determination, thought can achieve no final definition of its own situation and thus cannot transcend the history in which it finds itself as it turns back upon that which gives it its impetus.'[4] Such an analysis of finitude is not a naïve one. The finitude of Being is not simply an empirical finitude. Finitude is neither the finite, nor simply the negation of the infinite. It is a critique of totality. It is a critique of science. It proposes that Being's finitude is inaccessible by most of the means by which thought seeks to grasp it, and turns to the opening of questioning itself as a priority. Finitude is at once *after-and-never-yet-after* insofar as it seeks on principle to return any thought to the time-of-its-own-happening.

Given this intellectual context, it seems that thought is confronted with at least a double problem today. On the one hand, we are confronted with what seems to be the patent evidence from an enormous range of events that we live, at the beginning of the 21st century, in an unprecedentedly turbulent world. To advert to the essays collected in this volume and to the editors' expressed aims, climate change, algorithmic capitalism, and technological innovation go beyond any prior challenges that humanity has faced. On the other hand, the inherited tools that we have to think such phenomena present as not only insufficient, but possibly as part of the problem itself. Yet—and this has been essential to Heidegger's contribution—we cannot simply, by force of will or desire, think that we can think our way out of this double-bind. If we do indeed need to actualize a thinking that is *after* finitude, we must be aware that it was the thought of finitude that has radicalized the problematic of the *after* as such.

So what then would it mean to be after finitude at all? What does the title of the conference, this book, and perhaps this project even mean: *Aesthetics After Finitude*? First of all, it is an allusion to Quentin Meillassoux's *After Finitude*, as well as to an entire milieu of radical thought, to Graham Harman and Object Oriented Philosophy (OOP), François Laruelle and his non-philoso-

---

4. C. Fynsk, *Heidegger: Thought and Historicity*, Ithaca and London, Cornell University Press, 1993, pp. 16-17.

phy, Ray Brassier and *Nihil Unbound*, Reza Negarestani and *Cyclonopedia*, to Nick Land, whose *Fanged Noumena* exerts a powerful if occult force upon a wide range of contemporary thinkers.[5] Behind these, moreover, is an entire host of tutelary figures, from C.S. Peirce and A.N. Whitehead through Wilfred Sellars and beyond.

To the extent that Meillassoux's book provides the keynote reference for the present collection, *Aesthetics After Finitude* should also be understood as *Aesthetics After After Finitude*, as the editors themselves note in their Introduction. But this phantom 'after' is not *written* as such; it is patent but suppressed, as befits the structure of allusion. Moreover, this should alert us to the meta-nominal aspect of the title: the reflexive incorporation of another title within it, at once marked and unmarked. Yet this also provokes a question: is this title a statement or a question? Does it announce: *here is* aesthetics-after-finitude, this is what aesthetics looks like *after finitude* or rather *after after finitude*; or rather *is there* aesthetics after finitude? In the second case, there is a suppressed question mark, a punctuation mark that is present-in-absence.

'After' implies, and this is part of the intention behind the nomination, a temporal reference. 'After finitude' implies that finitude is finished. Finitude has proven to be—perhaps unsurprisingly—finite. Finitude was finite in time; it had its time (finite), and now it's gone. Hence: what do we do now, in the time after finitude? Presumably, we're now in the in-finite or at least the non-finite, which certainly poses some further questions. After all, finitude is not simply done away with by the infinite. Finitude is by definition a subset of the infinite, included in the infinite. Yet if we were just continuing to enjoy finitude-after-finitude, one wouldn't presumably need to have any discussions about it, we could just keep doing what we've always done. So the title proposes a discussion of the non-finite aftermath of finitude. Part of the problem would immediately seem to be that 'infinite' has traditionally been equivalent to 'everything': what do we do now, then, but everything? So perhaps we need to ask more about this equivalence. Perhaps the infinite is not simply endless.[6]

The title may also imply that the time after finitude is infinite. But is that so? What happens if, 'after finitude,' we've really hit the time of the infinite? That doesn't necessarily mean, however, that infinitude is infinite in time. In fact, the 'after' might seem to preclude an infinitude of time after the infinite; the time of the infinite has already been limited by the time of the finite that it comes after. The time of the infinite may not be infinite. In which case, there would be a strong sense in which infinitude itself would still be finite. After finitude, then, would be finitude, just more of it, more intense finitude. Which might imply that

---

5. See, *inter alia*, Q. Meillassoux, *After Finitude: An Essay on the Necessity of Contingency*, trans. Ray Brassier, London, Continuum, 2008; G. Harman, *Guerilla Metaphysics: Phenomenology and the Carpentry of Things*, Chicago, Open Court, 2005; F. Laruelle, *Principles of Non-Philosophy*, trans. N. Rubczak and A.P. Smith, London, Bloomsbury, 2013; R. Brassier, *Nihil Unbound*, Houndmills, Palgrave, 2007; R. Negarestani, *Cyclonopedia*, Melbourne, re.press, 2008; N. Land, *Fanged Noumena*, Falmouth, Urbanomic, 2011.

6. As one of the editors of the present volume commented here: 'the prefix in is significant here too. In doubles in English as a verb formative but, equally, a substitute for the negative un, from Latin ante-. What is nice about the word infinity is that the paradox of the concept is allegorized in the lexeme, specifically in this Janus faced prefix.'

finitude was or is or will itself be endless, that is, already infinite. Or, conversely, that infinity and time necessarily part company; if there is to be infinity, then
it cannot be in time. It is not a priori clear that an infinite time is the equivalent of eternity. Just because something lasts for ever doesn't make it eternal: as
any good theologian might tell you, God is eternal but you yourself have only
the chance at everlasting life…the life *after* this life, which is not true life but its
antechamber.

Aesthetics has historically always been attentive to the problem of 'after.' In
being a discourse regarding the operations of formal invention in the regime of
the senses, aesthetics has always also had to deal with the problem of time-as-
form-giving. Here, again paradoxically, 'after' has meant in aesthetics not only
temporally belated, but *formally* belated as well. 'After Poussin' means, for example: in the style of Poussin; or, alternatively, a new work created on the basis of a
work of Poussin's. Thus 'after finitude' can mean: *in the style of finitude.* 'Aesthetics
after finitude' would then demand not infinity, but a continuation or extension
of aesthetics in the style of finitude.

We can then again reinterpret the project as asserting: 'there are perhaps
many possible styles, such that finitude is one of them, and the one that we are
adopting here.' Even more strongly, there's a rather mournful edge to 'after finitude': we've lost finitude, it's gone, and now we're chasing after it, hunting its
traces. Where has finitude gone? How do we get it back? 'Aesthetics After Finitude' might then mean: although we are seeking to come to terms with, even
affirm, the present, in which we are post-finitude, what we really want is to get
back to finitude so we can have our aesthetics again. Or again: our aesthetics
is modelled on finitude. So the temporality of the 'after' is also a question of a
principle of the creation and transmission of forms: what does 'after' mean for
form? Is form necessarily finite? Or must form and finitude divide after finitude?

After finitude therefore denominates and participates in an event of oxymo-
ron, contradiction, and paradox. It is also, as the contributors to this volume
all insist in their own ways, *after* what Meillassoux calls 'correlation.' That is:
finitude was the last recourse of a subjacent correlationism that ruled all modern philosophy, at once illicitly limiting itself as it retained the privilege of an
anthropological bond. Such correlationism is a humanism, that is, a kind of
self-denying humiliation of thought and its objects in the name of a covert yet
grotesque inflation of humanity. Yet the greatest problem with finitude is that—
despite the sophisticated analyses it presented regarding time and being—it *was
never really an after* after all. While the philosophies of finitude proposed themselves as a philosophical reaction to and affirmation of the Copernican Revolution in natural science, they in fact accomplished quite the opposite, a Ptolemaic counter-revolution, to invoke Meillassoux. Finitude was the reinsistence of *the
before* posturing as *the after.* As such, it integrally installed the relation of the *for
us* as its non-negotiable condition and ideal. To be after finitude therefore also
means to generalize the *not-for-us* of thought. *After finitude* must be *not-for-us* because we must now affirm our own cosmic deracination, our own irremediable
levelling in existence.

And this is why the absolute exigency of an inhuman speculation as absolute and real is the governing motif of these investigations. Moreover, as the editors admirably posit, part of the challenge is that the cosmic deracination attendant on the *after* be given its properly aesthetic freighting. Yet this means that aesthetics is no longer a science of feeling, sensibility, or sense, but ensnarled in imperceptible batteries of polysonic decorporations. These essays, in other words, and in line with their own professed inspirations and the challenges of their often-anonymous materials, are offering a kind of philosophical therapy. Philosophy has been from its foundations such a therapy: Socrates has been a long time sick, as the phrase has it; Wittgenstein wanted to show the fly the way out of the fly-bottle. Here, the treatment will and must be played out in the absence of the for-us, in the often savage speculations regarding hyperstition, the hyperfly, the hyperlaruellean, the hypermillennial, the hypergeological, the hypersynthetic, the hypertransfinite, the hypercyclonic, the hyperalgorithmic, the hypermallarmean, the hyperaccelerationist, the hypertiamatic, the hyperchimerical, the hypergardic. *Aesthetics After Finitude* proffers a hypertherapeutics of the afterthought among the madness of the molecules. Thinking big requires feeling small.

So *Aesthetics After Finitude* seeks to cure us of ourselves by really unleashing our own finitude, in all senses of that phrase. After the end of a thought of finitude which itself had declared the end of the end, we find the thought of the after as activating an absolute end. The end of correlationism is not only a destruction, but a consummation of that which correlationism sought to think. One consequence of the critique of correlationism must be the true assumption of our own finitude. If one can see this elaborated with the utmost clarity throughout the contributions to this volume, we could also invoke Brassier's genial move as exemplary: taking contemporary science seriously entails dealing with the absolute necessity of universal extinction.

As Brassier puts it in the conclusion to his brilliant book:

> In becoming equal to it [the trauma of extinction], philosophy achieves a binding of extinction, through which the will to know is finally rendered commensurate with the in-itself. This binding coincides with the objectification of thinking understood as the adequation without correspondence between the objective reality of extinction and the subjective knowledge of the trauma to which it gives rise. It is this adequation that constitutes the truth of extinction. But to acknowledge this truth, the subject of philosophy must also recognize that he or she is already dead, and that philosophy is neither a medium of affirmation nor a source of justification, but rather the organon of extinction.[7]

If I have any complaints about such a position, it is that this practice of philosophy has sutured itself too directly and lovingly to contemporary physics. As Brassier announces regarding the destiny of science: 'the point is not just that science enriches and amplifies our understanding of reality but that it uncov-

---

7. Brassier, p. 239.

ers the truth.'[8] Confusing the refusal of ineffability with a particular image of science, Brassier's magnificent statements—such as 'I am a nihilist because I believe in truth'—remain superb interventions into contemporary thought, yet only have pertinence on the basis of his prior collapsing of an old conception of truth into a particular figure of knowledge. I don't think anybody has to believe—however authentically nihilistic such a belief may present itself as being—that science uncovers truth. However, I do believe we have to agree that science establishes what counts as knowledge. What's the difference? Whether there is one ring to rule them all. This is precisely where aesthetics can intervene to snap apart such contingent competing collages of belief. What the current collection does through its very attentiveness to *aesthetics* is supplement and extend such work as Brassier's by effectively de-suturing truth from knowledge again. If there is indeed a general political point to aesthetics after finitude, it is surely this: to ensure that the after is in the end the without-master.

But what I finally wish to emphasize in these heterogeneous writings is an experience—or, more precisely, the *contemporary non-experience of the loss of all possible experience as an atemporal after*—to which they all testify, but which none of them directly discuss. This experience is in some sense a loss of the real—not just of any real, but a loss of the real of time as loss. This is a cut between modernity, for which time crystallizes in historical sites, and the contemporary, for which the loss of the real of time is embodied in atemporal and inhuman articulations. Of course, time still passes, vulgarly, experientially, non-linearly, kairotically, differentially repetitively, intermittently, what have you. But the loss of the real of time revivifies a kind of spontaneous speculative naivety regarding the irreducibility of objects (OOO and OOP) and a concomitant if contradictory tendency to revive one or another master of thought (e.g., physics for Brassier, logic or mathematics for Meillassoux). Yet between this Scylla and Charybdis, a new aesthetics of the aftermath. Speculation is to the present what melancholia was for modernity—the attempt to present in thought the trace of an irreducible in-temporal difference as the exhibition of action-in-inaction.

The classical melancholic was immobilized by the overwhelmingness of what-was-gone—the void of the past deactivating the forces of the present beyond any possible explanation—as a kind of zombie of being. Whether that persecutory past had ever existed at all is unlikely; whatever the case, the key was that it marked the present with its vitiating absence. Hence the pure time-mark expressed by the melancholic: that there is time turns time against time within time by intensifying the impotence of the living body. The melancholic enacts and expresses the inability to act destined by the flaming brand of temporality. Then, afterness was the real essence of being-time: that is, finitude. But now we are after after. When that happens (or rather doesn't happen), the only discourse able to introduce a comparable immixture of consistency and paradox, in-action and fabulation, is fantastic speculation on the basis of rigorous impersonal knowledges.

8. R. Brassier and B. Ieven, 'Transitzone/Against an Aesthetics of Noise,' NY, 5 October 2009, http://ny-web.be/transitzone/against-aesthetics-noise.html, accessed 1 March 2016.

Still: the future is obliteration and oblivion, extinction and extermination. It swallows all speculation whole. Thinking at its geophysical and energetic limit, where past-time's exhaustion receives the final consummation from the future's inevitable apocalypse, the present presents as if it were already after. Today we are living—and dying—in and as the Phantom of the After. This book is a *Necronomicon* for its summoning.

Editors

AMY IRELAND

Amy Ireland is an experimental poet and theorist attuned to the darker labyrinths of creative production. She is writing a PhD on xenopoetics at the University of New South Wales, where she also teaches and lectures on creative writing and co-convenes the philosophy and aesthetics research cluster *Aesthetics After Finitude*. Her research focuses on questions of agency and technology in modernity, and she is a member of the technomaterialist transfeminist collective 'Laboria Cuboniks'. Recent work can be found in AUDINT (Toby Heys, Steve Goodman and Eleni Ikoniadou) (eds.), *Unsound/Undead* (Minneapolis: Univocal, 2017); Amy Ireland, Tim Matts and Tony Yanick (eds.), *Dark Glamor: Accelerationism and the Occult* (New York: Punctum Books, 2016); Armen Avanessian and Helen Hester (eds.) *Dea Ex Machina* (Berlin: Merve, 2015); Edia Connole and Gary J. Shipley (eds.), *Serial Killing: A Philosophical Anthology* (Schism, 2015), as well as *Seizure*, *Rabbit Poetry Journal, e-flux*, and *Flash Art*. Amy is an instructor at the *New Centre for Research and Practice*, a member of York University's *Sonic Research Initiative*, and has worked closely with the *Performing Arts Forum* (PAF) in France. She has exhibited and performed creative work in venues across Sydney, London, Toronto and Paris, and has brought to life numerous rogue publications, some of which can be found in the National Library of Australia.

BAYLEE BRITS

Baylee Brits writes about the way that scientific processes (quantitative methodologies), artefacts (the document or data) or symbols (natural and transfinite numbers) form and deform aesthetic innovation in literature, performance and visual art. Her broader project looks at the reciprocal influence between scientific and artistic experimentation, focussing on literary modernism and the modern mathematical concept of the transfinite. She is currently working on a project on the virtual and the generic in world literature. She has published in *Textual Practice*, *Reconstruction*, *The Parish Review, Parrhesia* and several book anthologies.

PRUDENCE GIBSON

Prudence Gibson is author of *Janet Laurence: The Pharmacy of Plants* (UNSW Press 2015), and *The Rapture of Death* (Boccalatte Publishing 2010). She teaches in creative writing at the University of New South Wales and has published seven academic peer-review journal essays and seven short stories published in fiction journals, *Antipodes, Eureka Street, Etchings Journal* and *Blood*. Gibson has published over 380 articles, reviews and catalogue essays on art for Artlink, Australian

Art Collector, Vogue, The Australian, Art Monthly, The Conversation and other platforms. She has curated exhibitions *The Carpentry of Speculative Things* (Alaska Projects 2013) and *The Pharmacy of Love and Hate* (MCA Artbar 2013), with an exhibition *Aesthetics after Finitude* 2015 at UNSW. Her research interests include plant philosophy, experimental art writing and hybrid creative/academic writing.

Contributors

Lendl Barcelos is a ,kataphysician, artist and philosopher. Hen is a research-er at the Audio Culture Research Unit at Kingston University in London, UK. Hens work has appeared internationally via The Passive Collective, TATE Brit-ain, OR Gallery (Berlin), V4ult, /V\inibar (Stockholm), Performing Arts Fo-rum, MIT Press and Her Royal Majesty. Hen is part of ASOUNDER and the collaborative artist o[rphan]D[rift>]. Hen tends to laugh and play at dériving words.

Justin Clemens is the author of many books, including *Psychoanalysis is an An-tiphilosophy* (Edinburgh UP 2013) and *The Mundiad* (Hunter 2014). He is currently working on an Australian Research Council project on contemporary Australi-an poetry. He teaches at the University of Melbourne.

Marc Couroux is an inframedial artist, pianistic heresiarch, schizophonic ma-gician, teacher (York University, Visual Arts) and author of speculative theo-ry-fictions. His work has been exhibited and performed internationally (Am-sterdam, Berlin, Chicago, Glasgow, London) and published by Manchester University Press. With Asounder, a sonic tactic collective, he coordinated the (un)sound occupation workshop (collapsing sound and politics) in Toronto in 2013. He is a founding member of The Occulture (with Eldritch Priest and Da-vid Cecchetto), a Toronto collective investigating the esoteric imbrications of sound, affect and hyperstition through (among other constellating ventures) Tun-ing Speculation: Experimental Aesthetics and the Sonic Imaginary, an ongoing workshop with yearly iterations, and the Sounding the Counterfactual stream at the 2014 London Conference in Critical Thought. His hyperstitional doppel-gänger was famously conjured in Priest's Boring Formless Nonsense (Blooms-bury, 2013).

Christian R. Gelder is undertaking a Master of Arts in English at The Uni-versity of New South Wales.

Adam Hulbert teaches media at UNSW. He's a sound artist and a member of the Australian Forum for Acoustic Ecology and the Aesthetics After Finitude collective. He hosts the Philip K. Dick Philosophical Podcast.

Tessa Laird is a Melbourne-based artist and writer from Aotearoa New Zealand. She received her Doctorate from the Elam School of Fine Arts in 2012 and her colour studies were published by Clouds as *A Rainbow Reader* in 2013. She is currently lecturing in Critical and Theoretical Studies at the School of Art, VCA, Melbourne, and writing a book on bats for the Reaktion Animal series.

Laura Lotti is a PhD candidate at the School of the Arts and Media, UNSW. She holds a Bachelor and a MSc in Economics at Bocconi University, Milan, and a MA in Digital Media at Goldsmiths, University of London. Her research investigates the intersection between economic calculation, algorithmic computation, and social exchange, and the interplay between aesthetics and control in algorithmic environments.

Stephen Muecke is Professor of Ethnography at the University of New South Wales, Sydney, where he is part of the Environmental Humanities program. He has written extensively on Indigenous Australia, especially in the Kimberley, and on the Indian Ocean. He is a Fellow of the Australian Academy of the Humanities. Recent books are *The Mother's Day Protest and other Fictocritical Essays* (Rowman and Littlefield International, 2016) and a new edition of *Paddy Roe, Gularabulu: Stories from the West Kimberley* (University of Western Australia Press, 2016).

Thomas Sutherland recently completed his PhD in the Media and Communications program at The University of Melbourne, Australia. His research focuses upon the interstices between metaphysics and media theory, and has been published in journals including *Theory, Culture & Society, Time & Society, Third Text, Parrhesia*, and *Environment and Planning D: Society and Space*.

Simon O'Sullivan is Professor of Art Theory and Practice in the Department of Visual Cultures at Goldsmiths College, University of London. He has published two monographs with Palgrave, *Art Encounters Deleuze and Guattari: Thought Beyond Representation* (2005) and *On the Production of Subjectivity: Five Diagrams of the Finite-Infinite Relation* (2012), and is the editor, with Stephen Zepke, of both *Deleuze, Guattari and the Production of the New* (Continuum, 2008) and *Deleuze and Contemporary Art* (Edinburgh University Press, 2010). He also makes art, with David Burrows, under the name Plastique Fantastique—and is currently working on a collaborative volume of writings, with Burrows, on *Mythopoesis–Myth-Science–Mythotechnesis: Fictioning and the Posthuman in Contemporary Art*.

Chris Shambaugh is an MA student in Philosophy at The New School for Social Research. He holds an MSc in Literature and Modernity from The University of Edinburgh and a BA in Philosophy from the Colorado College. He is currently interested in hyperstition, pessimism, and pragmatism.

Douglas Kahn is Professor at the National Institute for Experimental Arts, University of New South Wales, Sydney. He is author of Earth Sound Earth Signal: Energies and Earth Magnitude in the Arts (University of California Press, 2013) and Noise, Water, Meat: A History of Sound in the Arts (MIT Press, 1999), and co-editor of Wireless Imagination: Sound, Radio and the Avant-garde (MIT Press, 1992), Source: Music of the Avant-garde, 1966-1973 (University of California Press, 2011), and Mainframe Experimentalism: Early Computing and the Foundations of the Digital Arts (University of California Press, 2012). He was the recipient of an Australian Research Council Future Fellowship and a Guggenheim Fellowship.